Immigration Law and

the US–Mexico Border

THE MEXICAN AMERICAN EXPERIENCE

Adela de la Torre, EDITOR

Other books in the series:

Immigration Law and the US–Mexico Border

¿Sí se puede?

**Kevin R. Johnson
and Bernard Trujillo**

The University of Arizona Press   Tucson

The University of Arizona Press
© 2011 The Arizona Board of Regents
All rights reserved

www.uapress.arizona.edu

Library of Congress Cataloging-in-Publication Data
Johnson, Kevin R.
    Immigration law and the US–Mexico border ¿Sí se puede? / Kevin R. Johnson, Bernard Trujillo.
        p. cm. — (Mexican American experience)
    Includes bibliographical references and index.
    ISBN 978-0-8165-2780-9 (pbk.)
    1. Emigration and immigration law—United States.   2. Illegal aliens—United States.   3. Border security—Mexican-American Border Region.   4. United States—Foreign relations—Mexico.   5. Mexico—Foreign relations—United States.
    I. Trujillo, Bernard, 1966–   II. Title.
    KF4819.J6435   2011
    342.7308'2–dc23

                                                                2011024944

Publication of this book is made possible in part by the proceeds of a permanent endowment created with the assistance of a Challenge Grant from the National Endowment for the Humanities, a federal agency.

♾

Manufactured in the United States of America on acid-free, archival-quality paper containing a minimum of 30 percent post-consumer waste and processed chlorine free.

16   15   14   13   12   11   6   5   4   3   2   1

To my parents, Kenneth Johnson (1936–2010) and Angela Gallardo (1938–2007), both of whom taught me about the very best of the United States and Mexico.
—Kevin R. Johnson

For my father and mother, and for my wife, Victoria.
—Bernard Trujillo

■ CONTENTS

■ ILLUSTRATIONS

Figures

Tables

■ PREFACE

Over the past two hundred years, immigration has been a hot button issue on the American political scene in times of crisis. Anxieties over politics, economics, race and ethnicity, national identity, world events, and the status of US society in general have often been accompanied by public concern with immigration and the quantity and quality of immigrants coming to the United States.

There can be no question that immigration is one of the major policy issues that the nation must address in the twenty-first century. Today, people from radically different political persuasions agree on the need to "fix" the "broken" US immigration laws to address serious deficiencies and improve border enforcement. The ideas for reform run the gamut from more—and more—enforcement, including monumental efforts to close the borders, or even a moratorium on immigration, to more generous laws that provide, for example, for "earned legalization" of undocumented immigrants, a guest worker program, and perhaps even more liberal admissions of foreign workers to better accommodate the nation's labor needs.

The dawn of the new millennium saw considerable—and often very heated—debate over immigration reform. Pundits such as CNN's Lou Dobbs, who abruptly left the network in fall 2009, and other commentators decried the negative impacts that "illegal aliens" were having on the "American way of life." Advocates of immigrants strongly disagreed. In spring 2006, tens of thousands of people took to the streets in cities across the United States to protest draconian immigration legislation passed by the US House of Representatives and demanded nothing less than simple justice for undocumented immigrants.

Unfortunately, as we discuss in chapter 12, a political stalemate developed, and comprehensive immigration reform subsequently failed in the US Congress—at least through the period in which this book was being written. "Amnesty" became nothing more than a dirty word among some policy makers and segments of the public; more enforcement through, among other things, an extension of the fence along the US–Mexico border was the only immigration reform measure that could carry the day.

Recent developments, however, including the 2008 election of President Barack Obama, the son of a Kenyan and supporter of comprehensive immigration reform, have again placed immigration reform on the national agenda. As this book goes to press, immigration reform continues to be debated in the halls of Congress and in cities and towns across the United States. Only time will tell, however, whether Congress will ultimately enact immigration reform legislation, and if so, what it will entail.

This book focuses on what for many is the core of the entire immigration debate in modern America. Immigration to the United States from Mexico affects US citizens, including US citizens of Mexican ancestry; Mexican nationals; federal, state, and local governments in the United States; and the Mexican government. For generations, migrants in significant numbers have come to the United States from south of the border. Perhaps not surprisingly, migration from Mexico has generated considerable controversy in US society. The racial, cultural, linguistic, and other differences of the migrants at times have triggered unquestionably negative reactions, if not xenophobic outbursts.

In this book, we seek to explain the basic features of US immigration law and policy in an understandable way, paying special attention to how law and policy affect legal regulation of Mexican migration to the United States; the status of the Mexican-born population in the United States; the status of the Mexican American population in the United States; and relations between the governments of the United States and Mexico.

In looking at immigration from these vantage points, we explore two fundamental questions: (1) Why should Mexico and its citizens care about US immigration law and policy? (2) Why should Mexican Americans care about US immigration policy?

Chapter 12 sketches some of the reform possibilities, with a brief discussion of the current complex politics of immigration in the United States.

We have designed the book as an introductory reader on US–Mexico migration for college and university undergraduates as well as for a more general audience. This proved to be a formidable endeavor for two law professors, more familiar with writing about the technicalities of law for lawyers and law professors than writing for a general readership. Although we have striven to simplify where appropriate, we both hope that we have neither oversimplified nor left matters too complex. The reader is the best judge of our success.

Students and teachers can keep up to date on current issues in immigration law by visiting the ImmigrationProf blog (lawprofessors.typepad.com/immigration), which is managed by four law professors, including Kevin R. Johnson, one of the founders of the blog.

Kevin R. Johnson
Bernard Trujillo

■ ACKNOWLEDGMENTS

I thank my family, Virginia Salazar, Teresa, Tomás, and Elena, for supporting all that I do. Thanks to Donarae Reynolds, Glenda McGlashan, and Nina-Marie Bell for editorial and related support. Maryam Sayyed (UC Davis 2010), Janet Kim (UC Davis 2011), Aida Macedo (UC Davis 2011), Joanna Cuevas Ingram (UC Davis 2012), and Michael Wu (UC Davis 2012) provided invaluable research and editorial assistance. Tomás Salazar Johnson provided thoughtful and careful proofreading and editorial assistance. Teresa Salazar Johnson gave us permission to use her photographs from a photography and ethnography class at UC San Diego.

Thanks to Adela de la Torre for the encouragement to write this book and for her generous support throughout the publication process. Thanks also to the Mabie-Apallas Chair and the UC Davis School of Law for financial support.

Kevin R. Johnson

I would like to thank Victoria Trujillo, Jay Conison, JoEllen Lind, Tina Duron, Amelia Peterson, Gabe Franco, Kathryn McEnery, Mitch Gilfillan, Allison Horton, Gabriel Gutierrez, Jennifer Morris Gutierrez, Andrew Huber, and Matthew Skilling.

Bernard Trujillo

Immigration Law and

the US–Mexico Border

Introduction

It has always been easier, it always will be easier, to think of someone as a *noncitizen* than to decide that he is a *nonperson*.
—Alexander M. Bickel, *The Morality of Consent* (emphasis added)

Make no mistake about it: *Illegal aliens* are the carriers of the new strain of human–swine avian flu from Mexico.
—Michael Savage, *The Savage Nation* (emphasis added)

This book in essence contends that the "problem" of undocumented immigration from Mexico to the United States, which dominates any discussion of immigration in this country, is a product of US immigration laws. There are simply too few legal avenues for low- and moderately skilled workers to migrate lawfully from Mexico to the United States. Consequently, undocumented migrants violate the law to work. Moreover, US immigration laws and their enforcement have disparate impacts based on race and nationality, in no small part because of the high demand for migration to the United States by many low- and moderately skilled workers from the developing world.

Despite the disparate impacts of the laws, the courts in the United States have traditionally played an extremely limited role in reviewing the immigration laws. Congress—and a political process that sporadically lashes out at immigrants—has "plenary power" over immigration. The president has great discretion to enforce the immigration laws. Ultimately, this dynamic has negatively affected immigrants by contributing to the passage by Congress of punitive laws directed at them, enforced by the president, and unchecked by the judiciary.

Moreover, as we discuss throughout this book, there is a long history of discrimination against US citizens of Mexican ancestry in the United States. Mexican Americans, US citizens as well as immigrants, are often stereotyped as "foreigners" subject to the full force of US immigration laws and their enforcement. Unfortunately, the ancestry of Mexican Americans often limits their full acceptance into American society.

Finally, despite the United States and Mexico sharing a nearly two-thousand-mile land border, the immigration rules that apply to **nonciti-zens** from Iceland generally apply with equal force to noncitizens from Mexico. The laws fail to consider the special relationship forged over centuries between the United States and Mexico, including the long history of migration from Mexico to the United States, which has often been expressly or tacitly encouraged by the US government and employers. Immigrants—especially undocumented ones—from Mexico in the United States are often demonized in their new country, both in the communities in which they live and in the public debate over immigration.

To clarify the public debate over immigration in the United States, chapter 1 offers critical background. As we shall see throughout this book, immigration law and policy throughout US history have generated great public concern and controversy. In particular, as we discuss in chapter 2, migration from Mexico to the United States has often been a hotly contested and controversial issue, especially beginning in the twentieth century, after the continental United States had been largely settled.

The migration of people who are perceived to be of different races, cultures, and religions than the norm in the United States has often generated concern among the general American public. Change alone brought by the migration of people into a community can cause uneasiness, if not fear and loathing. Throughout US history, different waves of immigrants—Germans, Irish, Chinese, Japanese, southern and eastern Europeans, Arabs and Muslims, and Mexicans—have all sparked controversy among the general public, often for remarkably similar reasons, such as being seen as racially, culturally, and economically different as well as being seen as "unassimilable" to the American way of life.

In this chapter, we step back to look at the broader contours of the debate over immigration in the United States, with a special emphasis on immigration from Mexico. We offer a number of different perspectives on migration from Mexico to this country.

■ The "Alien" in the American Imagination

The controversy over immigration to the United States begins with the basic terms used in the discussion of immigration. At first glance, this might seem trivial but ultimately has great practical consequences. The word "alien" is a term of art used extensively in discussing the legal, political, and social rights of noncitizens in the United States.[1] By definition, "aliens" are outsiders to the national community. Even if they have lived in this country for many years, have had children here—who, under the law, are US citizens—and work and have developed deep community ties in the United States, noncitizens remain "aliens," an institutionalized "other," different and apart from "us" in law and society.

The classification of persons as aliens, as opposed to US citizens, has significant legal, social, and political importance. Citizens have a large bundle of political, social, economic, and civil rights, many of which are guaranteed by the US **Constitution**; aliens have a much smaller bundle of rights, thereby enjoying far fewer constitutional and statutory protections.

Citizens can protect themselves in the political process through voting and enjoy other political rights, such as jury service. In contrast, aliens, no matter what their ties to the community, enjoy very limited political rights. They generally cannot vote and, under US immigration laws, risk deportation if they engage in certain political activities that, if they were citizens, would be constitutionally protected. Noncitizens cannot sit on juries deciding the fate of fellow noncitizens charged with crimes, which thereby ensures that the jury in most cases will *not* reflect a genuine cross-section of the community.

Perhaps most importantly, aliens can be deported and banished from the country (and from family, friends, job, and community) while US citizens can never be. For example, under US immigration laws, an alien convicted of possession of a few grams of marijuana—whatever his or her ties to this country, even those developed over an entire adult life in the United States— may be deported, while a US citizen convicted of mass murder can never be.

The concept of the "alien" has more subtle social consequences as well. Most importantly, it reinforces and strengthens negative sentiments toward immigrants, which in turn influence US responses to immigration and human rights issues. Aliens have long been unpopular in the United States, though the particular group subject to the most antipathy—what one might call the "demons of the day"—has varied over time. As we discuss in chapter 3, early in this nation's history, Federalists pressed for passage of the now infamous Alien and Sedition Acts to halt the migration of radical and subversive ideas from France and to cut off the burgeoning support for the Republican Party offered by new immigrants.

Animosity toward other groups of aliens has occurred sporadically in US history. Benjamin Franklin decried the "criminal" (and, in his view, racially different) German immigrants flooding Pennsylvania in colonial times. Viewed as racially inferior, Irish immigrants in the 1800s generated great hostility and suffered widespread discrimination. Near the end of the nineteenth century, Chinese immigrants suffered violence and bore the brunt of a wave of draconian federal immigration laws notoriously known as the **Chinese exclusion laws**. Animosity directed at Japanese immigrants, as well as citizens of Japanese ancestry, culminated in their exclusion from the United States and their internment during World War II. Mexican immigrants were once disparaged—even in polite company—as "wetbacks." Today, Mexican immigrants are among the most disfavored in the United States, along with Arabs and Muslims, who find themselves demonized as "terrorists," especially after the events of September 11, 2001.

As these historical events suggest, perceived racial difference has influenced the social and legal construction of "the alien." Over time, the term has increasingly become associated with people of color from the developing world who, at least in the United States, are racial minorities. Some **restrictionist** laws, such as those passed by Congress in the late 1800s barring virtually all Chinese immigration, were expressly race based as well as class conscious (Chinese laborers were the primary focus of the exclusions laws). Before 1952, the law barred most nonwhite immigrants from naturalizing to become citizens, thereby forever relegating noncitizens of color to an alien status and effectively defining them as permanent outsiders in US society.

The word "aliens" today is often nothing more than code for immigrants of color, which has been facilitated by the changing racial demographics of immigration. Today, "illegal alien" is often used—especially by self-proclaimed opponents of immigration—to refer to **undocumented immigrants** from Mexico.

Many knowledgeable observers have expressed general concern with "alien" terminology in the US immigration law. Gerald Neuman has noted, "It is no coincidence that we still refer to noncitizens as 'aliens,' a term that calls attention to their 'otherness,' and even associates them with nonhuman invaders from outer space."[2] Gerald Rosberg acknowledged that "the very word, 'alien,' calls to mind someone strange and out of place, and it has often been used in a distinctly pejorative way."[3]

However, despite the concerns, the term is regularly used in discussions of immigration. This is the almost inevitable result of "alien" being the nucleus of the comprehensive federal immigration law, the **Immigration and Nationality Act (INA)**. Indeed, at a fundamental level, "alien" is the very DNA of the INA. The INA succinctly provides that an "alien" is "any person not a citizen or national of the United States."[4] The alien/citizen distinction has great practical importance for immigration laws; its rules for admission and removal primarily apply to aliens, not to US citizens.

Today, academics generally consider the concept of "race" and "races" to be social constructions rather than anything fixed by biology or science.[5] However, surprisingly little has been written about how the alien is socially and legally constructed as well. The truth of the matter is that the alien is made up out of whole cloth. It is only what we say it is. The alien represents a body of rules established by the courts and Congress and reinforced by popular culture. Society, often through the law, defines who is an alien, an institutionalized "other," and who is not. It is society, through Congress and the courts, that determines which rights to afford aliens. Nothing is predetermined. All the legal and other baggage attached to the alien is the product of the human imagination.

There is no inherent requirement that society establish a category of aliens at all. We as a nation could dole out political rights and obligations depending on residence in the community, which is how the public education and tax systems generally operate in the United States. Some commentators have advocated extending the franchise to noncitizen residents of this country, a common practice in many states and localities in the United States at the beginning of the twentieth century.

Many alternatives to the term alien exist, including "human," "person," "immigrant," "undocumented" or "unauthorized immigrant" or "undocumented worker." "Alien" has many negative connotations and, similar to the social construction of races, the construction of the alien has justified our legal system's restrictive approach, offering noncitizens extremely limited rights. References to the "alien," "aliens," and "illegal aliens" as societal others thus helps make the harsh treatment of people from other countries seem reasonable and necessary.

Consider the terms of the public debate. Today's faceless "illegal aliens" are invading and wreaking havoc on the nation; "they" must be stopped or "we" will be destroyed. Such images, which Lou Dobbs for years sensationalized almost nightly on CNN, have helped animate and legitimate the political movement to bolster enforcement of the border between the United States and Mexico and to crack down on immigration and immigrants in general.

The images that "alien" terminology creates have more far-reaching, often subtle, racial consequences. Federal and state laws regularly, and lawfully, discriminate against aliens. In contrast, governmental reliance on racial classifications ordinarily is unconstitutional.

Because a majority of immigrants are people of color, alienage classifications all too frequently serve as substitutes, or proxies, for discrimination based on race. Alienage discrimination, although overinclusive because it includes persons who are not minorities (put differently, not all "aliens" are people of color), allows one to disproportionately disadvantage people of color. We see this in operation in modern times, with the blaming of "illegal aliens" for the social ills of the United States, accompanied by a spike in hate crimes directed at Latinas/os, including US citizens as well as legal immigrants.

As the increase in hate crimes demonstrates, the terminological issue is not simply a word game. "Alien" terminology serves important legal and social functions. In the quote that prefaces this chapter, Alexander Bickel perhaps said it best in the context of analyzing citizenship: "It has always been easier, it always will be easier, to think of someone as a noncitizen than to decide that he is a *nonperson*."[6]

Aliens are partial members of the community with limited membership rights, which includes being potentially subject to treatment, such as deportation, that US citizens could *never* receive. An extreme example drives this point home. The US Supreme Court has held that, at least in certain circumstances, aliens may be detained indefinitely, consistent with the US Constitution. Citizens, of course, could never be subject to such treatment.

The value of US citizenship is nothing new to American law. Long ago, the Supreme Court held that Dred Scott, a black man, was not a citizen and therefore could not sue for his freedom in the federal courts. By denying citizenship to Dred Scott, the Court denied him a right—access to the federal courts—to which US citizens are ordinarily entitled, thereby highlighting the fact that freed slaves generally were not considered full members of US society.[7]

Consider the linkage between alien status and citizenship under modern immigration laws. The INA definition of an "alien" as not a US citizen or national is bland, yet the word "alien" alone evokes rich imagery. One thinks of frightening (and often predatory) space invaders portrayed regularly in science fiction TV programs and movies.

Popular culture reinforces the idea that aliens may be killed with impunity, and if we do not, *"they"* will destroy the world as we know it. Some of the synonyms for alien are particularly instructive in this regard: foreigner, interloper, intruder, invader, outsider, squatter, stranger—all terms that suggest the need for harsh treatment. In effect, the term "alien" serves to dehumanize people and legitimate their ill treatment, legally and otherwise. We have few, if any, legal obligations to alien outsiders to the community, although we have obligations to persons. Persons have rights—including basic human rights—while aliens generally do not.

The term "alien" not only intellectually legitimizes the mistreatment of noncitizens but it helps to mask true human suffering. Persons have human dignity, and their rights should be respected. Aliens deserve neither human dignity nor legal rights. By distinguishing between aliens and persons, society is able to reconcile the disparate legal and social treatment afforded the two groups.

Consider this phenomenon concretely. If we think that persons who come to the United States from another nation are hard-working and "good," it is difficult to treat them punitively (as our immigration laws do). We generally would not refer to these good folks in ordinary conversation as "aliens" or "illegal aliens." If we think about them only as faceless masses of aliens, as criminals who take "American" jobs, sap limited public resources, and damage the environment, it is far easier to rationalize the harsh treatment of human beings.

Legal Rights of "Aliens" and "Illegal Aliens"

Terminology plays a prominent role in the legal system's treatment of noncitizens, especially the limits on their legal rights. One justice of the US Supreme Court recognized the subtle yet discernible impact the terminology denoting different categories of "aliens" has on their treatment under the law. In a case involving the rights of immigrants, Justice William Douglas dissented: "We cannot allow the Government's insistent reference to these Mexican citizens as *'deportable aliens'* to obscure the fact that they come before us as *innocent persons* who have not been charged with a crime."[8]

The most damning terminology for noncitizens is "illegal alien," unquestionably one of the most unpopular groups of aliens in the United

States today. Restrictionists often rant about the evils of illegal aliens on talk radio. Although "alien" is the centerpiece of the INA, "illegal alien" is not defined by the omnibus federal immigration law. "Illegal alien," rather, is a deeply pejorative term that implies criminality, thereby suggesting that persons who fall into this category deserve severe punishment, not any kind of legal protection. "They" are "illegal" as well as "aliens." Despite its severely negative connotations, "illegal aliens" is common, if not standard, terminology in the modern debate over undocumented immigration.

The "illegal alien" label, however, suffers from numerous inaccuracies and inadequacies. Many nuances of US immigration law make it extremely difficult to distinguish between an "illegal" and a "legal" immigrant. For example, as we discuss in chapter 7, a person living without documents in this country for a number of years may be eligible for *relief from removal* and to become a **lawful permanent resident (LPR)**. He or she may have children born in this country, who are US citizens by operation of the Fourteenth Amendment, as well as a job and community ties here. It is difficult to contend that this person is an "illegal alien," indistinguishable from a person who entered without inspection the day before yesterday.

The vaguely defined, but emotionally powerful, "illegal alien" terminology also fails to distinguish between the different types of undocumented persons in the United States. There are persons who cross the border without inspection; another group of noncitizens enter lawfully but **overstay** or otherwise violate the terms of their business, tourist, student, or other temporary visas. This distinction is important because border enforcement measures, such as border fences and increased numbers of officers along the border, will have little impact on noncitizens who enter legally but overstay their visa. This helps reveal how "illegal alien" in public discussion ordinarily refers to a person who enters without inspection, often a national of Mexico. This is not surprising because the furor over illegal aliens often represents an attack on undocumented Mexicans, if not on lawful Mexican immigrants and Mexican American citizens, which is a central theme of this book.

In this vein, history teaches that it is difficult to limit anti-alien sentiment to any one segment of the immigrant community, such as undocumented immigrants. This is evidenced by the slow reduction of public benefits to all categories of noncitizens in the 1990s. On the heels of the passage of **Proposition 187** by the California voters in 1994, which focused on limiting benefits to *undocumented* persons, Congress enacted welfare "reform" legislation in 1996 that greatly limited *legal* immigrants' eligibility for public benefit programs.

Mean-spirited characterizations of aliens have real-life consequences. As we discuss in chapter 10, anti-immigrant rhetoric in cities and counties across the United States has escalated in the last few years. Not

California's Proposition 187 (1994)

California's Proposition 187 is nothing less than an immigration milestone of the 1990s and marked the beginning of an increasingly anti-immigrant period of US history. The measure, approved by California voters by a 2–1 margin, would have stripped undocumented immigrants of all public benefits, including a public school elementary and secondary education for undocumented children. The terminology in regard to immigrants used by its proponents is telling:

> Some supporters of Proposition 187 expressed hopes and aims well beyond simply fiscal ones. One of the initiative sponsors, Ron Prince, baldly asserted that "illegal aliens are killing us in California.... Those who support illegal immigration are, in effect, anti-American."[1]

One argument in support of Proposition 187 in the voters' pamphlet demonstrates the deeply negative feelings about immigration and immigrants: "Proposition 187 will be the first giant stride in ultimately ending the ILLEGAL ALIEN invasion."

The Proposition 187 media director for Southern California expressed even more disturbing and inflammatory concerns:

> Proposition 187 is ... a logical step toward saving
> California from economic ruin.... By flooding the state with 2 million illegal aliens to date, and increasing that figure each of the following 10 years, Mexicans in California would number 15 million to

(continued)

20 million by 2004. During those 10 years about 5 million to 8 million Californians would have emigrated to other states. If these trends continued, a Mexico-controlled California could vote to establish Spanish as the sole language of California, 10 million more English-speaking Californians could flee, and there could be a statewide vote to leave the Union and annex California to Mexico.

One of the initiative sponsors went even further and conjured up disturbing imagery from another era in advocating passage of the initiative: "You are the posse and the SOS [Save Our State, the supporter's name for the initiative] is the rope."

1. Kevin R. Johnson, "An Essay on Immigration Politics, Popular Democracy, and California's Proposition 187: The Political Relevance and Legal Irrelevance of Race," *Washington Law Review* 70 (1995): quotations on 629, 653–54, emphasis added; footnotes omitted. ■

coincidentally, hate crimes against all Latinas/os—not just immigrants—living in the United States have risen dramatically. In 2008, Latina/o immigrants were killed in vicious attacks in rural Pennsylvania and suburban New York. The facts surrounding the 2008 killing of a lawful *Ecuadoran* immigrant, Marcelo Lucero, in Long Island, are chilling. A group of young men allegedly began the events of a hate-filled evening with the ominous statement: "Let's go find some Mexicans." The *New York Times* later reported: "Every now and then, perhaps once a week, seven young friends got together ... to hunt down, and hurt, Hispanic men. They made a sport of it, calling their victims 'beaners,' ... prosecutors said."[9] Not long before the killing of Marcelo Lucero, the local county executive had blamed undocumented immigrants for fiscal, economic, and various social problems.

As the campaign surrounding Proposition 187 suggests, the negative images of the alien, often fed by restrictionist groups and politicians seeking punitive immigration measures, carry the day in the political process. "The discourse of legal [immigration] status permits coded discussion in which listeners will understand that reference is being made, *not to aliens in the abstract, but to the particular foreign group that is the principal focus of current hostility.*"[10]

An important first association between aliens and racial minorities can be seen in the foundational immigration cases allowing for the exclusion and deportation of Chinese laborers in the late 1800s, which we discuss in chapter 3. Not long after, in the early part of the twentieth century, some states passed laws known as the "alien land laws" that, through incorporation of the immigration and nationality laws, effectively barred persons of Japanese ancestry from owning real property.

As mentioned above, in the modern debate about immigration, the alien has increasingly become associated with racial minorities. The words "alien" and "illegal alien" today carry subtle racial connotations. The dominant image of the alien is often that of an undocumented Mexican or some other person of color, perhaps a Haitian, Chinese, or Cuban person traveling by sea from a developing nation. Treating racial minorities poorly on the grounds that they are "aliens" or "illegal aliens" allows people to reconcile the view that they "are not racist" while pursuing policies that punish certain groups of persons viewed as racially or otherwise different.

Although the term "illegal alien" is seemingly race neutral, it is relatively easy to discern which noncitizens are the ones that provoke concern. Study of the use of the terminology in context reveals that, particularly in the Southwest, the term refers to undocumented Mexicans and plays into popular stereotypes about Mexicans as criminals. The terminology more effectively masks nativist sympathies and downright racism than the popular vernacular that it replaced—"wetbacks," which is even more closely linked to Mexican immigrants.

The link between illegal aliens and Mexican citizens often goes unstated but is clear to the listener, whether it be a fellow anti-immigrant traveler or a person of Mexican ancestry. Indeed, the courts, with little explanation, often have approached the "illegal immigration problem" as an exclusively Mexican problem. For example, the late Justice William Brennan, a liberal on many social issues, writing for the US Supreme Court, suggests the equation in his mind between illegal aliens and Mexican immigrants:

Employment of *illegal aliens* in times of high unemployment deprives citizens and legally admitted aliens of jobs; acceptance by *illegal aliens* of jobs on substandard terms as to wages and working conditions can seriously depress wage scales and working conditions of citizens and legally admitted aliens; and employment of *illegal aliens* under such conditions can diminish the effectiveness of labor unions. These local problems are particularly acute in California in light of the significant influx of *illegal aliens* from neighboring Mexico.[11]

■ The Supreme Court: Migration from Mexico as a "Colossal Problem"

In focusing on the "illegal alien" as Mexican, US Supreme Court **decisions** are replete with negative imagery about undocumented immigration from Mexico. Such immigration, in the Court's view, is a "colossal problem" posing "enormous difficulties"[12] and "formidable law enforcement problems."[13] One justice observed that immigration from Mexico is "virtually uncontrollable."[14] Chief Justice Warren Burger stated that the nation "is powerless to stop the tide of *illegal aliens*—and *dangerous drugs*—that daily and freely crosses our 2000-mile southern boundary [with Mexico]."[15] Justice William Brennan, in analyzing the lawfulness of a workplace raid in Southern California, stated that "No one doubts that the presence of large numbers of undocumented *aliens* in the country creates law enforcement problems of *titanic proportions*."[16] Chief Justice William Rehnquist reportedly referred to Mexican immigrants as "wetbacks" in a conference with his fellow justices in discussing an immigration case.

Ignoring the heated debate among social scientists about the contribution of undocumented immigrants to the economy, the Supreme Court stated unequivocally in 1975 that undocumented Mexicans "create significant economic and social problems, competing with citizens and legal resident aliens for jobs, and generating extra demand for social services."[17] Such perceptions inspired Chief Justice Burger to include an extraordinary appendix to an **opinion** describing in remarkable detail "the illegal alien problem," which focused exclusively (and quite negatively) on unauthorized migration from Mexico into the United States.[18]

Similar concerns about "illegal aliens" from Mexico and other developing nations consciously and unconsciously influence policy makers. For example, in arguing for an overhaul of immigration enforcement in 1981, then-attorney general William French Smith proclaimed that "we have lost control of our borders,"[19] by which he specifically meant the US–Mexico border. Similar perceptions have prompted more recent congressional action designed to bolster border enforcement to the south. While the government fortifies the southern border with Mexico, reports of undocumented immigrants being smuggled across the northern border with Canada fail to provoke comparable public concern.

Concern with "aliens" and "illegal aliens" from Mexico is the primary lens through which many Americans view immigration today. The following pages offer facts about Mexican migration to the United States and outline various perspectives on US–Mexico migration, "aliens," and "illegal aliens."

■ Mexico as a Sending Country

Although immigrants from around the world come to the United States, Mexico is the country that sends the most. This is in part due to geography. Mexico and the United States are neighbors that share a land border of almost two thousand miles. In addition, economic disparities exist between the two nations, although the Mexican economy has experienced significant growth in recent years, and the disparities between the United States and Mexico have consequently decreased over time.

Over the last decade, somewhere in the neighborhood of a million immigrants—out of a total US population of more than 300 million (or less than .5 percent)—have lawfully come to the United States every year.[20] Roughly one-fifth of the lawful immigrants each year come from Mexico.

Table 1.1 shows the top five sending countries of lawful permanent residents to the United States in fiscal year 2008.

Table 1.1   Top five countries that send lawful permanent residents to the United States

COUNTRY	IMMIGRANTS	PERCENTAGE OF TOTAL (%)
1. Mexico	189,989	17.2
2. China, People's Republic	80,271	7.3
3. India	63,352	5.7
4. Philippines	54,030	4.9
5. Cuba	49,500	4.5

Source: US Department of Homeland Security, Office of Immigration Statistics, "US Legal Permanent Residents: 2008," (Mar. 2009) (Table 3), at 4, available at www.dhs.gov/xlibrary/assets/statistics/publications/lpr_fr_2008.pdf

Today, according to the best estimates available, roughly 11–12 million undocumented immigrants—about 4 percent of the population—live in the United States.[21] About 60 percent, or approximately 7.2 million, are from Mexico. Countries throughout Central America, the Caribbean, South America, and Asia also send significant numbers of undocumented immigrants to the United States.[22]

Despite the growing concern with immigration, the percentage of immigrants in the United States today—although numerically much greater than past epochs—is not all that different as a percentage of the total US population from that in the early twentieth century. Indeed, the percentage of immigrants out of the total US population is equaled, and in some instances surpassed, by similar percentages in the early twentieth century.[23] Growing pains resulted from the number of immigrants who settled in the United States during this period of US history; however, each wave of immigrants was more or less integrated into US society.

■ Demographics of the Mexican Ancestry Population in the United States

Here are some basics about the total population of persons of Mexican ancestry in the United States. "A record 12.7 million Mexican immigrants lived in the United States in 2008, a 17-fold increase since 1970. Mexicans now account for 32 percent of all immigrants. . . . More than half (55 percent) of the Mexican immigrants in this country are unauthorized. . . . The current Mexican share of all foreign born living in the United States—32 percent—is the highest concentration of immigrants to the United States from a single country since the late 19th century."[24]

The rise in Mexican migration has fueled a general growth in the Latina/o population in the United States. "According to the US Census Bureau, Latinas/os [today] are the largest minority group in the United States, comprising approximately 44.3 million people or roughly 14.8 percent of the total US population. . . . The Pew Hispanic Center estimated that, in 2005, approximately 40 percent of the Hispanic population was foreign born. The Census estimates that about a quarter of all Latinas/os in this country are not US citizens. In 2003, 33.5 million foreign-born people lived in the United States, with more than one-half born in Latin America."[25]

Because roughly one-quarter of all Latinas/os in the United States are not citizens, they cannot vote. The number of voting-eligible Latinas/os is further diminished by those under eighteen years old, which is a larger percentage of the Latina/o community than of others. Thus, the voting power of Latinas/os does not necessarily match the raw numbers of Latinas/os in the United States, a significant factor if one seeks to change US immigration laws and enforcement policies through political means. We discuss the impact of US immigration laws on Latina/o voting power in chapter 12.

Importantly, the last two decades have seen a significant change in the settlement patterns of Mexican immigrants in the United States. Mexican immigrant communities have emerged in places in the Midwest, South, and Northeast like Postville, Iowa; Rogers, Arkansas; Prince William County, Virginia; and Hazleton, Pennsylvania, which have not historically been destination points for Mexican immigrants. Immigrants have settled in these localities because of the high demand for relatively unskilled labor in agriculture, poultry and meat, and other industries. As we shall see in chapter 10, the new settlement patterns have at times resulted in social tensions.

■ Immigration and Immigration Policy: A Mexican Immigrant Perspective

Contrary to the claims of restrictionists who complain about migrants coming to secure public benefits or to commit crime, the great weight of scholarly research concludes that Mexican immigrants come to the United States primarily for employment opportunities and to rejoin family. More economic opportunities exist in this country than in Mexico. Put simply, migration from Mexico is in large part a labor migration. There is much demand for low-skilled labor in the United States, and workers, with legal immigration status or not, can land jobs. Few avenues for low-skilled citizens to immigrate lawfully to the United States exist under US immigration laws, thereby creating incentives for undocumented migration. In addition, political and other freedoms in the United States attract migrants.

Importantly, economic opportunities exist for Mexican immigrants in this country whether or not they are documented. The employment of undocumented immigrants in the United States has some labor market impacts. Unfortunately, the segregation of the labor markets along immigration status lines today in important ways resembles the systematic segregation of whites and African Americans in the days of **Jim Crow**. A separate and unequal labor market exists for undocumented immigrants, who are predominantly people of color.

US immigration laws have historically operated—and continue to operate—to prevent many poor and working people of color from migrating lawfully to the United States. Although Congress in 1965 eliminated blatant racial exclusions from immigration laws, many provisions of current US immigration laws that limit entry into the United States continue to have racially disparate impacts. Everything else being equal, people from the developing world—predominantly "people of color" as that category is popularly understood in the United States—find it much more difficult under US immigration laws to migrate to this country than similarly situated noncitizens from the developed (and predominantly white) world.

Consequently, for many prospective immigrants lacking realistic legal avenues, economic incentives exist to migrate or stay unlawfully in the United States. Given those incentives, it should be no surprise that we today have an estimated 12 million undocumented immigrants living in the United States, with close to 60 percent from Mexico. Many of them toil in a separate, largely racially segregated, labor market. Ultimately, we see a labor control system, with immigration law integral to its creation and maintenance, akin to some of the devices that existed in the Jim Crow South in the wake of the abolition of slavery.

What causes the flow of undocumented immigrants from Mexico and other developing nations to the United States? Under US immigration laws, as discussed in chapters 5 and 6, unskilled workers without relatives in this country have few legal avenues to lawfully immigrate here. Employment visas are generally reserved for highly skilled workers. Low- and medium-skilled workers lack practical lawful immigration opportunities. Despite the claims of restrictionists that "illegal aliens" should wait in line like everyone else, there is simply no line for many of them to wait in to lawfully immigrate to the United States. As a result, many of these prospective workers have the incentive to enter or remain in the country in violation of US immigration laws.

The exploitation of working-class undocumented immigrants in the United States continues virtually unabated. Unfortunately, undocumented workers often enjoy precious few protections under the law. The state of California, for example, has only a handful of personnel to enforce the state labor code in the vast Central Valley, the home of a thriving population of undocumented workers. In a case involving an undocumented worker from Mexico, the US Supreme Court greatly limited the relief available (and denied backpay) to an undocumented worker whose right to organize under federal labor law had been flagrantly violated by the employer.[26]

Undocumented immigrants who successfully make it to this country participate in a labor force with a racial caste quality, due largely to the operation of US immigration laws. Indeed, in the United States today, nothing less than dual labor markets exist. Undocumented workers—predominantly people of color—participate in one market, often without the protection of the minimum wage and other labor laws. Mexican and other Latina/o undocumented immigrants predominate in this secondary labor market. They are easily exploited, quickly disposed of, and generally extremely reluctant to complain about wages and conditions for fear that they will be deported.

Wage, labor, and other protections are but a faraway dream for many undocumented workers in the United States. By designating a population of undocumented immigrants, US immigration laws help to create a pliable labor force that employers often easily control and exploit. In another labor market, US citizens and legal immigrants enjoy the protections of the law.

In the old days, Jim Crow divided the job markets, with whites enjoying access to higher-paying jobs and African Americans relegated to the lower-wage market. Some fair-complected African Americans would seek to "pass" to secure jobs in the better-paying labor market reserved for whites. Today, undocumented immigrants at times attempt to "pass" as lawful workers by using false identifications and fraudulent Social Security cards to access the legal and legitimate labor market with higher wages ordinarily reserved for US citizens and lawful immigrants.

Aside from the dual labor market structure, another parallel between Jim Crow and the modern treatment of immigrants in the United States is facilitated by US immigration laws. As we discuss in chapter 10, over the last few years, several state and local governments have adopted measures that purport to regulate undocumented immigration and punish immigrants, in effect seeking to force them out of town. The debates over the local immigration measures in many ways resemble the kinds of vicious local debates—with race and racism at their core—over housing and school integration measures in the 1950s and 1960s.

Local ordinances that bar landlords from renting to undocumented immigrants, including ones adopted by the cities of Escondido, California; Hazleton, Pennsylvania; Valley Park, Missouri; and Farmer's Branch,

Texas, are a direct response to an increasing number of Latinas/os—not simply immigrants—moving into those cities. Some supporters of these laws seek to drive as many Latinas/os as possible out of town. This may sound familiar to those knowledgeable of housing discrimination and such things as restrictive covenants in housing deeds designed to exclude African Americans from white neighborhoods in the days of Jim Crow. In addition, states such as Arizona and Oklahoma have passed laws designed to sanction employers of undocumented immigrants and punish these immigrants.

With similar aims, some local governments have unsuccessfully attempted to address the efforts of day laborers, many of whom in some localities are undocumented immigrants from Mexico and Central America, to secure work. Ordinances have targeted day laborer pickup points, which can be found in cities and towns, large and small, across the United States. Home Depot stores across the country often serve as informal day laborer pickup points. These laborers are among the most vulnerable of all workers, often subject to exploitation, including nonpayment of wages and excessive hours in substandard working conditions.

Consider just two examples of local governments attempting to regulate immigration and the impacts of the Latina/o community generally. In 2007, Prince William County, Virginia, responded to an increase of Latinas/os by adopting a measure that, among other things, required police officers to check the immigration status of anyone accused of breaking the law, even for a broken tail light, if the officers for some reason believed that the person was in the country unlawfully. This is nothing less than an invitation to racially profile, a frequently criticized practice that plagues Latinas/os (as well as African Americans) in the United States. Fearful of the impacts of the new law, Latinas/os—citizens as well as noncitizens—reportedly have moved out of Prince William County to neighboring localities and states.

The upscale community of Escondido, California, less than one hundred miles from the US–Mexico border, is another local government that has tried to discourage undocumented immigrants from being visible in the city limits. The city passed an ordinance, which it later rescinded in the face of a formidable legal challenge, barring landlords from renting to undocumented immigrants. It also used traffic checkpoints to check driver's licenses (in California and most other states, undocumented immigrants are not eligible for driver's licenses) and aggressive enforcement of housing, zoning, and other ordinances to discourage undocumented immigrants from living there. Like other cities, Escondido officials considered a policy restricting drivers from picking up day laborers. A retired sheriff maintained that the city was doing nothing less than "looking for a way to reduce the number of brown people" in Escondido.[27]

Importantly, there is little indication that the labor provided by undocumented immigrants in cities with ordinances and policies like Prince William County and Escondido will not be in demand to maintain the homes and yards and provide child care services, as well as work in restaurants, hotels, construction, and service industries. The elimination of day laborer pickup points, for example, would likely drive the employment of these workers further underground. It would not, however, be likely to dramatically affect the informal labor market that thrives and helps satisfy the economy's thirst for inexpensive labor.

■ A Mexican American Perspective

Mexican Americans often have a deeply ambivalent view of immigration and immigrants from Mexico. At times, members of the established Mexican American community, like other groups of Americans, have expressed concern with the changes to communities brought by immigrants from Mexico. Tensions in East Los Angeles, California, and Phoenix, Arizona, for example, have grown with changes Mexican migrants have brought to the community. Complaints from Mexican Americans about immigration (like those of other Americans) run the gamut, from claims that the newcomers do not speak English to charges that too many live in one residence and fail to properly maintain the premises.

At the same time, Mexican Americans have a great concern with immigration and immigration enforcement. Importantly, Mexican Americans—like most Americans—do not generally support open borders with Mexico. However, many persons of Mexican ancestry—US citizens included—express concern about **racial profiling** in immigration enforcement, which we discuss in detail in chapter 9. In addition, some Mexican American families are concerned with the impacts of immigration law and enforcement on themselves, their family members, and their friends. Many families are composed of members with different immigration statuses; in 2008, for example, 4 million US citizen children had undocumented parents.

Some poor and working-class Mexican Americans also generally fear that immigrant workers will drive down wages. For all of the above reasons, many Mexican Americans have considerable concern with the level of immigration to the United States and, more generally, with immigration law and policy.

At times, Mexican Americans, including well-established US citizens, understand that the debate over immigration in the United States is often about popular fears about all persons of Mexican ancestry in the United States, not just about lawful and undocumented immigrants. In 1994, for example, polls showed that Mexican American citizens initially favored Proposition 187, California's anti-immigrant measure. However, as the campaign clearly became more anti-Mexican as well as anti-immigrant, US citizens of Mexican ancestry moved to oppose the measure. Mexican American voters ultimately opposed it by an overwhelming 2–1 margin, which was the reverse of the final overall vote. Similar patterns can be seen in other related ballot measures, as well as in debates over immigration reform in general.

The formation of Mexican American identity in the United States is an incredibly complex series of processes, which touches on immigration but goes well beyond the scope of this book.[28]

■ The US Government Perspective

As interpreted by the US Supreme Court, the US Constitution entrusts the federal government with regulating immigration. Federal law, specifically the comprehensive federal immigration law known as the Immigration and Nationality Act, generally governs the admission and removal of immigrants.

The federal government has general concerns with the uniformity of immigration and **naturalization** rules and moderation of at times negative domestic reactions to immigrants. Immigration law and policies, as well as the treatment of immigrants generally, can in certain circumstances affect the relations of the United States with foreign nations.

The national government also desires to maximize the economic benefits of immigration as well as its possible political implications. It receives substantial tax revenues from immigrants, including undocumented immigrants who pay taxes with the hope of sometime regularizing their legal status. (This can be accomplished through securing a Tax Identification Number; needless to say, the Internal Revenue Service accepts tax returns and taxes without questioning the immigration status of the filer.)

Undocumented immigrants who work with false Social Security numbers contribute billions of dollars each year to a system from which they in all likelihood will never collect benefits.

Border control and immigration enforcement are popular with the federal government in no small part because they are popular with the general public. The US government also has some interest in protecting human rights of noncitizens and has treaty obligations to not deport noncitizens fleeing torture and political and related forms of persecution to their native countries.

■ A Mexican Government Perspective

The Mexican government has many concerns with the migration of its citizens to the United States. We can expect the government to be concerned with the treatment and well-being of its citizens, in other words, the human rights of its citizens in the United States who are subject to various border enforcement measures.

Restrictionists often claim that the Mexican government is responsible for the migration of its citizens north; however, the Mexican government has limits on what it can do to prevent its nationals from leaving the country. It also feels pressure to save the lives of its citizens in their efforts to journey to the United States. Recall that the US government harshly criticized the old Soviet Union, and the Eastern bloc generally, for refusing to allow its citizens to emigrate to the West.

The Mexican government also has economic concerns with the migration of its nationals. Each year, billions of dollars in **remittances** from Mexican workers in the United States flow back to Mexico. Although remittances have fallen somewhat in recent years due to the economic downturn in this country, Mexico received in the neighborhood of $25 billion—a huge supplement to its economy—in 2007 from its citizens working in the United States. In this vein, "hometown clubs" have emerged through which migrants raise funds to send to their hometowns in Mexico and build roads, bridges, and other municipal improvements. The clubs, and remittances generally, greatly benefit the Mexican economy and reduce the fiscal (and political) pressures facing the Mexican government.

The Mexican government has political interests in the migration of its citizens to the United States as well. The flow of migrants out of the country serves as a sort of political safety valve, with some of the most unhappy people leaving the country to pursue economic opportunity, as well as political freedoms, in the United States. The **North American Free Trade Agreement**, for example, has caused adjustments in the Mexican economy that have resulted in migration pressures in recent years as well as increased internal dissent among certain segments of Mexican society. Immigration to the United States has thus helped to dampen political dissent in Mexico.

■ The Perspective of State and Local Governments

As we shall see in chapter 10, tensions over immigration, as well as the changes brought by immigrants, in recent years have been high in some state and local **jurisdictions**. Some of the concerns grew worse with the failure of Congress to address undocumented immigration and pass immigration reform in 2007. Fears grew as demographic changes resulting from migration affected areas of the United States that had not seen significant immigration from Mexico, such as parts of the East, Midwest, and South. Prince William County, Virginia, discussed earlier in this chapter, is one example. The state of Arizona, which passed a controversial anti-immigration law in 2010 that was largely struck down by a federal court, is another.

A number of concerns contribute to tensions at the state and local levels over immigration. First, controversy has emerged over the proper role of the state and local governments vís-a-vís the federal government in regulating immigration in recent years. State and local governments have moved to fill a perceived void and to rectify the failure of the US government to act on immigration enforcement.

Second, immigration imposes costs on state and local governments that are not always reimbursed by the US government, which is primarily in charge of regulating immigration and receives the bulk of the tax benefits. For example, state and local governments pay the bulk of the costs of elementary and secondary education, which must be provided to undocumented children, as well as emergency health care and services. In addition to receiving the bulk of tax contributions from immigrants (including roughly one-half of all undocumented immigrants), the federal government also receives Social Security contributions (amounting to billions of dollars each year in contributions from undocumented workers who will *never* be eligible for Social Security benefits).[29] The federal government also collects tax revenues from businesses that profit—and profit handsomely—from low-cost Mexican labor. The "fiscal disconnect" between federal and state and local governments exacerbates frustration with immigration and immigrants by the state and local governments, which in modern times are trying to balance tight budgets.

■ The Ordinary US Citizen Perspective

It is difficult to characterize the view of US citizens toward immigrants. On the one hand, the public has had open arms for the immigrants of the world, with the Statue of Liberty exemplifying this ideal. Many Americans sincerely believe in this heroic vision of America.

On the other hand, the United States at times has suffered from anti-immigrant backlashes, both historically and in more recent years. Immigrants have been blamed for the social problems of the day, whether it be the economy, social tensions, crime, disease, or related problems. These xenophobic outbursts are often most fiery when immigrants viewed as racially different are the predominant immigrants of the day.

Workers may also hold economic fears, namely that immigrant workers will depress wages as well as compete for scarce public benefits. Such fears increase in tough economic times. Some observers have claimed that African Americans are especially injured by inexpensive foreign labor. However, studies show that the negative impacts of immigration on workers are relatively small (at most 1–3 percent of a depression in real wages) and generally suffered by only the most vulnerable in the job market, those without high school diplomas.

As discussed previously, popular American culture often demonizes prospective immigrants of color—as well as those who reside here—as "aliens" or, even worse, "illegal aliens." Class as well as racial aspects of the stereotypical noncitizens contribute to the conventional wisdom that immigrants are a pressing social problem. The widespread perception is that all "illegals" are poor and unskilled, a stereotype that is not supported by the available empirical evidence. Nonetheless, *the term 'illegal alien' now . . . carries undeniable racial overtones and is typically associated with the stereotype of an unskilled Mexican male laborer.*[30] With both racial and class components, the stereotype helps to rationalize the calls for dehumanizing treatment of "illegal aliens" and aggressive enforcement of US immigration laws through, among other things, force, technology, and fences.

■ Concluding Thoughts

One thing is clear from US immigration history. The nation has been especially prone to anti-immigrant outbursts at times of social stress and turmoil. Untangling the myriad reasons for xenophobic outbursts is not easy. Both legitimate (economic cost) and illegitimate (racism) concerns have contributed to anti-immigrant sentiment.

There are many different perspectives on immigration to, and immigrants living in, the United States. Language and terminology are important as are care and sensitivity in considering the many issues surrounding, and perspectives about, migration from Mexico to the United States. Importantly, terminology—specifically, the references to "aliens" and "illegal aliens"—has direct and indirect impacts on the law, the immigration debate, and the treatment of noncitizens.

■ Discussion Questions

1. Is calling someone an "illegal alien" really any different from calling someone a "wetback"? Is there any other term that could be used in polite company that is as pejorative, distancing, and downright insulting as "alien" (besides "illegal alien")? With respect to terminology, what other term or terms might be better than "aliens" or "illegal aliens"? What about immigrant, undocumented immigrant, unauthorized worker, or human being? Is the term "anchor babies" (used by some to refer to the US-born and therefore US citizen children of undocumented immigrants) pejorative?

2. Should US immigration laws make distinctions between "aliens" and citizens in allocating the constitutional and other legal rights accorded to each group of persons? Why shouldn't all *residents* in the community have equal legal rights?

3. Why do so many Americans appear to be hyperconcerned over migration to the United States from Mexico as opposed to that from other countries, such as Canada, Germany, or Russia? Are the fears racial, economic, social, or cultural (or all of the above)? Are the fears generated by the magnitude of the migration from Mexico to the United States? Or are people simply resistant to particular kinds of change? Please explain and support your reasoning. Perspectives vary widely on the costs and benefits of migration from Mexico to

the United States. How can we as a society promote education, understanding, and common ground on the issue of migration from Mexico, as well as on immigration and immigrants generally? Such an understanding would seem to be necessary for immigration reform.

4. Immigrants have historically been scapegoated and demonized for the problems of the day in the United States. Immigrants, for example, often are blamed for "taking jobs" from US citizens in times of economic distress, being prone to criminal activity, and, as exemplified by the Michael Savage quote at the beginning of the chapter, spreading communicable diseases. Recall the flap in 2009 over the "swine" flu outbreak and previous grossly exaggerated claims by CNN's Lou Dobbs about immigrants spreading leprosy across the country. Why are persons of Mexican ancestry so often blamed for US society's problems?

5. Should the United States consider permitting the free migration of labor between Canada, Mexico, and the United States similar to the free trade of goods, services, and capital guaranteed by the North American Free Trade Agreement? See T. Alexander Aleinikoff, "Legal Immigration Reform: Toward Rationality and Equity," in *Blueprints for an Ideal Legal Immigration Policy*, Center Paper 17, Richard D. Lamm and Alan Simpson eds. (Washington, D.C.: Center for Immigration Studies, 2001). Explain your reasoning.

■ Suggested Readings

Bender, Steven W. 2003. *Greasers and Gringos: Latinos, Law, and the American Imagination*. New York: New York University Press.

Bosniak, Linda. 2006. *The Citizen and the Alien: Dilemmas of Contemporary Membership*. Princeton, N.J.: Princeton University Press.

Gutierrez, David. 1995. *Walls and Mirrors: Mexican Americans, Mexican Immigrants, and The Politics of Ethnicity*. Berkeley: University of California Press.

Ngai, Mae. 2004. *Impossible Subjects: Illegal Aliens and the Making of Modern America*. Princeton, N.J.: Princeton University Press.

■ Notes

Epigraphs: Alexander M. Bickel, *The Morality of Consent* (New Haven, Conn.: Yale University Press, 1975), 53; Michael Savage, *The Savage Nation*, a talk radio show, April 2009.

1. Parts of the discussion of alien terminology in this chapter have been adapted from Kevin R. Johnson, "'Aliens' and US immigration laws: The Social and Legal

Construction of Nonpersons," *University of Miami Inter-American Law Review* 28, no. 2 (1996–97): 263.

2. Gerald L. Neuman, "Aliens as Outlaws: Government Services, Proposition 187, and the Structure of Equal Protection," *UCLA Law Review* 42 (1995): 1425, 1428, footnote omitted.

3. Gerald M. Rosberg, "The Protection of Aliens from Discriminatory Treatment by the National Government," *Supreme Court Review* 1977 (1977): 275, 303.

4. Immigration and Nationality Act, § 101(a)(3), 8 USC § 1101(a)(3).

5. See Michael Omi and Howard Winant, *Racial Formation in the United States: From the 1960s to the 1990s,* 2d ed. (New York: Routledge, 1994).

6. Bickel, *The Morality of Consent*, emphasis added.

7. The Court further stated that African Americans "had no rights which the white man was bound to respect." *Scott v. Sandford*, 60 US 393, 407 (1857).

8. *Hurtado v. United States*, 410 US 578, 604 (1973), Douglas, J., dissenting; emphasis added.

9. Cara Buckley, "Teenagers' Violent 'Sport' Led to Killing, Officials Say," *N.Y. Times*, Nov. 20, 2008, A26.

10. Neuman, "Aliens as Outlaws," note 2, at 1440–41.

11. *United States v. Valenzuela-Bernal*, 458 US 858, 864n5 (1982).

12. *United States v. Cortez*, 449 US 411, 418 (1981).

13. *United States v. Martinez-Fuerte*, 428 US 543, 552 (1976).

14. *Plyler v. Doe*, 457 US 202, 237 (1982), Powell, J., concurring.

15. *United States v. Ortiz*, 422 US 891, 899 (1975), Burger, C. J., concurring in judgment; emphasis added; footnote omitted.

16. *INS v. Delgado*, 466 US 210, 239 (1984), Brennan, J., dissenting in part; emphasis added.

17. *United States v. Brignoni-Ponce*, 422 US 873, 878–79 (1975).

18. *United States v. Ortiz*, 422 US 891, 900 (1985) (Burger, C.J., concurring in judgment), excerpting *United States v. Baca*, 368 F. Supp. 398, 402–08 (S.D. Cal. 1973).

19. *Immigration Reform and Control Act of 1983: Hearings on H.R. 1510 Before the Subcomm. on Immigration, Refugees, and International Law of the House Comm. of the Judiciary,* 98th Cong., 1st sess. (1983), testimony of Attorney General William French Smith, 1.

20. See US Department of Homeland Security, *US Legal Permanent Residents: 2007* (March 2008), available at www.dhs.gov/xlibrary/assets/statistics/publications/LPR_FR_2007.pdf

21. See Jeffrey S. Passel, *The Size and Characteristics of the Unauthorized Migrant Population in the US 5* (Pew Hispanic Center, Mar. 7, 2006). The number decreased to an estimated 11.1 million in March 2009. See Jeffrey Passel and D'Vera Cohn, *US Unauthorized Immigration Flows are Down Sharply Since Mid-Decade* (Pew Hispanic Center, Sept. 1, 2010), available at http://pewhispanic.org/reports/report.php?ReportID=126.

22. See Jeffrey S. Passel and D'Vera Cohn, *A Portrait of Unauthorized Immigrants in the United States 21* (Pew Hispanic Center, Apr. 14, 2009), available at http://pewhispanic.org/files/reports/107.pdf.

23. See Migration Policy Institute, *Size of the Foreign-Born Population and Foreign Born as a Percentage of the Total Population, for the United States: 1850 to 2006* (2007), available at www.migrationinformation.org/datahub/charts/final.fb.shtml.

24. Pew Hispanic Center, *Fact Sheet: Mexican Immigrants in the United States, 2008* (Apr. 15, 2009), at 1–2, available at http://pewhispanic.org/files/factsheets/47.pdf.

25. Kevin R. Johnson, "A Handicapped, Not 'Sleeping,' Giant: The Devastating Impact of the Initiative Process on Latina/o and Immigrant Communities," *California Law Review* 96 (2008): 1259, 1266, footnotes omitted.

26. *Hoffman Plastic Compounds, Inc. v. NLRB* 535 US 137 (2002).

27. Anna Gorman, "Undocumented? Unwelcome," *L.A. Times*, July 13, 2008, B1, quoting Bill Flores, retired sheriff.

28. See generally Kevin R. Johnson, *How Did You Get to Be Mexican?: A White/Brown Man's Search for Identity* (Philadelphia: Temple University Press, 1999).

29. See Kevin R. Johnson, *Opening the Floodgates: Why America Needs to Rethink Its Borders and Immigration Laws* (New York: New York University Press, 2007), 151–52.

30. Jayashri Srikantiah, "Perfect Victims and Real Survivors: The Iconic Victim in Domestic Human Trafficking Law," *Boston University Law Review* 87 (2007): 157, 188–89, emphasis added.

2

A Brief History of Mexico-US Migration Patterns

What's past is prologue.
—Shakespeare, *The Tempest*

When Mexico won her independence from Spain in 1821, her northern border included all or part of what are now the states of California, Nevada, Utah, Arizona, New Mexico, Colorado, Wyoming, Oklahoma, Kansas, and Texas. From 1836 until 1853, the United States accomplished a land grab of epic proportions. By 1853, nearly two-thirds of Mexican territory had been acquired by the United States.

This chapter briefly summarizes the history of migration between Mexico and the United States. That history properly begins with the tale of how the United States achieved its current geographic character at the expense of its neighbor to the south. Figure 2.1 depicts the northern territories of Mexico in 1821, when she became an independent state.

This chapter first examines how the United States acquired, by hook or by crook, most of Mexico's land. We will see how the Mexican territory of **Tejas**, now known as Texas, was occupied and finally taken by settlers from the United States. We then consider the project of US expansionism that sought to acquire, at first by negotiation and ultimately by conquest, the lands from California to Colorado. Finally, we examine the migration patterns from Mexico to the United States during the twentieth century, and conclude by summarizing demographic patterns depicting Mexicans residing in the north at the beginning of the twenty-first century.

Tejas

We are all familiar with newspaper headlines sounding the sensational alarm: "ILLEGAL ALIENS INVADE TEXAS!!!" In this case, however,

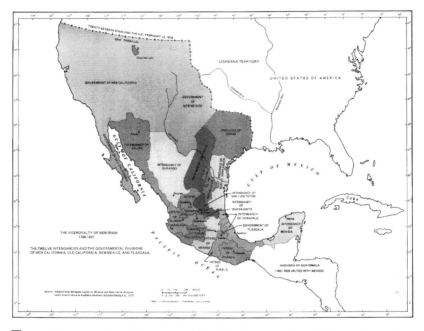

■ 2.1. The vice royalty of New Spain, 1786–1821. *Source:* Reprinted with permission from *The Atlas of Mexico* (Austin: Bureau of Business Research, 1975), p. 26. Copyright by the University of Texas Board of Regents.

the headline would have been in Spanish, Texas would have been spelled "Tejas," the year would have been 1830, and the undocumented foreign nationals would have been Anglos moving south into Texas territory belonging to the nation of Mexico.

Mexico initially adopted a lax policy of border control. Only three years after emerging as an independent nation, Mexico had passed the **Immigration Act of 1824**, permitting foreign migration into its northern territories. What followed was a concerted and sustained flow of American settlers into Mexican lands. Mexico then became alarmed by the aggressive and hostile nature of the settlers and in 1830 passed a decree curtailing immigration into the Tejas territory. Despite the new law, the flow of Anglo settlers, now consisting largely of unlawful entrants (who today might be called undocumented immigrants), continued unabated.

In 1835, the settlers in Tejas declared independence from Mexico. After several battles, including the infamous Battle of the Alamo and the decisive battle at San Jacinto, Texas won independence from Mexico and

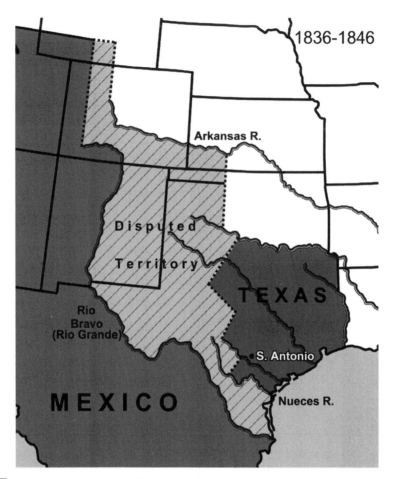

1836-1846

Arkansas R.

Disputed

Territory

TEXAS

Rio
Bravo
(Rio Grande)

S. Antonio

MEXICO

Nueces R.

2.2. Map of the Republic of Texas, 1836–1846, including land Mexico lost to Anglo settlers (Texas), disputed territory, and lands still held by Mexico. *Source:* Illustration by authors, based on maps found at en.wikipedia.org/wiki/Texas Annexation, en.wikipedia.org/wiki/Gadsden_Purchase, and en.wikipedia.org/wiki/United_States_territorial_acquisitions.

established the Lone Star Republic. Figure 2.2 displays the land Mexico lost during the Texas episode.

After the declaration of Texas's independence, a dispute continued over the location of its southern border. Mexico claimed that Texas territory was bordered by the Nueces River (north of present-day Corpus Christi), while Texas claimed its territory was bounded by the Rio Grande (known as the Rio Bravo in Mexico), about 150 miles farther south. This disputed territory would become very important to the start of the US–Mexican War in 1846 and would be resolved only by the war itself.

The Treaty Territories

After the loss of Tejas, Mexico wished to avoid further erosion of its territories. A New York newspaper plainly stated: "Let the tide of emigration flow toward California and the American population will soon be sufficiently numerous to play the Texas game."[1] Eager to preserve the remainder of its northern territories, Mexico from 1836 to 1846 undertook a program of deliberately populating the areas that now comprise California and New Mexico. To that end, the Mexican government made large *empresario* land grants, encouraging Mexicans to move to the northern territories. Consequently, many Mexicans, referred to as **Norteños**, relocated to the territories of California and Nuevo Mexico.

In 1844, James K. Polk was elected president of the United States on a platform of "Manifest Destiny," promising the westward expansion of the United States. Within a year, Texas was admitted as a state to the Union. In 1845, President Polk sent a mission, headed by John Slidell, to Mexico to bargain for the purchase of California and New Mexico, and to settle the disputed Texas boundary. The Mexican government rebuffed the Slidell mission, refusing to discuss the sale of its territory.

President Polk ordered American troops into the disputed Texas territory between the Nueces River and the Rio Grande. On April 25, 1846, there was a skirmish between the American and Mexican soldiers. President Polk famously declared, "American blood had been spilt on American soil." The US Congress quickly declared war on Mexico.

The war against Mexico was unpopular in many quarters of the United States. Many saw it as an unjust provocation, designed simply to acquire land by force from a weaker nation. Others were concerned that the newly acquired land would result in the establishment of new slave states, thus altering the delicate political balance on the United States' most controversial issue of the day: slavery.

No less a figure than Abraham Lincoln weighed in against the justness of the US war of aggression on Mexico. In 1847, Lincoln began his first (and, perhaps because of his courageous rejection of the war, his only) term representing Illinois in the US House of Representatives. The freshman member of Congress wrote what was known as the Spot Resolutions, in which he demanded that President Polk produce evidence of the exact spot on which American blood was shed. The House never considered, much less debated, the resolution.

Guadalupe Hidalgo

Gadsden Purchase

■ 2.3. Land Mexico ceded to the United States through the Treaty of Guadalupe Hidalgo (1848), and some of the lands ceded through the Gadsden Purchase (1853). *Source:* Illustration by authors, based on maps found at en.wikipedia.org/wiki/Texas Annexation, en.wikipedia.org/wiki/Gadsden_Purchase, and en.wikipedia.org/wiki/United_States_territorial_acquisitions.

Lasting from 1846 to 1848, the US–Mexican War resulted in a humiliating defeat for Mexico. To end the hostilities, Mexico and the United States negotiated the **Treaty of Guadalupe Hidalgo**, which, besides ending the war, ceded a tremendous amount of Mexican territory to the United States. Figure 2.3 shows the area of present-day United States that changed hands as a result of the treaty.

The war also settled the disputed Texas border (see figure 2.2) in favor of the United States.

In 1853, the last bit of land changed hands, as the US government initiated the **Gadsden Purchase** (see figure 2.3 for area of Gadsden Purchase in

New Mexico and Arizona) for the purposes of constructing a transcontinental railroad through the southern United States.

In summary, the US government conducted its land grab from Mexico in four parts:

1. 1836 Texas insurrection, with the land entering the United States in 1845;
2. the disputed southern border of the Texas territories, with the US–Mexican War finally settling these claims in favor of the United States in 1848;
3. the lands ceded by Mexico to the United States in 1848 by the Treaty of Guadalupe Hidalgo; and
4. the Gadsden Purchase of 1853.

From 1836 to 1853, the United States thus acquired nearly two-thirds of Mexico's entire territory. With the land came people, including the Norteños who had come north only a few years before the outbreak of war. The treaty included a provision in which Mexicans living on ceded territory could either become citizens of the United States or move south of the newly resettled border.

Treaty of Guadalupe Hidalgo (1848), Article IX
How Mexicans Remaining in Ceded Territories May
Become Citizens of the United States

Mexicans who, in the territories aforesaid, shall not preserve the character of citizens of the Mexican republic, conformably with what is stipulated in the preceding article, shall be incorporated into the Union of the United States, and be admitted at the proper time (to be judged of by the congress of the United States) to the enjoyment of all the rights of citizens of the United States, according to the principles of the constitution; and in the mean time, shall be maintained and protected in the free enjoyment of their liberty, and property, and secured in the free exercise of their religion without restriction. ■

■ Mexican Migration Patterns in the Twentieth Century

At the start of the 1900s, worsening economic conditions in Mexico caused a sharp increase in the number of Mexican migrants making the journey to the United States. In 1910, the Mexican Revolution ousted the government of Porfirio Díaz, causing another steep rise in immigration as thousands of Mexicans migrated north. The US Congress imposed immigration restrictions in 1917 and restricted immigration to only those immigrants who were able to read and write in at least one language.

During World War I, substantial labor migration from Mexico to the United States filled labor shortages. By the 1920s, approximately 10 percent of all immigration to the United States was from Mexico. Many of these immigrants settled in the Southwest, working for railroads, mines, factories, and farms. During the 1920s, the United States experienced the first large wave of Mexican immigrants drawn by the promise of political and economic opportunity but also fulfilling the nation's growing thirst for inexpensive labor. By 1924, however, the US government began to more aggressively patrol its southern border with Mexico, through the newly created Border Patrol.

During the Great Depression, immigration slowed with the end of employment opportunities combined with anti-Latina/o sentiment within the United States. Previously, Mexicans had provided relatively inexpensive labor in jobs that, according to some observers, many Americans did not want. With the severe economic downturn, however, Mexicans became viewed as a drain on the economy because, although they held less-skilled positions, they remained employed while many Americans became unemployed. In 1929, the State Department began to restrict Mexican immigration through increased enforcement measures. During this time, the enforcement of literacy requirements and public charge provisions limited migration from Mexico.

During the 1930s, state and local governments, with the assistance of the US government, "returned" to Mexico many persons of Mexican ancestry—including many US citizens as well as immigrants—as part of a "voluntary" repatriation program. However, this program proved anything but voluntary. Legal immigrants and US citizens of Mexican descent were forcibly sent to Mexico. Despite the large numbers of immigrants the United States received from many different nations, the repatriation program was limited only to persons of Mexican ancestry.

With the start of World War II, the United States once again experienced an increase in demand for labor and thus for immigrant workers. Because there were far more jobs than workers, Mexican workers were brought in to fill the United States' employment needs under a guest worker arrangement known as the **Bracero Program**. Instituted in 1942, the program could be viewed as a sort of early **nonimmigrant visa** policy. Under this program, the US government admitted temporary entry of nearly 4 million Mexican workers. The workers often accepted this contract employment at relatively low wages by US standards. Consequently, braceros became the preferred source of labor for many agricultural jobs.[2]

Although by its terms, the Bracero Program required Mexican workers to later return to Mexico, it soon became clear that the program did not work as planned. Many farms became dependent on the relatively inexpensive labor provided by Mexican workers. Laborers became accustomed to living and working in the United States, and many did not return to Mexico. Unfortunately, money withheld from the braceros' pay to facilitate their return to Mexico was "misplaced," and many braceros never received the cash.

By the 1950s, opposition had grown to both the Bracero Program and Mexican migration generally. This movement crystallized around the claims that Mexican workers depressed American wages, displaced US citizen workers, and endangered workers by accepting substandard labor conditions. From these debatable claims, **Operation Wetback** was born in 1954.[2] The Immigration and Naturalization Service (INS) raided farms in an effort to deport undocumented workers. Because farmers were concerned with a possible labor shortage, the US government doubled the number of braceros admitted annually into the United States to more than 400,000.[3] In 1954, the number of undocumented workers apprehended totaled more than 1 million for the first time in the history of the United States. The tension between popular anti-Mexican sentiment on the one hand and official importation of bracero labor on the other was unsustainable. Finally, in 1964, under continuous criticism, the US government officially ended the Bracero Program.

The end of the Bracero Program was not the end of migrant workers in the United States. Despite the prevalent use of undocumented Mexican migrant workers, growers insisted there was a shortage of farm workers. With the realization that the need for temporary workers had not disappeared, the United States began admitting workers under a new category of visa, the **H-2A visa.** Temporary visas in the H category were developed to comprise a wide variety of temporary workers, including noncitizens in specialty occupations and in occupations where US workers were in short supply, farm workers and nonagricultural workers, trainees, and families of H visa holders.

Under the H-2A visa subcategory, a noncitizen is allowed to enter the United States to work for a limited time. The program placed bureaucratic requirements on farmers, who claimed that the requirements were oner-ous, to prove that domestic workers were not available. As a result, fewer of these visas were issued than the agricultural market demanded.

Beginning in 1963, the US government imposed more stringent numeri-cal restrictions on visas. The restrictions included a cap of 120,000 on visas issued to immigrants from the Western Hemisphere, and forced Mexicans to compete with immigrants from other countries in Latin America and the Caribbean, including **refugees** from Cuba, for a scarce supply of visas. These restrictions prompted a lawsuit against the INS alleging an unfair denial of visas based on the government's decision to set aside a portion of the visas for Cuban refugees. The Mexican plaintiffs prevailed, and an additional 144,946 visas were allotted above the hemispheric limitation and reserved specifically for citizens of Mexico. The additional visas were available from 1977 to 1981.

In the 1970s, political issues surrounding Mexican immigration once again rose to the forefront with an economic recession; unemployment rose, inflation increased, and wages plummeted. In addition, the United States experienced a new surge in immigration from Mexico, along with immigration from Asia and other parts of Latin America. In 1976, Con-gress responded with amendments to the Immigration and Nationality Act (INA). Under the amendments, only US citizens who had attained the age of twenty-one would be permitted to petition for legal permanent resident status for their parents. A per-country visa limitation was then imposed on countries in the Western Hemisphere, including Mexico, and these visas were further subjected to the visa preference system (discussed in chapter 5). This Western Hemisphere restriction seemed to directly target Mexi-cans, because they were the largest group affected by the new visa limits.

By 1978, the situation for Mexican immigrants grew more dire as new immigration amendments eliminated the hemispheric limits and insti-tuted a 290,000 worldwide immigration cap. This worldwide number was later reduced to only 270,000 visas in 1980. All these legislative changes dramatically shrank the pool of available visas.

During this period of decline in legal visas, Mexico experienced declin-ing economic opportunities. Consequently, many undocumented workers crossed the border into the United States looking for jobs. And, with the stringent visa limitations in place, the 1980s and 1990s saw a steady climb in the number of undocumented Mexican migrants, while the numbers for legal Mexican immigration remained stagnant. With this increase in undocumented migration, the United States essentially operated a clandestine **guest worker program**, with the "guests" being undocumented immigrants. Although efforts were made to increase border enforcement, more often than not, these security measures did not deter illegal immigration but instead simply pushed would-be illegal Mexican migrants away from large cities and into more rugged but largely unpatrolled terrain along the border (see chapter 9). The current undocumented migration allows

> the United States [to] have its cake and eat it too. US employers continued to enjoy ready access to Mexican workers, while the American public was reassured that the border was under control. For more than two decades the system worked well to select highly motivated workers at little cost to the government, ensure their arrival at US work sites at their own expense, and then encourage their relatively prompt return, once again at their own expense.[4]

Later, under the **Immigration Reform and Control Act (IRCA)** of 1986, amnesty was granted to approximately 1 million Mexican workers.

In the years that followed, the United States experienced only nominal increases in the amount of H-2A visas granted to Mexicans. These small increases in legal visas were wildly insufficient to satisfy the demand for migrant labor. Mexican workers who could not enter the United States by lawful means found, and were encouraged to find, other ways to enter. However, despite the increases, growers insisted that visa numbers in the hundreds of thousands would be needed to replace the work performed by undocumented Mexican workers.

In 1996, the US government worked to stem the growing population of undocumented migrants through the **Illegal Immigration Reform and Immigrant Responsibility Act**. This legislation set out to increase immigration law enforcement, heighten work site investigations, allow for expedited exclusions and deportations, increase detention as a means of immigration enforcement, and ban many public benefits for undocumented migrants.

Throughout US history, anti-Mexican sentiment, the need for migrant workers, and the desire to maintain secure borders have formed a potent combination. For example, Governor Pete Wilson of California capitalized on immigration as a political issue by supporting the guest worker programs of the 1980s but later championing Proposition 187, a voter initiative in California that purported to deny almost all public benefits, including education, to undocumented migrants (see chapters 1 and 10).

Later, in response to the tragic events of September 11, 2001, several security-related changes were made to immigration admission procedures. Most applicants are now required to appear for a personal interview at a US consulate in their native country. These requirements have resulted in significant delays in the visa application process. Only a few visa categories are exempt, namely foreign government officials, representatives of international organizations, and treaty traders and investors.

In the security-conscious climate that followed September 11, 2001, visa holders have also come under increased scrutiny at ports of entry. If an applicant's home country is designated on a Department of State country watch list or if the applicant has a name similar to those found on the "terror watch list," the applicant may be subject to lengthy interrogation at the port of entry. Moreover, all sixteen- to forty-five-year-old male visa applicants must submit a form DS-157. This new form is mandatory for all males of any nationality, not just those from countries suspected of terrorist ties.

The discrimination against Mexicans brought on by this tumultuous history continues today and is evident in the very different policies applied to noncitizens from Mexico and Canada. At the nation's northern border, Canadians are allowed to enter the United States at any point along a four-thousand-mile border for business or pleasure with relatively few restrictions for up to six months. At its southern border, the US government issues restrictive border-crossing cards mandating that the noncitizen stay within twenty-five miles of the border and return to Mexico within seventy-two hours.

The border between the United States and Mexico is half the length, nearly two thousand miles, of the border between the United States and Canada. We find the Mexican border adorned with stadium lights, barbed-wire fences, steel and concrete walls, Border Patrol agents, and even the National Guard. The northern border is treated much differently. There is, for example, no **Operation Gatekeeper** along the Canadian border, yet many observers contend that plenty of undocumented workers enter from Canada.

There are also more indirect methods of racial discrimination in immigration enforcement. For example, Roberto Martínez, former director of a border watch group, points to Border Patrol raids of farms and construction sites at which the only persons questioned about their immigration status are persons of Mexican descent. As a result, undocumented workers from Europe, Canada, and Ireland frequently escape arrest during the raids. Moreover, Martínez notes that in his personal experience on trains from Mexico to Los Angeles, the only passengers who are asked for their papers by the Border Patrol are persons of Mexican descent. This, he says, is the "racist part of immigration."[5]

■ Mexicans Living North of the Rio Bravo: Migration at the Beginning of the Twenty-First Century

We began this chapter by examining maps of land flowing from Mexico to the United States. We conclude by examining demographic data that are continuous with these geographic events. Figure 2.4 shows census

Hispanic Population in the US

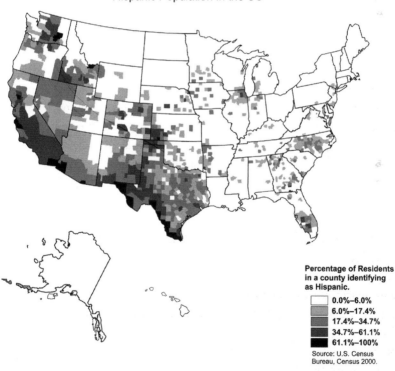

Percentage of Residents in a county identifying as Hispanic.

- 0.0%–6.0%
- 6.0%–17.4%
- 17.4%–34.7%
- 34.7%–61.1%
- 61.1%–100%

Source: U.S. Census Bureau, Census 2000.

The "Hispanic ethnicity" category on the Census includes Mexicans (7.3 percent of the total U.S. population in 2000), Puerto Ricans (1.2 percent), Cubans (0.4 percent) and a host of other Latin and South American ethnicities

■ 2.4. Hispanic population in United States by county, 2000. *Source:* From US Census Bureau, *Census 2000.* Available at www.censusscope.org/us/print_map_hispanicpop.html.

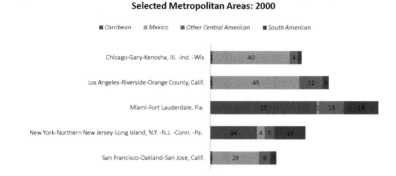

Percent of the Foreign Born Population from Latin America by Subregion for Selected Metropolitan Areas: 2000

■ Carribean ■ Mexico ■ Other Central American ■ South American

Chicago-Gary-Kenosha, Ill. -Ind. -Wis	40	4
Los Angeles-Riverside-Orange County, Calif.	45	12 3
Miami-Fort Lauderdale, Fla.	35	13 18
New York-Northern New Jersey-Long Island, N.Y. -N.J. -Conn. -Pa.	24 4 5 16	
San Francisco-Oakland-San Jose, Calif.	24 6 3	

■ 2.5. Foreign-born population from Latin America by subregion in select US metro areas, 2000. *Source:* US Census Bureau, "Coming From the Americas: A Profile of the Nation's Foreign-Born Population from Latin America (2000 Update)," PPL-145, table 5-2D, in *Census Brief: Current Population Survey*, issued January 2002, figure 2, p. 2.

2000 data representing which counties are most heavily populated by Hispanics.

Today, more than two-thirds of the Latina/o population lives in just eight states: California (24 percent), Texas (14 percent), Florida (9 percent), New York (7 percent), Arizona (5 percent), Illinois (4 percent), New Jersey (4 percent), and North Carolina (3 percent).

Figure 2.5 shows the population in certain US cities of immigrants from Latin America, including Mexico. The Pew Hispanic Center projects that if current trends continue, the US population will rise to 438 million in 2050, from 296 million in 2005, and 82 percent of the increase will be due to immigrants arriving from 2005 to 2050 and their US-born descendants.[6] Nearly one in five Americans (19 percent) will be immigrants in 2050, compared with one in eight (12 percent) in 2005. By 2025, the immigrant share of the population will surpass the peak during the great wave of immigration nearly a century ago.[7] Ultimately, the increase in the Latina/o population in the United States, driven in no small part by immigration, will likely have a political impact.

■ Concluding Thoughts

The changing geography of the past two centuries tells an important story. Unjust land transfers haunt US–Mexican relations and serve as a crucial subtext for immigration patterns.

After the borders moved south, the people moved, and still move, north. Those working in fields and yards beat out the verse with their feet and their hearts: "The land was ours before we were the land's."

■ Discussion Questions

1. Look at the three maps in this chapter that show land transfers from Mexico to the United States during the nineteenth century. Compare them with the map showing Hispanic population in 2000. Are there continuities between these geographic and demographic data?

2. Does a past history of interconnectedness between the United States and Mexico predict a future of continued migration? Is Mexican migration solely an economic phenomenon, or can a case be made that Mexican migration also has cultural and historical roots?

3. Can the United States learn from the failure of the Bracero Program to design a more just and efficient guest worker program? Can a guest worker program ever escape fatal flaws? Explain your reasoning.

■ Suggested Readings

Acuña, Rodolfo F. 2007. *Occupied America: The History of Chicanos*. 6th ed. New York: Pearson Longman.

Balderrama, Francisco E., and Raymond Rodriguez. 2006. *Decade of Betrayal: Mexican Repatriation in the 1930s*. Rev. ed. Albuquerque: University of New Mexico Press.

Calavita, Kitty. 1992. *Inside the State: The Bracero Program, Immigration, and the INS*. New York: Routledge.

Foley, Neil. 1997. *The White Scourge: Mexicans, Blacks, and Poor Whites in Texas Cotton Culture*. Berkeley: University of California Press.

García, Juan Ramon. 1980. *Operation Wetback: The Mass Deportation of Mexican Undocumented Workers in 1954*. Westport, Conn.: Greenwood Press.

Griswold del Castillo, Richard. 1990. *The Treaty of Guadalupe Hidalgo: A Legacy of Conflict*. Norman: University of Oklahoma Press.

Gutierrez, David G. 1995. *Walls and Mirrors: Mexican Americans, Mexican Immigrants, and the Politics of Ethnicity*. Berkeley: University of California Press.

Montejano, David. 1987. *Anglos and Mexicans in the Making of Texas, 1836–1986*. Austin: University of Texas Press.

Robinson, Cecil. 1989. *The View from Chapultepec: Mexican Writers on the Mexican-American War*. Tucson: University of Arizona Press.

Sanchez, George J. 1993. *Becoming Mexican-American: Ethnicity, Culture, and Identity in Chicano Los Angeles, 1900–1945*. New York: Oxford University Press.

Weber, David J. 2009. *The Spanish Frontier in North America*. New Haven, Conn.: Yale University Press.

■ Notes

1. Alfred Robinson to Thomas Larkin, New York, May 29, 1845, in *The Larkin Papers* 3, George Hammond, ed. (Berkeley: published for the Bancroft Library by the University of California Press, 1953), 205.

2. "Wetback" is a deeply pejorative (and racist) term used to describe undocumented immigrants. It literally refers to a person who crosses the border by way of the Rio Grande.

3. David M Reimers, *Other Immigrants: The Global Origins of the American People* (New York: New York University Press, 2005), 104.

4. Douglas S. Massey, Jorge Durand, and Nolan J. Malone, *Beyond Smoke and Mirrors: Mexican Immigration in an Era of Economic Integration* (New York: Russell Sage Foundation, 2002), 46.

5. Roberto Martínez, "Immigration and Human Rights on the US/Mexico Border," *Motion Magazine*, 1997, www.inmotionmagazine.com/border.html (accessed Mar. 13, 2009).

6. US Census Bureau, *2008 National Population Projections* (Washington, D.C., Aug. 2008).

7. Pew Hispanic Center, *US Population Projections: 2005–2050*, available at http://pewhispanic.org/reports/report.php?ReportID=85.

3

Federal Plenary Power
over Immigration

If . . . the government of the United States, through its legislative department, considers the presence of foreigners of a different race in this
country, who will not assimilate with us, to be dangerous to its peace and
security, ... *its determination is conclusive on the judiciary.*
—*Chae Chin Ping v. United States* (The Chinese Exclusion Case, 1889)

We understand the [Board of Immigration Appeals'] staggering workload.
But the Department of Justice cannot be permitted to defeat judicial
review by refusing to staff the Immigration Courts and the Board of
Immigration Appeals with enough judicial officers to provide reasoned
decisions.
—Judge Richard Posner, *Mekhael v. Mukasey*

The above quotes exemplify one of the more bizarre features of US
immigration law. The US government exercises extraordinary powers over regulating immigration, and the courts play an extremely
limited role in reviewing the constitutionality of that law. Such judicial
deference is hard to square with today's criticism by prominent federal
judges and commentators of the decisions of the agencies administering
the immigration laws for their poor quality, if not downright ineptitude.

In this chapter, we outline the history of the modern age of immigration regulation in the United States, specifically the comprehensive federal
regulation of immigration beginning in the late nineteenth century with a
series of laws infamously known as the Chinese exclusion laws. We then
explain the sources and contemporary state of the doctrine under which
the courts have ruled that Congress and the president enjoy *plenary power*
over immigration with little, if any, room for **judicial review**. We also provide a general overview of judicial review of immigration decisions under
the Immigration and Nationality Act (INA).

The **plenary power doctrine** as established by the Supreme Court in the Chinese Exclusion Case remains intact to this day—"good law," as a lawyer might aptly observe. The US Supreme Court has never overruled the decision, despite its being created to uphold a racist law. The doctrine currently in operation greatly restricts the rights available to noncitizens.

The plenary power doctrine was the legal underpinning for the tough border enforcement and security measures implemented as part of the "war on terror" after the tragic events of September 11, 2001. Those measures, although ostensibly directed at "terrorists" and "terrorism," ultimately had a dramatic impact on immigrants from Mexico and Central America, as well as on Arabs and Muslims who had nothing to do with terrorism. As we discussed in chapters 1 and 2, this is just the latest episode in a long history of US immigration laws and their enforcement detrimentally affecting persons of Mexican ancestry, both legal and undocumented immigrants as well as US citizens.

Change in federal plenary power over immigration to some extent is perhaps in the winds. State and local governments in recent years have increasingly attempted to intervene in the regulation of immigration and immigrants. Debate continues to be hot and heavy over the proper role, if any, of the state and local governments in immigration and related matters. Chapter 10 outlines the controversy over these roles. Despite the debate, the federal government undisputedly remains the primary source of immigration law and its enforcement in the United States.

■ US Constitutional Authority to Regulate Immigration

Today, the regulation of admission to, and removal from, the United States is primarily a function of federal law enacted by the US Congress. Administration and enforcement of the immigration laws passed by Congress is largely in the hands of the executive branch of the US government. Chapter 4 summarizes the functions of the various federal agencies that administer and enforce immigration law. Chapter 5 describes the procedure for admission of immigrants into the United States. Chapter 7 summarizes the law surrounding the removal of noncitizens from the United States.

As the US Supreme Court has interpreted the US Constitution, the federal government possesses primary—nearly exclusive—responsibility for regulating immigration into, and deportation from, the United States. Congress passes the immigration laws, and the courts ordinarily defer to the substantive immigration decisions of Congress, such as which categories of immigrants to admit to, and deport from, the country. To the extent it intervenes at all in immigration matters, the Supreme Court generally focuses on ensuring adherence to proper procedures for the admission and removal of noncitizens, such as compliance with the dictates of **Due Process Clause** of the **Fifth Amendment**, and the proper interpretation of the comprehensive federal immigration **statute**, the INA.

Oddly enough, no provision in the US Constitution unequivocally authorizes the federal government to regulate immigration and immigrants in the way that we see in modern times in the United States. Indeed, little in the Constitution directly pertains to immigration and immigrants. Immigration was apparently not a pressing concern to the framers of the US Constitution, who instead were understandably more concerned with establishing a system of government that would attract settlers to the US territories. Despite the general failure of the Constitution to address immigration, the conventional wisdom is that the federal government possesses the constitutional power to regulate it.

Scholars continue to struggle to find a constitutional provision that authorizes the general exercise of federal authority over immigration. Nonetheless, since the late nineteenth century, when Congress enacted immigration laws excluding, among others, most Chinese laborers from the United States, comprehensive federal regulation of immigration has been the norm.

Enumerated Powers

A fundamental principle of US constitutional law is that the federal government generally cannot exercise powers that are not expressly authorized by the US Constitution, which reserves most governmental powers to the states. The *enumerated powers* principle poses difficulties in attempting to find a constitutional justification for the federal government's authority to regulate immigration. Because in the late eighteenth century, immigration and migration implicated the movement of slaves, and thus the very institution of slavery, the framers were extremely reluctant to address the topic, and the US Constitution is largely silent on the subject of immigration.

The Naturalization Power

Article I, section 8, clause 4, of the US Constitution specifically grants Congress the power "[t]o establish a uniform Rule of Naturalization." Before ratification of the Constitution, states had greatly differing rules for granting citizenship. Some states granted citizenship immediately to those who landed on their shores while other states established a waiting period. To prevent the confusion that might arise from individual—and varying— state laws bestowing citizenship on foreigners, the Constitution expressly delegated the **naturalization power** to Congress. The result has been a single national set of naturalization rules that, generally speaking, have worked fairly well for the last two hundred years.

Unlike the general immigration power, Congress has exercised the naturalization power since early in this nation's history. The executive branch has primarily administered the naturalization rules established by Congress. Chapter 12 reviews the modern criteria for, and significance of, naturalization. US naturalization laws, although generous in important respects—for example, the five-year residency requirement for naturalization that has generally been the rule over the last two hundred-plus years—have not always been laudable. From 1790 to 1952, US naturalization law generally required that a person be "white" to naturalize, which denied US citizenship to many immigrants.[1]

Article I is limited to naturalization and does not expressly bestow authority on the national government over immigration generally. However, the rationale for a uniform system of naturalization of citizens would seem to apply to immigration generally. It is difficult to see how the nation as a practical matter could cope with a hodgepodge of varying state laws regulating admission to, and removal of immigrants from, the United States.

The Commerce Power

Article I, section 8, clause 3, of the US Constitution provides Congress with the power "to regulate Commerce with foreign Nations, and among the several States, and with the Indian Tribes." In the earliest immigration cases, the Supreme Court viewed the federal government's power to regulate immigration as based on the power to regulate commerce and invalidated state statutes that sought to regulate immigration through the imposition of taxes or other regulations on common carriers.

The Commerce Clause is an attractive constitutional justification for the federal power to regulate immigration. Migration and commerce, both international and domestic, are obviously linked. Immigration is often attributable to the movement of labor, which has distinct economic impacts on labor, consumer, and other markets. Moreover, the perceived economic benefits and costs of immigration are often employed to justify tighter or looser immigration laws.

Migration and Importation Clause

Article I, section 9, clause 1, of the US Constitution provides that "the Migration or Importation of such Persons as any of the States now existing shall think proper to admit, shall not be prohibited by the Congress prior to the year one thousand eight hundred and eight but a Tax or duty may be imposed on such Importation, not to exceed ten dollars for each Person." This clause has generally been interpreted as prohibiting Congress from ending the slave trade before 1808, a critical compromise in the framing of the entire Constitution.

As closely linked as it is to slavery, the Migration and Importation Clause is difficult to employ as a general constitutional justification for the federal regulation of immigration.

War Power

Under Article I, section 8, clause 11 of the US Constitution, Congress possesses the authority "to declare War." The Supreme Court has held that the War Power authorizes laws providing for the exclusion and expulsion of so-called enemy aliens, including the infamous Alien and Sedition Acts initially passed in the 1790s.[2]

There are obvious limits on the War Power as a justification for general immigration regulation by the federal government. Fortunately, it is relatively rare for war and peace to be directly implicated by the admission or removal of a specific immigrant or group of immigrants. As a practical matter, only a small number of this nation's admission and deportation decisions will ever truly implicate war or foreign relations. The War Power thus appears to be a less-than-compelling constitutional provision on which to justify the power of the national government to comprehensively regulate immigration.

As this review demonstrates, nothing in the US Constitution clearly enumerates the general federal power to regulate immigration, much less absolute authority in Congress to enact federal immigration laws. However, the naturalization, commerce, war, and related powers afforded to Congress under Article I, in combination, offer support for the enactment of federal laws regulating immigration.

■ Implied Powers in the US Constitution

The US Supreme Court has referred to several powers implied in the US Constitution in evaluating the national government's power to regulate immigration.

Foreign Affairs Power

Commentators often contend that the implied power of the executive branch over foreign affairs authorizes the federal regulation of immigration. In *Chae Chan Ping v. United States* (the Chinese Exclusion Case), the US Supreme Court in 1889 linked the power to regulate immigration with the power of the federal government to conduct foreign affairs: "The United States, in their *relation to foreign countries* and their subjects or citizens, are one nation, invested with powers which belong to independent nations. . . . For national purposes, embracing our *relations with foreign nations*, we are but one people, one nation, one power."[3]

Similar to the Constitution's treatment of the immigration power, it fails to expressly mention the foreign affairs power. The Supreme Court, however, has ruled that the US government possesses inherent sovereign powers over foreign affairs. Indeed, the federal government's exclusive power to conduct foreign affairs has led courts to invalidate *state* statutes that attempt to regulate immigration.[4] Similarly, in the 1993 decision in *Sale v. Haitian Centers Council, Inc.*, the Supreme Court upheld the US government's interdiction of Haitians fleeing political violence in their native land and emphasized, "We are construing treaty and statutory provisions that may involve *foreign and military affairs* for which the President has unique responsibility."[5]

Necessity and Structural Justifications
for Federal Regulation of Immigration

Some immigration scholars contend that because federal power over immigration is necessary to the implementation of the US Constitution, the power must by necessity be implied in the US Constitution.[6] To be a sovereign nation, they argue, the people must possess control over the national territory in order to define itself as a nation.

Although it is true that federal immigration regulation did not exist in its current form for the first century of the United States' existence, that was a different time. We have a nation today that no longer promotes the settlement of the great frontier and in which movement of people, generally speaking, is no longer as difficult and dangerous as in the past. There arguably is no real alternative except for the federal government to regulate immigration—especially in the modern world, with relatively easy travel and economic disparities creating significant migration pressures for the nation as a whole.

The Scope of the Federal Power to Regulate Immigration: The Plenary Power Doctrine

In the last decades of the nineteenth century, Congress passed a series of laws that comprehensively regulated immigration, largely in response to the migration of Chinese laborers to the United States. By the end of the century, the federal government was the firm master of immigration regulation. Despite the lack of clear authority under the US Constitution to regulate immigration, the Supreme Court has declared the scope of the federal power to do so to be broad and expansive, with the role of the judiciary in reviewing the immigration laws passed by Congress, and the implementation by the executive, exceedingly narrow.

The judicially created plenary power doctrine protects from judicial scrutiny the substantive decisions of Congress on the criteria regulating admissions of immigrants to the United States. In the Chinese Exclusion Case, the Supreme Court rejected a constitutional challenge to racial discrimination in the infamous Chinese Exclusion Act and emphasized that courts lack the power to review congressional exercise of its plenary power over immigration. Curiously, although it is quite difficult to identify a constitutional justification for the federal power to regulate immigration, the Court has implied that power and, at the same time, concluded that the authority is plenary, not subject to basic, or any, constitutional limitations.

Scholars have consistently criticized the plenary power doctrine, which allows noncitizens to be treated in ways that would be blatantly unconstitutional if they were US citizens. To date, there have been no successful challenges in the US Supreme Court to laws passed by Congress that refuse admission to classes of noncitizens or that authorize the removal of noncitizens from the United States.

Born with the emergence of the federalization of immigration, the plenary power doctrine was later aggressively invoked in Supreme Court cases decided during the Cold War with the former Soviet Union. The Court has upheld exclusions and deportations of certain races and nationalities and noncitizens with particular political views in addition to upholding indefinite detention of immigrants. In 1977, the Court unequivocally emphasized, *"Over no conceivable subject is the legislative power of Congress more complete than it is over' the admission of aliens."*[7]

After September 11, 2001, the Bush administration expressly—and aggressively—relied on the plenary power doctrine in targeting Arab and Muslim noncitizens through special rules and procedures put in place as part of a newly declared national security policy known as the "war on terror." Invoking the doctrine, the courts generally declined to intervene.

The Supreme Court has relied on the plenary power doctrine also to immunize from meaningful judicial review certain *federal* laws that discriminate against *legal immigrants* who live in the United States. For example, in finding that Congress could limit the eligibility of lawful immigrants for federal medical benefits, the Court emphasized, *"In the exercise of its broad power over naturalization and immigration, Congress regularly makes rules that would be unacceptable if applied to citizens."*[8]

In short, there is a long tradition of judicial deference continuing to this day to decisions made by Congress and the executive branch on issues of immigration and the treatment of immigrants. Ultimately, Congress and the executive branch, rather than the courts, generally have the final say on US immigration law and policy.

The courts ordinarily decline to interfere with the substantive decisions of the political branches of government. Judicial intervention in US immigration laws has ordinarily been limited to ensuring that proper procedural protections are in place in removal and other proceedings; the courts also work to ensure that the agencies in charge of immigration decisions comply with the dictates of the omnibus federal immigration law, the INA.

Constitutional Limitations on the Federal Power to Regulate Immigration and Immigrants

Consistent with limited judicial review of immigration legislation, noncitizens seeking admission into the United States have very few rights under the US Constitution. The US Supreme Court in 1982 restated the essence of the plenary power doctrine: "An alien seeking initial admission has *no* constitutional rights regarding his application, for the power to admit or exclude aliens is a sovereign prerogative."[9]

Noncitizens present in the United States, or lawful immigrants who are returning after a brief trip out of the country, have more rights than initial entrants but still not as many as US citizens.

■ Procedural Due Process

Aliens in removal (also known as deportation) proceedings have long been entitled to the protections of the Due Process Clause of the Fifth Amendment of the US Constitution: "No person shall be . . . deprived of life, liberty, or property, without due process of law." The US Supreme Court initially defined due process rights narrowly—for example, finding that a **deportation hearing** conducted in English for a Japanese noncitizen who did not understand English did not violate due process.[10]

The due process rights of noncitizens in deportation proceedings have expanded over time consistent with the general expansion of due process rights in the Supreme Court's decisions, in part because of the growing recognition of the weighty individual interests at stake in removal proceedings—family, friends, and community in the United States. Notice and an opportunity to be heard are core due process rights afforded to noncitizens facing removal.

The Lost Weekend: *Landon v. Plasencia* (1982)

Born in El Salvador, Maria Antonieta Plasencia had been admitted into the United States in March 1970 as a lawful permanent resident after marrying a native-born US citizen, Joseph Plasencia. The Plasencias established a household in downtown Los Angeles that included her four children from El Salvador; Joseph Plasencia had adopted them after marrying Maria.

On Friday, June 27, 1975, the Plasencias made the two-hour drive from Los Angeles to the border town of Tijuana, Mexico. Maria later explained that she hoped to see a dentist. At about 9:30 on Sunday night, Immigration and Naturalization Service (INS) agents arrested and detained Maria while she attempted to enter the United States by automobile with her husband and six undocumented immigrants—four young men and two women, from El Salvador and Mexico. The next morning, the INS served Maria, who did not read English, with a notice in English. The notice stated that she was charged with being inadmissible because she

(continued)

"knowingly and for gain, encouraged, induced, assisted, abetted, or aided any other alien to enter or to try to enter the United States in violation of law," and stated that an exclusion hearing in the immigration court would be held at 11:00 that same morning.

At that time, a noncitizen seeking entry into the country at the border was given an exclusion hearing; persons who faced removal from the interior of the country were placed in deportation hearings. The government bore the burden of establishing that a noncitizen should be deported from the United States; in exclusion proceedings, the noncitizen had the burden of proving admissibility. As a practical matter, it has always been much more difficult to deport a noncitizen already in the country than to exclude one stopped at the border.

The primary question for the exclusion hearing was whether Maria Plasencia had agreed to bring undocumented immigrants into the United States "for gain." Maria testified that her husband agreed to bring the Salvadorans across because he "just felt sorry for them" and "did it just for pity." The INS called three witnesses, all natives of El Salvador, who had used the minor alien identification cards of Maria's children in attempting to enter the country and claimed that they had provided small amounts of money to the Plasencias for gas.

The burden of proof greatly influenced the final outcome of Maria Plasencia's case in the immigration court. In the exclusion proceedings, Plasencia bore the burden of proof that she was entitled to enter the country and was not excludable. Maria's case for admission into the United States rested almost entirely on her and her husband's testimony.

The immigration judge ruled that Maria Plasencia did "knowingly and for gain encourage, induce, assist, abet, or aid nonresident aliens" to enter or try to enter the United States in violation of law. The Plasencias appealed. The Board of Immigration Appeals ruled that Maria Plasencia had been "accorded due process of law at every stage of the proceedings."

Plasencia next filed a petition for a writ of habeas corpus in federal district court. That court found that, in the case of a lawful permanent resident like Maria, entry and excludability could not be determined in an exclusion proceeding because it lacked the necessary procedural safeguards. The US Court of Appeals for the Ninth Circuit agreed.

On November 15, 1982, the Supreme Court, in an opinion by Justice Sandra Day O'Connor, issued its decision in *Landon v. Plasencia*. The Court reversed the Ninth Circuit's decision and held that the question whether Plasencia had entered the country could be determined in an exclusion hearing, but also that this hearing must comport with due process. The Court noted that Maria Plasencia had a "weighty" interest at stake because she "stands to lose the right 'to stay and live and work in this land of freedom'" and "may lose the right to rejoin her immediate family, a right that ranks high among the interests of the individual." It further observed that "the government's interest in efficient administration of the immigration laws at the border also is weighty."

On remand from the Supreme Court, the Ninth Circuit sent the case back to the district court. The INS appears to have never sought to remove Maria Plasencia from the country.

Source: Kevin R. Johnson, "Maria and Joseph Plasencia's Lost Weekend: The Case of *Landon v. Plasencia*," in *Immigration Stories*, David A. Martin and Peter H. Schuck, eds. (New York: Foundation Press; Eagan, Minn.: Thomson/West, 2005), 221. ■

In 1982, the Supreme Court held that a lawful permanent resident from El Salvador who had briefly left the country to travel for the weekend in Mexico was entitled to have her right to return decided in a hearing that comported with due process: "Once an alien gains admission to our country and begins to develop the ties that go with permanent residence, his constitutional status changes accordingly. Our cases have frequently suggested that a continuously present resident alien is entitled to a fair hearing when threatened with deportation."[11]

Substantive Due Process

So-called substantive due process rights are substantive rights to life and liberty guaranteed by the US Constitution, rather than simply procedural ones such as a right to a fair hearing. Noncitizens in the United

States—like, in certain respects, US citizens—enjoy limited substantive due process rights. For example, in *Reno v. Flores*, a case challenging the detention of undocumented children, the US Supreme Court rejected the substantive due process claim of unaccompanied noncitizen minors to be released to persons other than their parents, close relatives, or legal guardians. The parents, often undocumented, feared arrest and deportation if they picked up their children.[12]

In subsequent cases involving the detention of noncitizens, the Court has been inconsistent in the substantive due process rights afforded to noncitizens. In *Zadvydas v. Davis*, the Court refused to invoke the plenary power doctrine to shield from review the indefinite detention of noncitizens awaiting deportation and held that regular review for possible release was required.[13] Just two years later, however, the Court, in *Demore v. Kim*, upheld the mandatory detention of certain noncitizens pending their deportation.[14]

First Amendment

The free speech rights of immigrants in the United States under the **First Amendment** of the US Constitution ("Congress shall make no law ... abridging the freedom of speech, or of the press; or the right of the people peaceably to assemble, and to petition the Government for a redress of grievances") are somewhat uncertain. The US Supreme Court at times has emphasized that noncitizens living in this country enjoy First Amendment protections.[15] At other times, however, the Court has found that noncitizens could be deported for politically subversive speech. Importantly, "terrorist activity," a category that Congress has regularly expanded over the last twenty years, especially after the events of September 11, 2001, which can subject a noncitizen to exclusion and removal, now may include such things as monetary contributions to certain political organizations and leafleting for specific political causes.

The judicial hands-off approach to federal immigration laws may well have encouraged, and surely did not discourage, Congress to pass laws permitting the exclusion and deportation of noncitizens of certain political persuasions, including anarchists, labor leaders, and Communist Party members. In *Galvan v. Press*, the Supreme Court in 1954 upheld the deportation of Robert Galvan, an immigrant from Mexico who had entered the United States in 1918. Galvan had been a member and officer of the Spanish Speaking Club, which the US government had classified as a Communist

Party organization. The Court wrote, "Any policy toward aliens is vitally and intricately interwoven with contemporaneous policies in regard to the conduct of foreign relations, the war power, and the maintenance of a republican form of government, and *such matters are so exclusively entrusted to the political branches of government as to be largely immune from judicial inquiry or interference.*"[16]

The harshness of the ruling is apparent from Justice Hugo Black's stinging dissent:

> Petitioner has lived in this country thirty-six years, having come here from Mexico in 1918 when only seven years of age. He has an American wife to whom he has been married for twenty years, four children all born here [and thus US citizens], and a stepson who served his country as a paratrooper. Since 1940 petitioner has been a laborer at the Van Camp Sea Food Company in San Diego, California. In 1944 petitioner became a member of the Communist Party. Deciding that he no longer wanted to belong to that party, he got out sometime around 1946 or 1947.... During this period of his membership the Communist Party functioned "as a distinct and active political organization." ... Party candidates appeared on California election ballots, and no Federal law then frowned on Communist Party political activities. Now in 1954, however, petitioner is to be deported from this country solely for his lawful membership in that party.... *There is strong evidence that he was a good, law-abiding man, a steady worker and a devoted husband and father loyal to this country and its form of Government.*[17]

Until 1990, ideological exclusions remained part and parcel of US immigration laws, though Congress temporarily suspended them for a time in the late 1980s. Under those laws, the US government refused to allow many foreign nationals seeking to visit the United States, such as Hortensia Allende (widow of the former Chilean president), a member of the Palestine Liberation Organization, a high-ranking member of the Nicaraguan government under Sandinista leadership, and other notable public figures.

The **Immigration Act of 1990** modernized the exclusion grounds for membership in a totalitarian party, eliminated the exclusion for nonimmigrants, and significantly narrowed the grounds for ideological exclusion.[18] The act also restricted deportation on the grounds of a noncitizen's political views, with membership in a totalitarian party no longer a specific ground for deportation, and focused instead on the removal of noncitizens for "terrorist activities" or actions with serious foreign policy consequences.

The political views of noncitizens remain relevant, however, to a number of other immigration and nationality decisions under US law. For example, the naturalization statute long required that a noncitizen be "attached to constitutional principles," a requirement that was invoked to bar naturalization of lawful permanent residents who are conscientious objectors to military service and Jehovah's Witnesses who object to voting, participating in politics, and serving on juries. Several ideological bars to naturalization are related, including those pertaining to anarchists, Communist Party members, and those who advocate overthrow of the US government by force.

In a case involving Muslim supporters of a political group, the US Supreme Court in 1999 limited challenges in lawsuits to claims of selective enforcement of the immigration laws based on the exercise of free speech rights.[19]

Equal Protection of the Laws

The equal protection rights of noncitizens living in the United States under the Fifth and Fourteenth Amendments ("No state shall ... deny to any person within its jurisdiction the equal protection of the laws") are diluted when it comes to noncitizens. The US Supreme Court has invoked the plenary power doctrine to immunize from meaningful judicial review *federal* laws that discriminate against immigrants who live in the United States. In several cases, however, the Court has struck down *state and local* limitations on the rights of noncitizens on equal protection grounds, such as restrictions on fishing rights and the ownership of real property. The Court has also carefully reviewed state laws that discriminated against lawful immigrants. However, the Court has permitted state governments to impose citizenship requirements on state jobs that perform a "political function," such as public school teachers and police officers.

Discrimination based on status as an "alien" can have disparate impacts on particular national origin groups. This is especially the case given that the vast majority of today's immigrants are from Latin America and Asia. In *Cabell v. Chavez-Salido*, for example, the Supreme Court rejected an equal protection challenge to a California law requiring probation officers to be US citizens.[20] Based on the law, Los Angeles County refused to hire a lawful permanent resident from Mexico who had lived for more than twenty-five years in the United States.

The high-water mark of noncitizen rights under the **Equal Protection Clause** is *Plyler v. Doe*.[21] In that case, a 5–4 majority of the US Supreme

Court struck down a Texas law and held that undocumented children (who in Texas at that time were at least a majority of Mexican origin) could not constitutionally be denied access to elementary and secondary public schools. The Court found that the Texas law violated the Equal Protection Clause.

■ The "War on Terror" Measures and the Plenary Power Doctrine's Collateral Impacts

After September 11, 2001, the Bush administration instituted a "special registration" program—known as the **National Security Entry-Exit Registration System**—applicable to certain noncitizens from nations populated predominantly by Arabs and Muslims; in doing so, the administration emphasized, "The political branches of the government have plenary authority in the immigration area."[22] The courts thus refused to disturb the special registration program.

The invocation of the plenary power doctrine by the Bush administration in support of special registration is consistent with other claims by the administration that ordinary rules of law—and constitutional protections—do not govern the executive branch in the "war on terror." Immigrants from Mexico and Central America in the end were collateral damage in the various immigration measures put into place as part of that war.

Visa Processing and Monitoring

Most of the September 11 airplane hijackers apparently entered the country lawfully on student visas, which understandably provoked great public concern. The fears erupted into a national furor when the **Immigration and Naturalization Service (INS)** mailed visa renewals to two of the hijackers many months after their deaths. Efforts by the INS to improve the monitoring of temporary visitors on student and other visas became a high priority. In fiscal year 2008, Mexico was the leading nation of origin of nonimmigrants (generally speaking, temporary visitors), sending over 440,000 nonimmigrants to the United States.[23]

Tightened visa monitoring negatively affects Mexican citizens. Since September 11, Mexican students have faced difficulties in entering the United States. More generally, tighter enforcement at the border has slowed trade and migration within North America, with economic and related consequences for Canada, for the United States, and especially for Mexico.

Increased Immigration Enforcement

As part of efforts to fight terrorism after September 11, the US government pursued immigration enforcement policies adversely affecting immigrants generally, not simply Arab and Muslim noncitizens. The Justice Department, for example, announced its intention to enforce the requirement that noncitizens report changes of address within ten days of moving or be subject to deportation from the United States. The most dramatic change was the incorporation of the INS, housed in the US Department of Justice, into the new **Department of Homeland Security (DHS)**.

Until spring 2003, the INS was the primary federal agency in charge of administering and enforcing the INA. Since then, the DHS has been primarily charged with administering and enforcing the immigration laws. The jury remains out on whether the DHS is any better than the old INS at serving the needs of noncitizens and ensuring border enforcement and homeland security. Some commentators contend that the situation for noncitizens now is worse with the DHS mission of ensuring "homeland security" and fighting terrorism, with immigration enforcement dominating any other immigration objectives (such as the fair and efficient treatment of noncitizens in processing various applications). Immigration enforcement actions of agencies in the DHS, especially **Immigration and Customs Enforcement (ICE)**, are frequent subjects of criticism, a topic reviewed in chapter 9.

Citizenship Requirements

As a result of the tragedy of September 11, the nation saw new citizenship requirements for various jobs based on the untested assumption that US citizens are more likely to be loyal to the United States. The Aviation and Transportation Security Act, which placed airport security in the hands of the federal government, made US citizenship a qualification for airport security personnel.[24] Although noncitizens can be conscripted into the military, they can no longer work in airport security positions. The citizenship requirement injured many lawful immigrants who had previously held these low-wage jobs in airports across the country. Over 80 percent of the security screeners at San Francisco International Airport and an estimated 40 percent of those at Los Angeles International Airport were reportedly lawful immigrants who lost their jobs.

Immigration checks at airport businesses led to the arrests of undocumented persons at food and other airport establishments across the United States. Few were of Arab or Muslim ancestry, and many were from Mexico.

Increased Local Involvement in Immigration Enforcement

The regulation of immigration to the United States today is firmly in the hands of the federal government, although there has been increased state and local government participation in immigration enforcement in recent years. The war on terror pushed the federal government to reconsider its exclusive domain over immigration enforcement. As we discuss in chapter 10, it later showed a new willingness to delegate power to state and local law enforcement agencies to enforce the federal immigration laws.

State and local law enforcement authorities today are cooperating more with the federal government in immigration enforcement than in the past. Such enforcement has been on the rise under a provision of US immigration laws that permits the federal government to enter into agreements with state and local law enforcement agencies to enlist their assistance in enforcing the federal immigration laws.[25] Great concern has been expressed that, besides frightening immigrant communities from reporting crime and otherwise assisting law enforcement, state and local involvement in enforcement will exacerbate the existing problems with racial profiling.

State and local involvement in immigration enforcement warrants consideration because of the recurring pattern of civil rights violations of immigrants by state and local authorities. When given the opportunity, local governments have all too frequently fallen prey to the popular stereotype of all Latinas/os as suspected foreigners. For example, in an effort to rid the community of undocumented immigrants, police in a Phoenix, Arizona, suburb in 1997 violated the constitutional rights of US citizens and lawful immigrants of Mexican ancestry by stopping persons because of their skin color or use of the Spanish language. Over many decades, the Los Angeles Police Department's infamous Ramparts Division reportedly engaged in a pattern and practice of violating the rights of immigrants. One can expect additional civil rights violations when local law enforcement authorities, who are generally not well versed in immigration laws, are permitted to enforce those laws.

End of the Efforts to "Fix 96"

Before September 11, 2001, immigrant rights advocates believed it possible that Congress would ameliorate the harshest edges of the 1996 immigration reform legislation, some of the toughest immigration legislation in US history. Over several years, immigration rights activists had built broad

The Matter of Collado
Board of Immigration Appeals, Int. Dec. No. 3333 (Dec. 18, 1997)

In 1972, Jesus Collado, a seventeen-year-old, lawfully came to the United States from the Dominican Republic. He later had a consensual sexual relationship with a girlfriend who was four years younger, a minor. After his girlfriend's mother pressed criminal charges, Collado pled guilty to the equivalent of statutory rape. He served no prison time. When he pled guilty, Collado's crime did not constitute grounds for deportation from the country under the US immigration laws.

For close to twenty-five years, Collado committed no further crimes. He established a life in this country, married, raised US citizen children, and managed a restaurant. In 1997, he returned to the Dominican Republic on a two-week trip with his wife. Upon return to the United States, he was detained and placed in removal proceedings.

Reforms to the US immigration laws in 1996, which were particularly tough on "criminal aliens," made Collado deportable for his single misdemeanor offense in 1974 and subjected him to detention. After months of detention, he was ultimately able to successfully resist removal and remain with his family and community in the United States. Nonetheless, the case of Jesus Collado became the poster child for the excesses of the immigration reforms of 1996. ■

support for a series of immigration reforms to "Fix 96." All such legislative proposals died a quick death on September 11.

Until "comprehensive immigration reform" appeared on the horizon in 2006–07 (see chapter 12), immigrant advocacy groups had marshaled scarce political resources to attempt to thwart aggressive pieces of restrictionist legislative and regulatory measures that would adversely affect the immigrant community.

End of a Possible US–Mexico Migration Agreement

A far-reaching immigration reform possibility was moved to the back burner in the wake of September 11, 2001. Only days before that tragic day, the highest levels of the US and Mexican governments discussed dramatically changing the migration relationship between the two nations; both US President George W. Bush and Mexican President Vicente Fox expressed optimism about the possibility of a historic bilateral agreement addressing migration. The Mexican government supported a program that would allow for greater labor migration and the regularization of the status of many undocumented Mexican migrants in the United States, while the Bush administration hoped for, among other things, a revamped guest worker program.

After September 11, discussions between the two nations stopped in their tracks. A US–Mexico migration agreement restructuring migration between the United States and Mexico was one of the many casualties of the catastrophic events of that infamous day.

September 11 and the Comeback of Racial Profiling

Over the last few years, scholars and policy makers have critically scrutinized the use of racial profiling in criminal law enforcement, which in its most extreme form finds manifestation in police stops of African Americans, Latinas/os, and other racial minorities on account of their perceived group propensities for criminal conduct. Not long before September 11, the highest levels of the federal government publicly condemned racial profiling of African Americans by state and local government law enforcement on the nation's highways. Over time, public support appeared to coalesce around efforts to end racial profiling. Similarly, the courts, and to a certain extent the public, reexamined race-based enforcement of US immigration laws.

Unfortunately, governmental reliance on statistical probabilities at the core of racial profiling was resurrected after the September 11 attacks and found broad public support. Persons of apparent Arab ancestry and Muslim faith were questioned for possible links to terrorism, removed from airplanes, and generally subject to suspicion at every turn. Many commentators, and even some prominent academics, proclaimed that the reconsideration of racial profiling in law enforcement made perfect sense.

The federal government's profiling of Arabs and Muslims in the terrorist dragnet promoted the legitimacy of racial profiling at all levels of government. It also undermined federal efforts to pressure state and local law enforcement agencies to end the practice in criminal law enforcement.

In the end, racial profiling in the war on terrorism poses serious risks to all minority communities in the United States, not just Arab- and

Muslim-appearing people. Once government embraces the logic of race-based statistical probabilities as a law enforcement tool, the argument follows that probabilities may justify similar law enforcement techniques across the board, from terrorism to fighting crime on the streets to apprehending undocumented immigrants. As they were for many years, statistical probabilities can also be employed to justify focusing police action on African Americans, Asian Americans, and Latinas/os in cities and streets across the United States. The efforts to end racial profiling in ordinary criminal law enforcement clearly lost steam after September 11.

The federal government's multifaceted response to the horrible loss of life on September 11 has had, and will continue to have, a devastating impact on Arabs and Muslims in the United States. Although the harms to Mexican immigrants, as well as to other immigrant communities, are less visible, they also have suffered from the changes to immigration laws and enforcement.

As the largest single group of lawful and undocumented immigrants in the United States, Mexican noncitizens are particularly sensitive to immigration regulation and remain the group most affected by immigration reform. Similarly, Mexican American families who have immigrant members, who seek to bring family members to the United States from Mexico, or who are subject to racial profiling in immigration enforcement will be affected as well. Unfortunately, little attention has been paid to the impacts of the "war on terror" on persons of Mexican ancestry.

■ Deference to Administrative Agencies

We have discussed the plenary power doctrine and its limits on the power of the judiciary to review the immigration decisions of Congress and the executive branch. That doctrine is one way in which the courts generally defer to immigration laws. There is also the ordinary deference given to the decisions of administrative agencies, which are considered as having "expertise" in their subject areas, in the administration of these laws.

For the most part, administrative agencies within the executive branch of the US government administer and enforce US immigration laws, including exclusion and removal decisions and border enforcement generally. Specialized administrative courts decide most immigration matters. **Immigration courts**, part of the US **Department of Justice**, hold hearings, accept evidence, and decide removal and other immigration matters; the

Board of Immigration Appeals (BIA) is the administrative board that decides appeals of immigration court decisions.

The federal court of appeals considers appeals from the rulings of the BIA. In immigration cases, federal courts tend to defer to agency fact findings, legal conclusions, and applications of the law. Along these lines, general administrative law principles, as they emerged in the later part of the twentieth century, have called for significant deference to the legal determinations of administrative agencies.

In *INS v. Elias-Zacarias*, the Supreme Court articulated a strong form of deference to the fact finding of the BIA and held that, for a reviewing court to reverse a board fact determination, the **asylum** applicant must show that the evidence "was such that a reasonable fact finder would have to conclude that the requisite fear of persecution existed."[26] In 1996, Congress codified the Court's deferential holding into the immigration laws; subsequent legislation generally limited judicial review to *legal* questions.

An Example of Judicial Deference
to the Immigration Bureaucracy
INS v. Elias-Zacarias *(1992)*

Two masked guerillas armed with machine guns came to the home of eighteen-year-old Jairo Jonathan Elias-Zacarias in Guatemala. Because Elias-Zacarias refused to join their forces, the guerrillas promised to return. Fearing that the guerrillas would kill him, he fled the country. The immigration court and Board of Immigration Appeals denied Elias-Zacarias's claims for asylum and withholding of deportation. The US Court of Appeals for the Ninth Circuit found that Elias-Zacarias' asylum claim had merit: The guerrillas' threat constituted "persecution ... 'on account of political opinion' because the person resisting forced recruitment is expressing a political opinion hostile to the persecutors and because the persecutors' motive ... is political."

In an opinion by Justice Antonin Scalia, the Supreme Court reversed the Ninth Circuit decision. The Court emphasized that to "obtain judicial

(continued)

---

reversal of the BIA's determination, [an asylum applicant] must show that the evidence ... presented was so compelling that no reasonable fact finder could fail to find the requisite fear of persecution." Applying this narrow standard, the Court held that Elias-Zacarias failed to establish a well-founded fear of persecution on account of political opinion "with the degree of clarity necessary" to justify reversal of the board's ruling.

The Court rejected the conclusion that resistance to the guerrillas' conscription efforts constituted political persecution. According to the Court, a decision to remain neutral in the midst of hostilities might be based on "indifference, indecisiveness and risk-adverseness," rather than adherence to political belief. It was not sufficient that Elias-Zacarias feared that if he joined the guerrillas, the Guatemalan government would retaliate in the harshest ways against him and his family.

The Court further emphasized that the record lacked evidence suggesting that the guerrillas attributed any political views to Elias-Zacarias based on his refusal to join. Consequently, the "generalized 'political' motive" of the guerrillas failed to convince the Court that Elias-Zacarias established a "'well-founded fear' [of persecution on account of] political opinion."

Emphasizing that Elias-Zacarias faced "a well-founded fear that he will be harmed, if not killed, if [deported] to Guatemala," Justice John Paul Stevens dissented. ∎

The Supreme Court extended deference to certain *legal* interpretations of administrative agencies in the landmark decision of *Chevron USA v. Natural Resources Defense Council, Inc.*[27] In *Chevron*, the Court pronounced that the courts must defer to the agency's interpretation of a statute that Congress has delegated it the power to interpret. The courts often apply *Chevron*, as well as related forms of agency deference, to BIA interpretations of the INA. This is true even though, as discussed below, the BIA's decisions have been much criticized by courts and informed observers.

Deference to the legal conclusions of the agency is not automatic, however. In *INS v. Cardoza-Fonseca*, the Supreme Court rejected the BIA's interpretation of INA's provisions governing the evidentiary burden on an asylum seeker from Nicaragua in establishing a well-founded fear of persecution on account of political opinion.[28] Because the Court found that the agency's interpretation was contrary to the intent of Congress, it refused to apply *Chevron* deference and found that a more generous burden of proof applied to asylum claims than that endorsed by the BIA.

The Current Controversy over Judicial Review of Immigration Decisions

As we have seen, the courts afford considerable deference to the president and Congress on immigration matters. This may make sense if there is general confidence in the agencies making the decisions and in the political branches of government affording proper weight to the interests of noncitizens. Neither applies, however, to the administrative agencies that administer and enforce US immigration laws.

Given the longstanding problem with the inequitable administration and enforcement of immigration laws, one might think that the courts would intervene. Congress itself, however, has imposed significant limits on judicial review of immigration decisions, especially in immigration reform laws passed in 1996 and 2005. These limits—often derided as "court-stripping" provisions—have provoked considerable controversy. Congress intended the reforms, generally speaking, to eliminate perceived "excessive" delays and "frivolous" appeals, especially of disfavored groups of "aliens"—with a particular focus on "criminal aliens." As amended by Congress, the INA limits judicial review of immigration decisions in various significant ways.

A combination of recent developments has made judicial review of immigration decisions especially controversial. In 2002, Attorney General John Ashcroft reduced the number of members sitting on the BIA, the sole administrative appellate body in the immigration adjudicatory bureaucracy, from twenty-three to eleven, accelerated the review of cases, and increased the number of summary dispositions (i.e., rulings without oral argument and decided by less than a full board). In this reduction, the members of the BIA perceived as more liberal, not coincidentally, lost their jobs. Some influential commentators saw the various measures as a challenge to the independence of the BIA. The result of the so-called streamlining of the BIA has been a surge in the federal courts of appeals brought by noncitizens of BIA rulings ordering their removal from the country.

Like the old INS, the immigration courts and BIA have been the subject of sustained, often harsh, criticism. The courts have challenged the BIA for, among other things, a lack of independence and neutrality, poor quality rulings (most charitably attributed to overwork), bias against noncitizens, and simple incompetence, ineptitude, and sloppiness. Such criticism, not coincidentally, increased after the BIA changed its procedures to expedite its rulings.

Along these lines, a recent empirical study of the asylum adjudication system—the system that addresses claims of relief from removal from the United States because of past or well-founded fear of future persecution on account of political opinion, race, religion, nationality, and related grounds—revealed widely disparate results among immigration judges across the United States.[29] Such divergent decision making has been referred to as "refugee roulette." This characterization clearly fails to inspire confidence in the impartiality, fairness, and consistency of the decisions of the immigration courts. Along with the reversals in the courts, the evidence suggests a chronic problem in the quality of immigration court and BIA decisions.

In 2005, the criticism of immigration court decisions reached a crescendo when the *New York Times* ran a front page story about how immigration judges at times ordered the removal of noncitizens in mean-spirited and disrespectful ways.[30] The veracity and consistency of the critics of the immigration courts, along with the surrounding national publicity, ultimately provoked Attorney General Alberto Gonzales to instruct the immigration judges to clean up their acts.

Congressional Restrictions on Judicial Review

Over roughly the same time that criticism of administrative immigration adjudication was on the rise, Congress consistently limited judicial review of agency immigration decisions. In immigration reform legislation in 1996 and 2005, Congress dramatically restricted the authority of the courts to review the removal decisions of the immigration bureaucracy—in certain instances, purporting to eliminate all review by courts of certain deportation orders. After the 1996 reforms, litigation continued for years about what, if any, judicial review was permitted in removal cases in which Congress purported to eliminate *all* judicial review; the US government aggressively argued for limited, or no, judicial review in the cases of noncitizens convicted of certain crimes.

It might understandably strike the uninitiated reader as peculiar that Congress has consistently moved toward *less*—not *more*—judicial review at the same time that administrative immigration decision-making bodies have been subject to consistent—indeed, escalating—criticism. One could forcefully argue that careful judicial review is *most* necessary when the agency's competence, independence, and impartiality have been seriously questioned for a lengthy period.

Especially when critical decisions affecting an unpopular and disenfranchised minority are at stake, basic fairness concerns militate in favor of meaningful review by the courts of deportation orders. In such circumstances, limits on the power of courts to review administrative decisions adverse to noncitizens can only make matters worse for noncitizens, as well as for the perceived legitimacy of the agency's actions.

■ Constitutional Scope and Limits on Judicial Review of Immigration Decisions

The Supreme Court has interpreted the US Constitution as affording different degrees of judicial review for various types of immigration decisions. At one time, there were two types of proceedings. As traditionally known, **exclusion hearings** decided the claims of noncitizens seeking admission into the United States. **Deportation hearings** adjudicated efforts of the US government to remove noncitizens from the United States. Congress and the Supreme Court historically allocated different rights and protections to noncitizens in these hearings. Both groups of noncitizens possessed different bundles of constitutional rights, with few protections guaranteed to persons seeking initial admission into the United States.

Today, the INA refers to both types of hearings as **removal hearings**. Importantly, despite the lack of constitutional guarantees, immigrants excluded from the United States are generally afforded hearings to establish whether they are admissible. Immigrants in removal proceedings, including some seeking admission to the United States, generally have a right to a hearing that comports with the Due Process Clause.

Review of the Right to Enter

The Supreme Court's 1982 decision in *Landon v. Plasencia* is the most significant recent development in the due process rights of lawful permanent residents. The Court held that a lawful permanent resident denied entry after briefly leaving the country must have her right to return decided in a hearing consistent with the Due Process Clause. Congress in 1996 amended the INA so that returning lawful permanent residents seeking to enter the country would not generally be subject to the same procedures and **inadmissibility grounds** as first-time entrants.

Removal

"Aliens" physically present in the United States are entitled to a hearing that complies with due process—reasonable notice of the proceedings and an opportunity to be heard—before they can be deported. For that reason, deportation hearings are held before the removal of a noncitizen from the country.

Given the weighty interests at stake for the noncitizen, including living with family, friends, and community, removal hearings must comply with due process. The Supreme Court has repeatedly emphasized that the general rule is that the US Constitution requires *some* type of judicial review of a removal, or deportation, order by the immigration court and BIA.

■ The Immigration and Nationality Act Provisions on Judicial Review

The Immigration and Nationality Act provides for judicial review of removal orders by the BIA as well as various other immigration decisions. However, the precise nature of that review has changed over time. Today, BIA rulings are generally reviewable in the US Court of Appeals, not the US district courts (the trial courts of the federal system).

■ Limits on Judicial Review

Although removal decisions are ordinarily subject to judicial review, other immigration decisions are not. Importantly, denials by US State Department consular officers at US embassies in countries around the world of applications for immigrant visas are generally immune from judicial review. The rule of *consular absolutism* provides that a consular officer's decision to deny a visa necessary for entry into the United States is not reviewable by *any* court, and that any review is limited to appeals within the State Department. This rule can have onerous impacts on persons seeking entry under a visa that they claim to be entitled to but who are found by the consular officer to be inadmissible and thus refused a visa.

Another important limit of judicial review on immigration decisions involves removal of noncitizens convicted of certain crimes. Reflecting the fact that there are few defenders of "criminal aliens" in the political process, Congress has consistently imposed restrictions in the immigration laws on the judicial review of removal orders of this category of immigrants.

In addition, one of the most important limits on judicial review concerns the exercise of discretion by immigration officials. Many forms of relief from removal are at the discretion of the immigration court. Congress has provided that courts cannot review the discretionary elements of those decisions.

Decisions of **expedited removal** at ports of entry, added by 1996 reform legislation, are not subject to judicial review. Expedited removal generally applies to arriving noncitizens whom immigration inspectors believe to be inadmissible on documentary or fraud grounds and who are denied entry into the United States.

◼ Concluding Thoughts

Congress and the executive branch of the US government have extraordinary—denominated *plenary*—power over immigration. The courts have limited power to review the immigration decisions of the other two branches of government. Noncitizens possess certain rights, but the scope of those rights are more limited than those of US citizens. Immigrants facing removal from the United States have full due process protections and more rights than initial entrants into the United States. When all is said and done, the role of the courts is generally limited to protecting procedural rights of the noncitizen and ensuring compliance with the Immigration and Nationality Act.

◼ Discussion Questions

1. Why, unlike the treatment of other minority groups, don't immigrants generally receive constitutional protection from the courts in the United States?

Is it because of the workload of the courts, an insensitivity to the rights of immigrants, the complexities of US immigration laws, a combination of the above, or something else? Should the US courts meaningfully review the immigration decisions of Congress and the executive branch just as they review the constitutionality of other laws and their enforcement? Given the US courts' hands-off approach to the immigration laws and immigrants, can it fairly be said that the rule of law even applies to immigrants? Articulate the most persuasive justification for the courts' lack of meaningful review of immigration decisions of Congress and the executive branch.

2. Informed observers in recent years, including the US attorney general and respected court of appeals judges, have criticized the quality of the immigration court and BIA rulings. Since at least 1996, Congress has substantially restricted the jurisdiction of the federal courts to review the decisions of the immigration bureaucracy. In light of the many concerns expressed about the decision making of the immigration courts, why is Congress limiting, not expanding, judicial review of immigration decisions? Do the court-stripping provisions make any sense? Is more review of immigration decisions necessary and proper under the circumstances?

3. Given that the courts do not ensure constitutional protections to immigrants, and that noncitizens cannot vote to protect themselves in the political process, is it at all surprising that immigrants are regularly blamed for US society's problems, are often punished in the political process, and frequently encounter onerous and punitive immigration laws that are aggressively enforced?

4. What can immigrants and their allies in the United States do to protect themselves from the persistent attacks on the rights and remedies of noncitizens in the political process? Is political organization and activism of noncitizens and their supporters the answer?

5. Does nearly exclusive federal power over immigration make sense? Why not allow state and local governments to play some role in the regulation of immigration and immigrants? Explain your position.

■ Suggested Readings

Aleinikoff, T. Alexander. 2002. *Semblances of Sovereignty: The Constitution, the State, and American Citizenship*. Cambridge, Mass.: Harvard University Press.

Chin, Gabriel J. 1998. "Segregation's Last Stronghold: Race Discrimination and the Constitutional Law of Immigration," *UCLA Law Review* 46: 1.

Haney-López, Ian. 2006. *White by Law: The Legal Construction of Race*. 10th anniversary ed. New York: New York University Press.

Johnson, Kevin R. 2003. "September 11 and Mexican Immigrants: Collateral Damage Comes Home," *DePaul Law Review* 52: 849.

López, Gerald P. 1981. "Undocumented Mexican Migration: In Search of a Just Immigration Law and Policy," *UCLA Law Review* 28: 615.

Neuman, Gerald L. 1996. *Strangers to the Constitution—Immigrants, Borders, and Fundamental Law*. Princeton, N.J.: Princeton University Press.

■ Notes

Epigraphs: *Chae Chin Ping v. United States* (the Chinese Exclusion Case), 130 US 581, 606 (1889), emphasis added; Judge Richard Posner, *Mekhael v. Mukasey*, 509 F.3d 326, 328 (7th Cir. 2007).

1. See, for example, *Ozawa v. United States*, 260 US 178 (1922), holding that an immigrant from Japan was not "white" and thus was ineligible for naturalization; *United States v. Thind*, 261 US 204 (1923), same with respect to immigrant from India.

2. *Ludecke v. Watkins*, 335 US 160 (1948).

3. *Chae Chan Ping v. United States*, 130 US 581, 604, 606, 609 (1889), emphasis added.

4. See, for example, *Chy Lung v. Freeman*, 92 US 275, 280 (1875).

5. *Sale v. Haitian Centers Council, Inc.*, 509 US 155, 188 (1993), emphasis added.

6. See T. Alexander Aleinikoff, David A. Martin, Hiroshi Motomura, and Maryellen Fullerton, *Immigration and Citizenship: Process and Policy*, 6th ed. (St. Paul, Minn.: West Group, 2008), 207–10.

7. *Fiallo v. Bell*, 430 US 787, 792 (1977), citation omitted; emphasis added.

8. *Mathews v. Diaz*, 426 US 67, 79–80 (1976), footnotes omitted; emphasis added.

9. *Landon v. Plasencia*, 459 US 21, 32 (1982), citations omitted; emphasis added.

10. *The Japanese Immigrant Case,* 189 US 86, 100–02 (1903).

11. *Landon v. Plasencia,* 459 US 21, 32 (1982).

12. *Reno v. Flores*, 507 US 292 (1993).

13. *Zadvydas v. Davis*, 533 US 678 (2001).

14. *Demore v. Kim*, 538 US 510 (2003).

15. See, for example, *Bridges v. Wixon*, 326 US 135 (1945).

16. *Galvan v. Press*, 347 US 522, 531 (1954), emphasis added. Neither the Supreme Court's decision nor the record is clear on the precise nature of the Spanish Speaking Club.

17. Ibid., 347 US 522, 532–33, Black, J., dissenting; citation omitted; emphasis added.

18. Pub. L. 101–649, 104 Stat. 4978 (1990).

19. *Reno v. American-Arab Anti-discrimination Committee*, 525 US 471 (1999).

20. *Cabell v. Chavez-Salido,* 454 US 432 (1982).

21. *Plyler v. Doe*, 457 US 202 (1982).

22. Registration and Monitoring of Certain Nonimmigrants, 67 *Fed. Reg.* 52584, 52585 (Aug. 12, 2002), citations omitted.

23. See US Department of Homeland Security, *Nonimmigrant Admissions to the United States: 2008*, (Apr. 2009) table 3, at 5, available at www.dhs.gov/xlibrary/assets/statistics/publications/ois_ni_fr_2008.pdf.

24. Pub. L. No. 107–71, § 111(a)(2), 115 Stat. 597, 617 (2001).

25. INA § 287(g), 8 USC § 1357(g).

26. *INS v. Elias-Zacarias*, 502 US 478, 481 (1992), citation omitted; footnote omitted.

27. *Chevron USA v. Natural Resources Defense Council, Inc.*, 467 US 837, 865–66 (1984).

28. *INS v. Cardoza-Fonseca*, 480 US 421 (1987).

29. See Jaya Ramji-Nogales, Andrew I. Schoenholtz, and Philip G. Schrag, "Refugee Roulette: Disparities in Asylum Adjudication," *Stanford Law Review* 60 (2007): 295.

30. See Adam Liptak, "Courts Criticize Judges' Handling of Asylum Cases," *New York Times*, Dec. 26, 2005, A1.

4

The Administration and Enforcement of US Immigration Laws

It is one of the Maxims of the Civil Law, that definitions are hazardous.
—Samuel Johnson, 1751

We begin by examining administrative agencies as a general matter, before turning to immigration in particular. Next, we look at how the immigration agencies were substantially reorganized after the events of September 11, 2001. Then we explain the various immigration administrative agencies as they exist today and study their roles. Finally, we examine the very limited role the federal court system plays in the day-to-day regulation of immigration.

The US Congress regulates immigration primarily through a law passed by Congress known as the Immigration and Nationality Act (INA). The everyday implementation of that regulation is an incredibly complex job.

We have seen in chapter 3 how the federal government assumed primary responsibility for regulating immigration in the United States. In this chapter, we examine how the federal government administers and enforces the power to regulate immigration.

Administrative Agencies

Congress generally delegates the power to implement legislation to an administrative agency in the executive branch. Examples of such delegation include the fields of environmental protection, antitrust enforcement, and securities regulation. Immigration is another important area in which Congress has delegated regulatory power to administrative agencies.

An *administrative agency* is a legal creature housed in the executive branch of the federal government. The president and vice president of the United States, the president's appointees, such as the secretary of state and the attorney general, and their appointees, along with many federal employees who are not appointed by politicians, run the administrative agencies. Except for the president and vice president, leading officials in the executive branch are not elected by popular vote, but are instead appointed by the president. The president nominates each department secretary for confirmation by the US Senate and annually submits a budget for each department to Congress—as part of the system of "checks and balances" between government branches. Although many appointed officials in executive departments change with the political climate, general agency staff often provide years of dedicated public service and develop expertise in their fields.

Immigration is an area of US government in which no single administrative agency is responsible for all aspects of carrying out the law. People crossing at the US–Mexico border interact with staff from **Customs and Border Protection**, while a person submitting an application for permanent residence will work with **Citizenship and Immigration Services**. Persons facing removal are processed by Immigration and Customs Enforcement. All these bureaus are part of the Department of Homeland Security. Government offices responsible for immigration also include the Departments of State, Justice, and Labor. The work of all these departments is coordinated by the president as a function of the executive branch of government.

Reorganizing the Immigration Agencies after September 11, 2001

For many years, the most important administrative agency charged with implementing immigration regulations was the Immigration and Naturalization Service, known as the INS. The INS was part of the Department of Justice.

The events of September 11, 2001, resulted in a substantial reorganization of the administrative apparatus handling immigration. The **Homeland Security Act of 2002** created a new Department of Homeland Security (DHS), formally abolished the INS, and distributed most of the responsibilities of the old INS to the DHS.[1] Despite its abolition, one often hears reference to the INS (now sometimes referred to as the "legacy INS") as the agency responsible for Border Patrol and immigration.

The DHS also became the home of other agencies concerned with national security, including the US Customs Service (formerly housed in the Treasury Department), the Transportation Security Administration (from the Department of Transportation), the Coast Guard, and many others.[2]

Although the DHS is now entrusted with most immigration matters, we should remember that this department has a much broader purpose

Offices within the Department of Homeland Security

Directorate for National Protection and Programs
Directorate for Science and Technology
Directorate for Management
Office of Policy
Office of Health Affairs
Office of Intelligence and Analysis
Office of Operation Coordination
Federal Law Enforcement Training Center
Domestic Nuclear Detection Office
Transportation Security Administration
United States Customs and Border Protection*
United States Citizenship and Immigration Services*
United States Immigration and Customs Enforcement*
United States Coast Guard
Federal Emergency Management Agency
United States Secret Service

* indicates former INS ■

overall. As shown in the sidebar, the Department of Homeland Security is broadly responsible for matters of national security and effective national response to natural disasters, such as hurricanes and earthquakes.

Immigration Agencies Today

Are immigrants an opportunity and a potential boon for the United States? Or do immigrants pose a threat to American society? Should our immigration agencies provide a welcome mat, helping to integrate immigrants into the US economy and society? Or should our immigration agencies be a wall, keeping out those of whom we are suspicious? The tension between "immigrants as opportunity" and "immigrants as threat" is a theme that animates much of US immigration law and policy. The conflict between these two positions is on display in the makeup of the modern

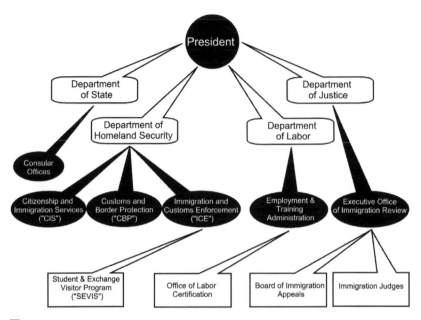

■ 4.1. Departments, agencies, and positions responsible for regulating immigration. Illustration by authors.

administrative state. Figure 4.1 shows the major administrative players in the regulation of immigration.

THE DEPARTMENT OF HOMELAND SECURITY. The DHS has the primary role in administering immigration regulation. We will focus on three main bureaus within the DHS: Citizenship and Immigration Services (CIS), Customs and Border Protection (CBP), and Immigration and Customs Enforcement (ICE). Following the analysis of "immigrant as opportunity" versus "immigrant as threat," CIS is charged to treat the immigrant as a potential boon, while both ICE and CBP regard the immigrant as a potential hazard.

CITIZENSHIP AND IMMIGRATION SERVICES. The primary function of CIS is to approve applications for lawful permanent residency and citizenship. As we discuss in chapter 5, this process involves separate tracks for family-based and employment-based applications. In family admissions, for example, CIS is the agency that interviews spouses who are applying for lawful permanent residence based on marriage to a US citizen. CIS also oversees the *adjustment of status* of noncitizens whose situations have changed after coming to the United States. For example, a foreign national may be admitted on a student visa but then take a job and adjust her status to an employment visa.

CIS also handles intercountry adoptions; reviews applications from asylum seekers and refugees through its Refugee, Asylum, and International Operations Directorate; operates a program to assist family historians in finding genealogy information; and issues temporary visas for foreign visitors, workers, and students. CIS operates an internal review mechanism for rejected lawful permanent resident (LPR) and citizenship applications. An ombudsman's office that responds to complaints about CIS programs reports directly to the secretary of homeland security. Finally, CIS administers a process through which individuals who are in the process of being removed (a function of the Department of Justice) can petition for citizen or LPR status in order to be granted a stay of this process, or *relief from removal.* All of these functions contribute to the welcome mat character of the CIS.

But the CIS also participates in the wall intended to keep out potentially dangerous foreign nationals. CIS works with the Federal Bureau of Investigation, the **Department of State**, and the **Social Security Administration (SSA)** on security screens in immigration applications. These screens may include fingerprinting, background checks, and name checks for some applicants. The purpose of these checks is to ensure that the applicant is not misrepresenting his or her identity for purposes of work eligibility or has not been previously identified as a security threat.

Electronic technology is deployed in many parts of the application process, reducing some of the delays for which the CIS and other legacy-INS processes are infamous. For example, in 2007 more than 150,000 security name checks had been pending for more than six months. A cooperative venture between the CIS and the FBI has reduced most of that backlog, and the FBI projects that in the near future, 98 percent of name check requests will be completed within thirty days and the rest within ninety days.[3] Similarly, the CIS now uses an electronic database of passport information from the Department of State to help confirm work eligibility for foreign applicants.

CUSTOMS AND BORDER PROTECTION. US Customs and Border Protection (CBP) has one of the most visible presences within the Department of Homeland Security, very much representing a wall preventing individuals from entering the US. CBP is the home of the Border Patrol, a large law enforcement agency that patrols the nation's land and water boundaries at and between more than three hundred ports of entry and along thousands of miles of border. In recent years, hundreds of miles of barriers and other fencing have been erected along the US–Mexico border. Members of the Border Patrol monitor the territories in between formal ports of entry, looking for migrants who have entered the country without documents.

CBP agents at ports of entry focus on potential criminal activity. They inspect cargo shipments for evidence of smuggled goods and narcotics and screen incoming individuals against lists of outstanding arrest warrants.

Basic Facts on Daily CBP Activity

- 1.1 million passengers and pedestrians processed
- 3,000 visitors ruled inadmissible
- 70,451 truck, rail, and sea containers inspected
- 256,897 incoming international air passengers processed
- 43,188 passengers/crew arriving by ship inspected
- 331,347 incoming privately owned vehicles inspected
- 73 criminal arrests
- 2,796 apprehensions at and in between the ports of entry for illegal entry
- 7,621 pounds of narcotics seized
- $295,829 in undeclared or illicit currency seized
- 4,125 prohibited meat, plant materials, and animal products, including 435 agricultural pests, at ports of entry seized
- 3 illegal crossers in distress or dangerous conditions rescued between ports of entry
- 1,275 canine enforcement teams deployed
- 18,276 vehicles, 275 aircraft, 181 watercraft, and 252 equestrian patrols deployed

Source: US Customs and Border Protection website, www.cbp.gov ■

In 2008, CBP reported admitting more than 1.1 million international travelers on a typical day in 2008 while refusing entry to less than 1 percent of all travelers who sought entry.

IMMIGRATION AND CUSTOMS ENFORCEMENT. ICE, an investigative branch of DHS, is designed to identify criminal activity and national security breaches by noncitizens. ICE has authority to monitor noncitizens once they enter the United States and may detain and initiate removal (deportation) proceedings against individuals who have entered the country without proper documents, who have failed to comply with the terms of their visa, or who break other US laws. It operates programs targeted at organized crime, drug smuggling, and human trafficking. ICE has the authority to monitor workplaces that might unlawfully employ noncitizens.

ICE's **Office of Detention and Removal Operations (DRO)** operates fifteen detention facilities called service processing centers (SPCs) in the United States and Puerto Rico and may also detain noncitizens in custody in state or local jails. DRO enforces administrative orders for the removal of noncitizens by managing the transportation of the foreign national and dealing with the foreign country that will receive the deported person.

ICE also manages the Student and Exchange Visitor Information System (SEVIS), an electronic database of information on the location and activities of more than 5 million foreign students, exchange visitors, and their dependents residing in the United States. ICE also authorizes schools to accept foreign students and visitors.

An interesting question is whether SEVIS, a prominent interface between foreign students and US immigration regulation, should be run by an agency whose official function is to be suspicious of immigrants. Some observers argue that foreign students provide a great boon to US research and economic development and that treating these students to the "wall" rather than the "welcome mat" may actually hurt US interests.

DEPARTMENT OF STATE. In addition to DHS, other cabinet-level agencies have significant roles in regulating and enforcing US immigration laws. The Department of State provides diplomatic services between the United States and foreign countries and is the source of nonimmigrant and immigrant visas for individuals wishing to enter the US for family, business, or travel reasons. A foreign national seeking a US visa will approach the US consulate's office (often attached to the US embassy) in the sending country. Consular officers have tremendous discretion in refusing visa applications. A remarkable feature of the system is the doctrine of *consular unreviewability,* which bars judicial review of visa application denials. The Department of State also issues annual reports on human rights in every country in the world. These reports often play important roles in adjudicating claims of noncitizens for relief from removal because they fear persecution on account of political opinion, race, religion, nationality, and related grounds in their native country.

A visa technically gives the holder permission only to travel to the US border and does not guarantee that the CBP inspector will grant admission. It is therefore possible for a foreign national to receive a visa from a State Department representative in the sending country, travel to the United States, and then be refused entry by the CBP.

DEPARTMENT OF LABOR. The **Department of Labor (DOL)** serves the dual purposes of protecting the interests of US workers and supplementing the national workforce with foreign labor as needed. The primary role of the DOL is to receive, and potentially monitor, attestations from US employers that they sought US citizens and nationals to fill job openings before ultimately offering positions to foreign nationals. This labor certification is necessary to secure a number of employment visas. The DOL also regulates the wages, housing, and transportation of the small number of temporary agricultural laborers who are in the United States on a **nonimmigrant visa** called the H-2A.

SOCIAL SECURITY ADMINISTRATION. The Social Security Administration (SSA) is an independent federal agency within the executive branch that is not part of any cabinet-level department. It provides financial benefits to elderly and disabled US residents meeting certain criteria. The SSA plays a collaborative role with the DOL, sharing information that helps verify work authorizations for immigrants and keeping track of immigrants' work status once they are employed. The SSA data are used to "match" a worker with a given Social Security number, thus allowing the government to discern whether a person is legally authorized to work. Unfortunately, the SSA database is notoriously inaccurate and has thus provided a fairly unreliable basis for ferreting out undocumented persons in the workforce.

DEPARTMENT OF HEALTH AND HUMAN SERVICES.   All applicants for permanent residency and some nonimmigrant visa applicants are required to be screened for serious medical conditions and contagious diseases. Standards for the medical exams are set by the Centers for Disease Control, Division of Global Migration and Quarantine, within the **Department of Health and Human Services (HHS)**. Actual exams are the responsibility of the Department of State (outside the United States) and Department of Homeland Security's CIS (within the United States).

A free-standing corps of trained health professionals serves the HHS's Public Health Service. Although working directly for HHS, they provide medical care on commission to non-HHS agencies in government in a variety of programs. The Division of Immigration Health Services within ICE (Department of Homeland Security) is one of these, providing medical care to individuals in ICE custody. Health services for refugees and children being resettled in the United States is managed by HHS directly within the Office of Refugee Resettlement, as part of HHS's Administration for Children and Families.

DEPARTMENT OF JUSTICE.   The Department of Justice (DOJ) serves as the federal government's law office. Under the direction of the attorney general, it has the primary responsibility of enforcing federal laws, including immigration laws.

Before the reorganization that took place in 2002, the DOJ was entrusted with the enforcement and administration of most US immigration laws. After 2002, the DOJ continued to exercise the adjudicative functions of immigration administration. The **Executive Office for Immigration Review (EOIR)**, located in the DOJ, is the administrative home of the immigration courts, scattered across the country. These courts conduct hearings and review ICE removal recommendations. Reviews of immigration court orders may be performed by the Board of Immigration Appeals (BIA), which is located on the outskirts of Washington, D.C. The EOIR also conducts administrative reviews of employer sanctions and document fraud cases.

The DOJ also contains one of the most well-known agencies of the federal government, the Federal Bureau of Investigation (FBI). The FBI gathers counter-terrorism and criminal intelligence that it shares with federal, state, local, and international law enforcement agencies. In its Criminal

Justice Information Services Division, the FBI maintains the Integrated Automated Fingerprint Identification System, the largest fingerprint and criminal history database in the world. It also identifies individuals known or suspected to be terrorists in the Terrorist Screening Database, a consolidated information tool created within its National Security Branch. Both databases are shared with the administrative agencies responsible for border security and application review. The FBI also investigates and assists ICE with the prosecution of immigration fraud and other violations of US immigration laws, as in the example in the sidebar.

DOJ Press Release

February 28, 2008

Sharon Man Convicted of Immigration Fraud

BOSTON, MA—A Sharon man was convicted today in federal court of fraud and misuse of documents required by the immigration laws, making false statements in a matter relating to the registry of aliens, and making false statements to Immigration and Customs Enforcement and Citizenship and Immigration Services ("Immigration Officials").

At today's plea hearing [at which the Defendant pled guilty], the prosecutor told the Court that had the case proceeded to trial the Government's evidence would have proven essentially the following:

MASOOD lied repeatedly, both orally and in writing, to Immigration and Customs Enforcement and Citizenship and Immigration Services ("Immigration Officials") concerning facts material to his eligibility to become a Lawful Permanent Resident ("LPR") of the United States, (commonly referred to as the holder of a "green card"), for which he had applied. In an application for LPR status submitted to the Immigration Service on or about December 18, 2002, in a document submitted in support thereof on January 31, 2005, and in interviews conducted under oath by immigration officials in matters relating to the registry of aliens on November 15, 2006, and February 13, 2003, MASOOD asserted that he had left the United States and returned to Pakistan during the two-year period from 1991 through 1993, as required as a condition of his Exchange Visitor visa. Moreover, he repeatedly asserted that, during that period of time, he had served as an Imam at a mosque in Faisalabad, Pakistan. MASOOD also lied about a prior arrest, which was material to the Immigration Service.

The defendant, MASOOD, came to this country as an economics student in 1987 pursuant to a J-1 visa. A J-1 visa is an Exchange Visitor visa, pursuant to a program which offers an opportunity to aliens who reside abroad to come to the United States to serve important interests for both countries. Because the purpose of this program is to benefit the home country and because the funding for the visitor is in part from the government, there are restrictions on a J-1 visitor from obtaining future US immigration benefits. Particularly, to ensure that meaningful exchange occurs, the Exchange Visitor program has a two-year home country physical presence requirement, which means that a J-1 visa-holder must return to his home country for two years before he is eligible to apply for future immigration benefits. In other words, an alien cannot become a legal permanent resident unless he complies with this requirement or gets a waiver.

The evidence demonstrates that MASOOD left his economics program at Boston University in 1991 without a degree, when his J-1 visa expired. However, instead of returning to Pakistan as he was required to do under the Exchange Visitor program, MASOOD continued to stay in this country illegally. In 1998, while an undocumented alien, MASOOD became the Imam of a mosque in Sharon. On the basis of that employment, in December 2002, he applied for legal permanent residency, and commenced the series of false statements which are charged in the indictment.

The evidence shows that the defendant lied repeatedly over several years about his compliance with the J-1 visa requirement, and in order to cover-up those lies, told fictional stories about what he did in Pakistan during the two years he was supposed to return to Pakistan. He also told fictional stories with shifting details about how he re-entered the United

(continued)

States. The evidence indicates that the defendant never left the United States after 1990 and that he lived, worked, had children and even received traffic tickets in the Boston area during the time that he claimed to have gone back to Pakistan. The evidence also shows that MASOOD lied about a number of additional facts for purposes of obtaining benefits in the United States such as for housing, public assistance, and a driver's license.

Judge Woodlock scheduled sentencing for May 22, 2008. MASOOD faces up to 10 years' imprisonment for each of the counts charging fraud and misuse of documents required by the immigration laws, and 5 years' imprisonment for the charges of false statements and false statements in a matter relating to the registry of aliens, to be followed by 3 years of supervised release, up to a $250,000 fine and a mandatory special assessment of $100 on each charge.

Source: DOJ press release at http://boston.fbi.gov/dojpressrel/pressrel08/immi grationfraud022808.htm. ■

Other major agencies within the DOJ responsible for aspects of immigration law include the Office of Special Counsel for Immigration-Related Unfair Employment Practices and the Trafficking in Persons and Worker Exploitation Task Force, both housed in the Civil Rights Division and responsible for prosecuting, on behalf of immigrants, violators of criminal and antidiscrimination laws, as well as the Office of Immigration Litigation, in the DOJ's Civil Division, which is responsible for the nationwide coordination of immigration matters before the federal district courts and courts of appeals.

■ Federal Court Review of Immigration Action

Access to the federal courts for review of administrative action is an important part of the US legal system. Unfortunately, judicial review of agency immigration decisions remains narrow.

Rulings of the BIA involving removal are regularly heard by the US federal courts of appeal. Appeals of their decisions may be taken by the US Supreme Court. Other decisions by immigration administrators rarely, if ever, see the light of a federal courthouse (see chapter 3). The INA (in various provisions colloquially described as "court-stripping" provisions) expressly limits judicial review of many immigration matters. For example, courts may not review certain criminal deportation decisions or decisions expressly authorized at the discretion of the attorney general. Thus, individuals do not have the right to challenge the decisions made daily by immigration officials, such as the denial of a visa application.

Even if court review were not expressly prohibited by statute, two other judicial doctrines award great deference to the administrative determination of immigration matters: the plenary power doctrine and the *Chevron* doctrine, which directs courts to generally follow agency interpretation of statutory language, thus creating a presumption in favor of the immigration agencies' interpretation of statutes.[4]

■ Concluding Thoughts

The day-to-day operation of immigration regulation is entrusted to several administrative agencies. These various agencies share power and responsibility for different parts of the immigration process.

A central question throughout the administration of immigration law is: Do immigrants cause problems or solve problems? Riven by this tension, the immigration administrative system exhibits a Jekyll-and-Hyde personality. The administrative system is split between acting as a wall to keep out troublemakers and drains on national resources and acting as a welcome mat to attract and develop new national resources.

■ Discussion Questions

1. Should the United States institute country-specific legal rules to better regulate the immigration from high-sending countries such as Mexico?

2. Is it appropriate for the Student and Exchange Visitor Program to be housed in Immigration Customs and Enforcement (ICE)? Does this signal that foreign students present an opportunity or a threat?

3. Do you think immigration should be managed by three separate bureaus (CBP, ICE, and CIS), or should management of temporary and permanent

admission to the United States be managed by one agency? Which one and why?

4. What role should judges exercise in reviewing administrative decisions about immigration? When should the courts defer, or not, to the judgment of the administrative agency? (See chapter 3.)

■ Suggested Readings

Krauss, Erich, and Alex Pacheco. 2005. *On the Line: Inside the US Border Patrol*. New York: Citadel.

Nafziger, James A. R. 1991. "Review of Visa Denials by Consular Officers." *Washington Law Review* 66: 1.

US Department of Homeland Security. 2009. *2008 Yearbook of Immigration Statistics*, at www.dhs.gov/xlibrary/assets/statistics/yearbook/2008/ois_yb_2008.pdf.

US Department of State. 2009. *Report of the Visa Office 2008*, at www.travel.state.gov/visa/statistics/statistics_4391.html.

■ Notes

1. Pub. L. No 107–296, 116 Stat. 2153 (2002).

2. See the DHS website at www.dhs.gov/xabout/history/editorial_0133.shtm for the history of the DHS and a chart of agencies moved into the department in 2003.

3. See the March 9, 2009, press release at the US CIS website: www.uscis.gov/portal/site/uscis.

4. *Chevron USA v. Natural Resources Defense Council, Inc.* 467 US 837 (1984).

5

Admissions

> Except as specifically provided [by the per-country limits], no person shall
> ... be discriminated against in the issuance of immigrant visa because of
> the person's race ... nationality ... [or] place of birth.
> —Immigration and Nationality Act

H ow do immigrants get into the United States? This chapter explains the various forms of admission into the country, that is, the routes by which noncitizens enter the country under US immigration laws. We look at four categories of foreign nationals who come to the United States:

1. those who have been admitted as immigrants;
2. those who have been admitted as nonimmigrants;
3. those who have been granted asylum and refugee status; and
4. those who are undocumented.

An examination of these categories demonstrates that US law preserves substantial racial and nationality discrimination, which creates barriers to entry for Mexican immigrants.

■ Immigrant Visas

US regulation of immigration tries to control the racial and ethnic composition of the incoming stream of migrants. Racial and ethnic engineering has been a hallmark of US immigration law from its earliest days. The most famous examples are the Chinese exclusion laws discussed in chapter 3. Another important example is the **National Origins Act**, passed in 1924, which established a quota system for the admission of foreign nationals based on the 1890 census. The system was designed to keep constant the ethnic makeup of the US population. Under the National Origins Act formula, the proportion of the incoming stream of migrants from a region was capped to match the proportion of the US population from that region. In a country already dominated by settlers from western Europe, this national origins formula effectively guaranteed that the ethnic status quo would remain stable and unthreatened by immigration-driven population changes. The quota system discriminated against immigrants from southern and eastern Europe, many of whom came to the United States in the early years of the twentieth century.

Versions of quotas explicitly based on national origins persisted until 1965, when US immigration law received a radical legislative makeover. Although the express aim of the 1965 amendments was to abolish unfairness in the admission of migrants, elements of ethnic social engineering remained, most notably within the per-country limits and the diversity visa category, both of which we discuss later in this chapter. (Immigration admissions are governed by the omnibus federal immigration law, the Immigration and Nationality Act [INA], which has been discussed extensively throughout this book.)

Congress annually allots 675,000 visas for legal permanent residency, also known as green cards. These visas are distributed among three groups: (1) applicants who seek admission based on family connections (480,000 visas per year); (2) applicants who seek admission based on employment (140,000 visas per year); and (3) winners of the "diversity" lottery (55,000 visas per year). This lottery tries to award visas to applicants coming from a country that Congress believes is "underrepresented" in the incoming immigrant stream.

Of the 480,000 family-based visas distributed annually, many (by law, a minimum of 226,000 per year) are awarded to "immediate relatives of citizens," a category that gives visas to the spouses and children of US citizens, and in some cases, to the parents of US citizens. The "immediate relatives of citizens" category is very popular; it is the quick and ready route to a green card for those foreign nationals who marry citizens. Included in the 480,000 annual cap are also green cards distributed among the family-based preference categories.

Congress has also imposed an annual per-country limit on the number of visas. Every sending nation is limited to a total of 7 percent of the annual number of visas. The per-country limit means that the same number of visas is available to applicants from high-demand countries (such as Mexico and China) as is available to applicants from low-demand countries (such as Luxembourg). The limit has the effect of punishing immigrants from high-demand countries, creating waiting lines much longer than the lines of low-demand countries. The United States thus distributes visas in a manner that is insensitive to demand.

Family Visas

The most popular means of admission for **family-based immigration** is as immediate relatives of US citizens. This category includes spouses of the citizen, unmarried children who are under twenty-one years old, and parents of a citizen (when the US citizen is over twenty-one years old).

The INA also includes four "preference categories" for family-based admission. These include (1) unmarried sons and daughters of US citizens and spouses and unmarried children (under age twenty-one) of lawful permanent residents; (2) unmarried adult children (over age twenty-one) of lawful permanent residents; (3) married sons and daughters of US citizens; and (4) brothers and sisters of US citizens.

Immigration law also allows the immediate family, including minor children, of the applicant to enter as "following to join," that is, a family member following to join the immigrant who has successfully acquired a green card.

When a marriage will result in immigration benefits, the law is fairly careful to test the bona fides of that marriage. Many Americans are concerned about sham marriages that are designed only to acquire immigration benefits. When a citizen marries a foreign national, a green card will be granted to the foreign national on a conditional basis. After two years, the couple will have to show that they are still married. Only then will the conditional green card become an unconditional green card. The couple will have to submit a substantial documentary record attesting to the authenticity of their marriage. Immigration authorities may decide to interview the couple and may even separate the spouses and interview them individually in an effort to uncover a sham marriage.

Sometimes, the marriage has broken up but the law still provides lawful immigrant status to the foreign national. This is called *self-petitioning* because the foreign national petitions for immigration benefits by him- or herself, rather than jointly petitioning for those benefits with a spouse. One common occasion of self-petitioning is when the immigrant spouse has been a victim of domestic violence. In such cases, the law allows the foreign national to remain in the country without having to cooperate with the abusive spouse.

When a family member in the United States begins the process of petitioning for an immigrant relative, a common first question is, "How long do I have to wait before the visa is available?" For applicants entering via one of the preference categories, this question is best answered by reference to the Visa Availability Chart compiled by the Department of State.[1]

The chart operates like a "Now Serving" notice at a delicatessen; a glance at the chart shows which immigrants are currently at the front of the line to receive visas. The differing times to entry result from the **per-country ceilings** that apply across the board to all nations, regardless of the demand among its citizens to immigrate to the United States.

The chart shows that the waiting time varies by sending country. Immigrants from some countries have substantially longer to wait than immigrants from other countries. Thus, US immigration laws, although not discriminatory on their face on the basis of race or nationality, have disparate impacts on certain racial groups and nationalities.

One of the April 2009 charts looks like table 5.1. The numbers down the first column refer to the preference category for which the foreign national has applied (e.g., "Family-based, 1st" refers to unmarried sons and daughters of US citizens). The notations across the top refer to the sending country from which the foreign national is applying. There are special waiting lines for the highest sending countries (e.g., Mexico), and then a general waiting line for all the other countries.

From the chart, we can see the wide disparity in waiting times between a Mexican applicant and an applicant from, let us say (drawing an example from the "all other nations" column), Switzerland. The Mexican applicant is standing in a much longer line than applicants from the rest of the world. Table 5.2 gives us a sense of the relative waiting times.

Table 5.1   US Department of State visa chart, April 2009

PREFERENCE CATEGORY: FAMILY BASED	CHINA (MAINLAND BORN)	INDIA	MEXICO	PHILIPPINES	ALL OTHER NATIONS
1st	15Aug02	15Aug02	08Oct92	01Aug93	15Aug02
2A	15Aug04	15Aug04	01Jan02	15Aug04	15Aug04
2B	01Sep00	01Sep00	01May92	15Jan98	01Sep00
3rd	22Aug00	22Aug00	22Oct92	15Jun91	22Aug00
4th	08Jan98	15Apr98	22Apr95	22Jun86	15Apr98

Source: Bureau of Consular Affairs, US State Department.

Table 5.2 Visa waiting period comparison between Swiss and Mexican immigrants

FAMILY BASED	SWISS IMMIGRANT	MEXICAN IMMIGRANT
1st	6 years 7 months	16 years 5 months
2A	4 years 7 months	6 years 3 months
2B	8 years 6 months	16 years 11 months
3rd	8 years 5 months	16 years 5 months
4th	11 years	14 years

Table 5.2 refines the comparison in waiting times between our hypothetical applicants from Mexico and Switzerland. For example, Swiss applicants who applied six years and seven months ago for a visa as an unmarried son or daughter of a US citizen are now receiving those visas. Mexican applicants who applied at the same time for the same sort of visa have nearly ten more years to wait.

Tables 5.1 and 5.2, moreover, do not tell the entire story. These tables give a snapshot of the relative length of the waiting lines, but do not tell us about the rate at which the lines are moving over time. Even there, applicants from Mexico are at a severe disadvantage, since the Mexican waiting line moves much more slowly than the others.

Mexico demands US visas at a higher rate than other countries. Because of the per-country limits, a Mexican applicant bears the burden of an onerous delay, which applicants from most other countries do not have to bear. When we hear the phrase that the aspiring Mexican immigrant should "get in line, like everybody else," we should remember that the structure of immigration law makes the Mexican line unlike everybody else's. The onerous and unique burdens we place on Mexicans' lawful entry may predictably increase the likelihood of unlawful entry.

Employment Visas

The INA allots 140,000 visas annually for **employment-based immigration**, primarily to allow high-skilled workers a permanent legal footing in this country. There are five categories of employment-based immigration: (1) immigrants with extraordinary ability; (2) immigrants with advanced degrees; (3) immigrants who are skilled or other workers; (4) special workers; and (5) immigrants who commit to investing and creating jobs.

Many of the employment-based visas require a **Department of Labor (DOL)** certification. Labor certification shows that the secretary of labor has determined that (1) no native worker could fill the position; and

(2) employing an immigrant in the specified job will not adversely affect the working and wage conditions of similarly employed people already in the United States.

The purpose behind labor certification is to ensure that the United States does not employ an immigrant when there is a native worker who could do the job. In the past, this certification made it difficult to admit immigrant workers. Now, the secretary of labor will typically accept an affidavit from the employer. The DOL reserves the right to investigate the truthfulness of the affidavit, but for the most part, the DOL has been rather trusting of employers' attestations.

The DOL certification process is designed to make employers look first to native workers to fill jobs and to turn to foreign nationals only when no native fits the bill. The reality, however, is much different.

Studies done in 1996 show that of the 42,150 applications that received DOL certification that year, 99 percent of those immigrants were in the United States at the time the application was filed. Seventy-four percent were already working for the applying employer; 16 percent of those already working were working illegally for the employer; 11 percent never worked for the employer again after getting legal permanent resident status; and 17 percent left the employer six months after getting legal permanent resident status. Based on these statistics, one may conclude that the DOL certification process is perfunctory at best and a sham at worst.

Many laborers from Mexico would fall into the category of low-skilled workers, and the INA provides few lawful ways for these types of workers to enter. In chapters 6 and 8, we discuss the impacts of the limited lawful routes to admission that US immigration law provides for low-skilled workers.

Diversity Visas

Fifty-five thousand green cards per year, or about 8 percent of the entire annual allotment, are distributed by lottery. The stated goal of the **diversity lottery** is to secure visas for applicants from sending countries that Congress would like to see better represented in the incoming stream. The actual effect of the diversity lottery is to favor applicants from Europe and Africa over applicants from high-demand countries in Asia and Latin America. One could argue that applicants from Mexico, who cannot enter the lottery at all, are particularly disserved by this means of distributing visas.

If an applicant's nation is eligible for the diversity visa, the particular applicant is eligible to qualify for the visa. To qualify, an immigrant needs to have either a high school education or, in the last five years, two years of work experience in a job that requires two years of training or experience. This extremely low threshold shows how easy it is to qualify for a diversity visa, but only if you come from a country that Congress has declared desirable.

■ Nonimmigrant (Temporary) Visas

The holder of a nonimmigrant visa (NIV) is typically in the United States for a limited time, to perform some specific task. The nonimmigrant category is for persons who desire to come to the United States for a temporary stay, such as to vacation, to study, or to visit temporarily for business. An NIV allows a noncitizen to request entry upon their arrival for a period ranging from one day to a few years. Typically, applicants for an NIV must show that they have a home in the sending country to which they intend to return. The immigrant category, on the other hand, is for those who wish to live permanently in the United States.

The greatest difference between NIVs and the green cards held by lawful permanent residents is that green cards are generally permanent while nonimmigrant visas are only temporary. A lawful permanent resident is entitled to many of the rights and obligations of US citizenship and is considered a permanent resident of the United States. A green card may be revoked only if certain laws or regulations are violated. By contrast, the government can very easily take a nonimmigrant visa away. In addition, a green card is often referred to as a path to citizenship due to the holders' ability to naturalize after a certain length of time. However, regardless of the length of time held, an NIV will never allow the possessor to obtain US citizenship.

The NIV category is particularly important for those interested in migration from Mexico to the United States. Some of the proposed immigration reforms seek to better manage Mexican labor migration through a temporary worker program.

A person's nationality may also affect his or her entry into the United States. Under the Visa Waiver Program, for example, noncitizens from a list of approved countries, which tend not to be developing nations with high demand for immigration to this country, may be granted entry into the United States without a visa for up to ninety days. On the flip side, persons from certain high-traffic countries, such as Mexico, will find it harder to obtain entry into the United States.

An NIV allows the applicant to request entry into the United States for pleasure, temporary work, business, medical attention, or a number of reasons other than permanent relocation. If you have traveled abroad, you may have already encountered nonimmigrant visas. They are issued at US consulates in the sending country of the noncitizen.

At the consular office, a nonimmigrant may experience the first impediment to entering the United States. Consular officers play a central role in the immigration process because they make many low-visibility decisions regarding eligibility. Eligibility may depend on the availability of a visa, the visa status requirements, the excludability of the applicant, and, in some instances, whether a waiver of excludability is warranted.

Once obtained, an NIV represents only the holder's right to request entry to the United States for a specific purpose and duration. Often this right is represented simply as a stamp placed on a page of the applicant's passport. Thus, although a visa allows a noncitizen to travel to the United States, it does not guarantee entry.

Upon arrival in the United States, a border agent will review a noncitizen's visa application and determine the noncitizen's eligibility for nonimmigrant status. When approval for entry is obtained, the nonimmigrant's status, length of stay, and any other limitations will be reflected on his or her arrival departure card (form I-94) regardless of what the visa application states. This process differs from the grant of a visa because a visa only allows the holder to *request* entry to the United States, and the form I-94 *admits* a nonimmigrant for a certain period.

In addition to varying widely in purpose, nonimmigrant visas vary in the length of stay lawfully allowed. The immigration official determines the expiration of status for each nonimmigrant who arrives. Nonimmigrant visas can be issued for any length of time up to a certain maximum allowed by law and, depending on the type of visa, may be issued for up to ten years. However, this only means that you have the right to request entry during that period, not that you are allowed to stay for that period. For example, tourist visas are normally allowed an entry period of no greater than six months, but many foreign tourists do not intend nor are they granted permission to stay in the United States for that long. While tourists represent a shorter admission period, diplomats, government officials, business travelers, and noncitizens affiliated with international organizations may be allowed an entry period of up to ten years.

Many visas have a set expiration date, but others may be of indefinite duration. For example, a student form I-94 may state "D/S" for the duration of status. This designation means that a student may stay in the United States only while actively pursuing the academic program for which they entered the United States. Thus, a graduation, a change in academic programs, or a decrease in academic schedule may result in an expectation that the student depart within a short time.

Another limitation placed on visa entry is the number of entries that may be made on a particular visa. Most visas are issued as multiple entry visas, which allow a visa holder to go in and out of the country an unlimited number of times. But single entry visas allow a noncitizen holder to enter the United States only once. Upon departure, the noncitizen will not be allowed to return again on the same visa, regardless of the amount of time left before the visa's expiration.

In addition to limitations placed on visas, various penalties exist for a nonimmigrant who overstays a visa. In general, nonimmigrants are given forty-eight hours past the expiration of their form I-94 to leave the country. If a nonimmigrant overstays without a compelling reason—usually cancelled airline flights, sickness, or other emergencies—their later requests for entry to the United States may become more complicated. For example, persons who overstay for six months up to one year may not reenter the United States for three years. Those who overstay beyond one year may not reenter the United States for ten years.

Despite these penalties, nonimmigrants admitted to the United States can extend their stay or adjust their visa status prior to expiration in various ways. Most of these changes can be accomplished while in the United States. An extension of a stay usually requires proof that a nonimmigrant intends to stay in the United States in the same capacity. Likewise, a nonimmigrant applying for a change of visa status must show proof of eligibility for that particular status.

There are a variety of nonimmigrant visas available under US immigration law. Each category of nonimmigrant visa is recognized by both its name and a letter-number combination. For example, the most popular type of nonimmigrant visa, the one for business or pleasure, is denoted as a B visa. Thus, the B visa contains two subdivisions, one for noncitizens

Nonimmigrant Visas

Current nonimmigrant visas available include

- foreign government officials, such as ambassadors and diplomats
- visitors in transit
- ship crew members
- treaty traders and investors
- students
- representatives of international organizations
- temporary workers
- foreign journalists and other media representatives
- fiancés of US citizens
- intercompany transferees
- NATO representatives, resident members, and staff
- trade visas under NAFTA
- athletes, entertainers, fashion models, and artists
- international cultural exchange visitors
- religious workers
- witnesses and informants
- victims of trafficking and domestic violence

Source: Immigration Classifications and Visa Categories, www.uscis.gov. ■

visiting temporarily on business (B-1) and another for temporary visitors for pleasure (B-2). These and other types of visas each fall under an expansive twenty-five-category list of nonimmigrant visas.

In total, the United States has approximately twenty nonimmigrant categories that allow the admission of noncitizens to work for temporary periods. As noted above, visas range from those for ambassadors to those for noncitizens with a bachelor's degree.

Despite this large range of categories, most legal Mexican nonimmigrants to the United States enter on either an H-2A visa as farm workers or an H-2B visa as unskilled non-farm workers. Both the H-2A and H-2B visa categories require certification by the US Department of Labor that no American workers are able to fill the position. The overall purpose of these programs is to provide necessary temporary labor and not to allow persons to settle in the United States. Each worker is expected to leave upon discharge, upon mechanization of the position, or upon elimination of the positions from the trade or industry. There is no annual cap on H-2A visas, but data from 2002 to 2006 show that only about 30,000 of these are distributed per year. There is an annual cap of 66,000 on H-2B visas. Thus lawful access to the low-skilled labor market is limited to about 100,000 visas per year, a ridiculously low number given typical market demand for such labor.

■ Consular Nonreviewability

Applicants for visas frequently face the possibility of denial. In fiscal year 2008, for example, US consuls denied visa applications to 1,545,597 potential nonimmigrants, or roughly 23 percent of all nonimmigrant visa applicants.[2] Despite the relatively high denial rate, a consular officer's decision is not reviewable and therefore effectively final. Nonreviewability is a longstanding judicial rule that has established a hands-off approach in which courts will not review the factual findings made by the consular office in its decision to deny a visa. The rationale for the nonreviewability doctrine can be described as follows:

> To allow an appeal from a consul's denial of a visa would be to make a judicial determination of a right when, in fact, a right does not exist. An alien has no right to come to the United States and the refusal of a visa is not an invasion of his rights. Permitting review of visa decisions would permit an alien to get his case in United States courts, causing a great deal of difficulty in the administration of the immigration laws.[3]

Although each visa denial must be accompanied by an explanation of the legal basis for the denial, it is clear that consular officers maintain a high degree of discretion in this area. Even though consular decisions may in some instances be entitled to an informal review within the consular post, a nonimmigrant applicant is afforded no independent protection against arbitrary or erroneous decisions. As a result, many instances of abuse have been documented, and nonreviewability remains a common focus of legislators and legal practitioners.

Refugees and Asylum Seekers

The US immigration system is structured to receive migrants who are fleeing political and related forms of persecution. These migrants typically arrive at the border or points of entry without documentation. The US government is obligated to identify such migrants and admit them into the country.

US immigration law distinguishes between three categories of forced migration: (1) conflict-induced displacement; (2) development-induced displacement; and (3) disaster-induced displacement. Development-induced displacement occurs when people are forced to move from infrastructure development like a dam or urban-clearing project. Disaster-induced displacement occurs as a result of a natural disaster.

For our purposes, we are particularly interested in the first category: migrants who flee conflict and seek safety in the United States. These are people who are forced to flee their homes for one or more of the following reasons, when the state authorities are unable or unwilling to protect them: armed conflict, including civil war; generalized violence, including gang violence; and persecution on the grounds of nationality, race, religion, political opinion, or social group.

Within these reasons for displacement, several categories arise. The two we most closely examine here are refugees and asylum seekers. Refugees are defined by the 1951 United Nations Convention Relating to the Status of Refugees.[4] The convention defines refugees as "a person residing outside his or her country of nationality, who is unable or unwilling to return on account of a well-founded fear of persecution on account of race, religion, nationality, membership in a political social group, or political opinion." The United Nations Protocol Relating to the Status of Refugees ensured the international protection of refugees beyond those persons displaced by World War II.[5]

The INA requires the attorney general to withhold the removal of a noncitizen who is subject to persecution in his or her home country. This type of protection is commonly called **nonrefoulement**, a French term. Protection from refoulement has extended beyond the convention to nearly all facets of international law. These protections were implemented in the United States through the Refugee Act of 1980, which amended the INA to make nonrefoulement mandatory for the attorney general instead of discretionary.

Withholding of removal gives fewer rights than the protections provided by asylum. Work authorization is provided and limited access to public services is permitted. The biggest differences relate to family members and change in status. A simple withholding of removal does not permit the refugee to bring in immediate family members. It also does not provide for adjustment to lawful permanent resident status. However, refugees who qualify for LPR status through marriage or employment may adjust their immigration status. Despite these restrictions, nonrefoulement is mandatory and, unlike asylum, a form of relief within the discretion of the agency.

In 1980, Congress amended the INA and created the form of relief known as asylum. A person granted asylum is called an asylee. To be granted protection, an asylum applicant must establish past persecution or a well-founded fear of future persecution. This is a subtle difference from the withholding of removal requirement, which reads, "would be threatened." This statutory language is not the only difference between asylum and withholding. Beyond the differences mentioned above, noncitizens granted withholding of removal may lose their status if the fear of persecution ends (because of, for example, an end to armed conflict or a regime change).

Asylum protection, refugee status, and withholding of removal all share the common element of persecution on account of race, religion, political opinion, nationality, or membership in a particular social group. The subtle differences among the three forms of relief can be seen when the texts are placed side by side.

Applicants seeking refugee status must report to a US consulate office outside the United States and meet the criteria of residing outside his or her country of nationality and being unable or unwilling to return because of a well-founded fear of persecution as defined by the INA. Once eligibility is established, the refugee must also fall into a class that is considered a special humanitarian concern by the United States. They must not have resettled in another country, and they must be admissible under INA § 212(a), 8 USC § 1182(a). Although they cannot be turned away as a "public charge," a "responsible person or organization" must sponsor refugees.[6] The sponsor must also provide transportation for the refugee. Sponsors are typically relatives or nonprofit organizations.

By meeting the above criteria, the refugee is eligible to complete forms I-590 (registration for classification as a refugee), G-325 (biographical

Asylum, Refugee, and Withholding of Removal

Asylum INA § 208(b)(1)(A), 8 USC § 1158(a)(1)(A)	"The Attorney General *may* grant asylum to an alien ... if the ... alien is a refugee."
Refugee INA § 101(a)(42), 8 USC § 1101(a)(42)	"Any person ... who has a *well-founded fear of persecution* on account of race, religion, nationality, membership in a particular social group, or political opinion."
Withholding of Removal INA § 241(b)(3), 8 USC. § 1231(b)(3)	"The Attorney General may not remove an alien to a country if the Attorney General decides that the alien's *life or freedom would be threatened* in that country because of the alien's race, religion, nationality, membership in a particular social group, or political opinion." ■

information), and FD-258 (applicant card). Finally, the refugee must submit to a medical examination and wait for admission.

The president of the United States, after consulting with Congress, is given the power to determine what humanitarian concerns are in the national interest. The president is also charged with setting a cap on both overall and regional refugee applications. Upon completion of the paperwork, the refugee is placed on a waiting list for the refugee's humanitarian group. The waiting list is ordered by the applicants' filing dates but can be adjusted by the Department of Homeland Security (DHS) if conditions deteriorate. A refugee has four months to enter the United States once his application has been approved. If the refugee's application is denied, there is no process to appeal the decision.

Protections under withholding of removal are generally the same as asylum protections. The applicant is allowed to stay in the United States and is eligible for employment. Keep in mind that successful applicants cannot be removed to the persecuting country, but they can be removed from the United States to a third, nonpersecuting country.

The standard of proof for withholding of removal, a mandatory form of relief, is higher than for asylum, a discretionary form of relief. If the applicant is successful in showing his or her claim to relief, the court is required to withhold removal.

■ Immigration Courts

Asylum is one area in immigration law in which the noncitizen has access to adjudication by an immigration court. Removal proceedings in the immigration court are conducted in two stages: (1) master calendar hearing; and (2) individual merits hearing. At the master calendar hearing, the judge will decide if enough facts exist to hear the individual case. If denied asylum by the immigration court, the noncitizen may appeal to the Board of Immigration Appeals (BIA).

The BIA is part of the larger Executive Office for Immigration Review (EOIR), which, in turn, is located within the Department of Justice. The BIA was created under regulations promulgated by the attorney general. Despite being the "board" of appeals, 2002 legislation made it possible for one member of the BIA to hear a case. There are only six circumstances in which an appeal is before a three-member panel. An affirming decision by a single member does not require an opinion, and nearly one-third of all cases before the BIA are affirmed without one. The large number of cases decided without an opinion has increased the rate of appeals to the federal courts of appeals.

There are some limits to the types of cases that can be appealed. Final removal orders against citizens for crime-related activities "shall not be subject to review by any court."[7] However, questions of constitutional scope or questions of law can be appealed to the federal courts of appeal. Decisions based on the discretion of the attorney general are barred from review.

It is difficult to determine the chances that an asylum claim will be successful. A relatively low percentage of asylum claims are granted. Current and exact statistics on Mexican asylum claims are hard to uncover because data for Mexican applicants are not kept by the US government. The most accurate data come from a Freedom of Information Request by the independent website www.asylumlaw.org.

Between January 1, 2000, and August 31, 2004, almost 300,000 asylum applications were filed. Of these, about half made it to the immigration judge decision process. Of these roughly 150,000 claims for asylum, only 2,714 were made by Mexicans and were decided on by an immigration judge. Only 9 percent of these applications were granted. Thus, over this four-year period, only 246 Mexicans successfully applied for asylum.

Compare this to Chinese applicants during the same time frame: 31,749 Chinese applied for asylum and 14,437 were granted asylum (a 45 percent grant rate). Among Latin American countries, only Nicaragua has a lower grant rate (7 percent) than Mexico.

Recent reports show an increase in asylum applicants from Mexico due to the violence in the country. Only time will tell whether the rate of approval of Mexican asylum applications will increase.

■ Undocumented Foreign Nationals

Although the title of this chapter is "Admissions," we would be remiss if we did not address the sizable population that does not formally seek admission (i.e., **entrants without inspection,** or EWIs), or the population of migrants who were lawfully admitted but have fallen out of status (**overstays**), or those who have been ordered removed, but remain *absconders* or *fugitives.* We will refer to people in these groups as undocumented foreign nationals (UFNs).

For purposes of this book, we are particularly interested in the characteristics of the undocumented Mexican population in the United States. In this chapter we explore the Mexican UFN population generally. Chapter 8 looks specifically at Mexican undocumented immigrants in the US labor force.

Approximately 11.9 million UFNs were living in the United States in March 2008. The size of the UFN population has increased by more than 40 percent since 2000, when it was 8.4 million. In 2005, the Pew Hispanic Center estimated 11.1 million UFNs were in the United States. The most recent estimate, 11.9 million, indicates that UFNs make up 4 percent of the US population. The size of the UFN population appears to have declined slightly since 2007, presumably due to the downturn in the US economy. Figure 5.1 demonstrates the steady rise of the UFN population from 2000 to 2008.

The nationalities of the 11.9 million UFNs living in the United States in March 2008 is displayed in figure 5.2. We see that 7 million UFNs hail from Mexico. Taken together, UFNs from Mexico and Latin America represented 81 percent of the UFN population in 2008.

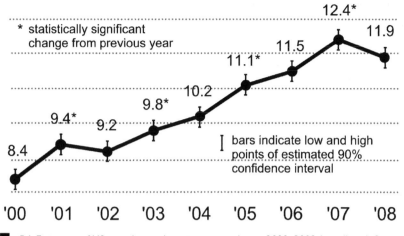

* statistically significant change from previous year

I bars indicate low and high points of estimated 90% confidence interval

'00 '01 '02 '03 '04 '05 '06 '07 '08

5.1. Estimates of US unauthorized immigrant population, 2000–2008 (in millions). *Source:* Illustration by author based on data found in Jeffrey S. Passel and D'Vera Cohn, *Trends in Unauthorized Immigration: Undocumented Inflow Now Trails Legal Inflow* (Pew Hispanic Center, October 2, 2008), figure 1, p. ii. Used by permission.

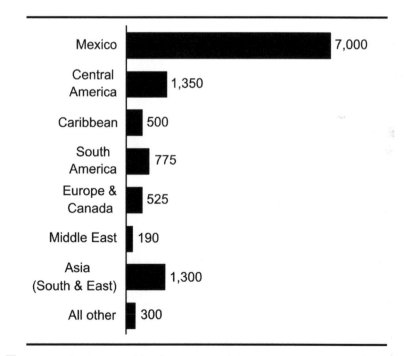

5.2. Unauthorized foreign-born immigrants, (in thousands). *Source:* Adapted from Jeffrey S. Passel, *A Portrait of Unauthorized Immigrants in the United States* (Pew Hispanic Center, April 14, 2009), figure 30, p. 21. Used by permission.

About 1.3 million undocumented immigrants from Asia resided in the United States in 2009, representing about 11 percent of the total. Europe and Canada accounted for 525,000, or about 4 percent, of all undocumented immigrants. Finally, the Middle East, Africa, and all other countries accounted for about 490,000, or about 4 percent, of the undocumented population. We look more deeply at the demographic characteristics of the UFN population in chapter 8.

◼ Concluding Thoughts

This chapter has laid out the means by which noncitizens are admitted into the United States on permanent and temporary bases, as well as key characteristics of the population of undocumented foreign nationals. We have seen that the road to entry is substantially conditioned by racial and ethnic considerations that disfavor noncitizens from Mexico.

◼ Discussion Questions

1. What are the pros and cons of the per-country ceiling on the distribution of visas? Does the ceiling unfairly discriminate against prospective immigrants from Mexico (and other nations whose citizens have a high demand for immigration to the United States)?

2. Should the allocation of visas under US immigration law be more sensitive to demand? Specifically, should more visas be available to migrants from countries where there is a greater demand for visas? How might the distribution of the current US visa system, which is not sensitive to demand, contribute to undocumented migration?

3. Should the doctrine of consular nonreviewability be abolished? Is the doctrine contrary to the rule of law and general presumption of judicial review of agency decisions?

4. Does the United States need a diversity lottery? What purpose does it serve? What are its costs?

5. How might a temporary worker program be fashioned to accommodate Mexican nationals who seek to work in the United States? Can we really expect temporary workers to leave the country after their labor is completed?

Suggested Readings

Higham, John. 2002. *Strangers in the Land*, 4th ed. New Brunswick, N.J.: Rutgers University Press.

Hing, Bill Ong. 2004. *Defining America Through Immigration Policy*. Philadelphia: Temple University Press.

Legomsky, Stephen H. 1993. "Immigration, Equality and Diversity." *Columbia Journal Transnational Law* 31: 319.

Massey, Douglas S., Jorge Durand, and Nolan J. Malone. 2002. *Beyond Smoke and Mirrors: Mexican Immigration in an Era of Economic Integration*. New York: Russell Sage Foundation.

Ramji-Nogales, Jaya, Andrew I. Schoenholtz, and Philip G. Schrag. 2007. "Refugee Roulette: Disparities in Asylum Adjudication." *Stanford Law Review* 60: 295.

Trujillo, Bernard. 2000. "Immigrant Visa Distribution: The Case of Mexico." *Wisconsin Law Review* 2000, no. 3: 713.

Walker, Kathleen C., and Katherine E. Urban. 1998. "Visa Processing at the US Consulate in Ciudad Juarez, Mexico." *Interpreter Releases* 75 (July 27): 1009.

Notes

Epigraph: Immigration and Nationality Act, § 202(s)(1)(A).

1. Visa bulletin: http://travel.state.gov/visa/bulletin/bulletin_1360.html.

2. US Dep't of State, Bureau of Consular Affairs, *Report of the Visa Office 2008*, (2008), table 1, table 20. More than 6.6 million nonimmigrant visa applications were received, 2,083,726 were determined ineligible, and only 538,129 were able to overcome this determination. The most common reason for denial was a failure to establish eligibility for a nonimmigrant visa under INA § 214(b), 8 USC § 1184(b).

3. Luke T. Lee, *Consular Law and Practice*, 2d ed. (Oxford: Clarendon Press; New York: Oxford University Press, 1991), 222.

4. United Nations Convention Relating to the Status of Refugees, 19 UST 6223, 189 UNTS 150 (entered into force Apr. 22, 1954). The convention provides two basic guarantees: (1) no refugee may be returned to his or her country of nationality if the refugee has a well-founded fear of persecution on account of one of the five enumerated grounds; and (2) lawfully admitted refugees are granted full access to civil and political rights.

5. United Nations Protocol Relating to the Status of Refugees, 606 UNTS 267 (entered into force Oct. 4, 1967).

6. 8 CFR § 207.2(d).

7. INA § 242(a)(2)(C), 8 USC § 1252(a)(2)(C).

Inadmissibility

An alien seeking initial admission has *no* constitutional rights regarding his application, for the power to admit or exclude aliens is a sovereign prerogative.
—*Landon v. Plasencia*

The list of grounds for exclusion of noncitizens from admission into the United States in the Immigration and Nationality Act "is like a magic mirror, reflecting the fears and concerns of past Congresses."
—*Lennon v. INS*

US immigration laws create general rules for admission to and removal from the United States but generally fail to make any special rules recognizing the special relationship between the United States and Mexico, neighboring nations that share a land border extending thousands of miles and that saw a dramatic increase in social and economic intercourse over the twentieth century. One might think that the unique history of US–Mexico relations might have an impact on the treatment of Mexican nationals under US immigration laws. That, however, is not the case.

The Treaty of Guadalupe Hidalgo, which ended the US–Mexican War in 1848, and the North American Free Trade Agreement fail to address migration between the two nations (see chapter 2).[1] As a result, there are generally no special rules that govern migration between the United States and Mexico.

This chapter briefly outlines two important treaties between the United States and Mexico and their failure to address immigration between the two nations. It then considers grounds for denying admission to noncitizens who are eligible for a visa.

■ Treaty of Guadalupe Hidalgo

Much of what is now the American Southwest became part of the United States under the Treaty of Guadalupe Hidalgo after the US–Mexican War ended in 1848. Although not dealing generally with the migration of persons from Mexico to the United States, the treaty addressed the citizenship rights of Mexican citizens living in the large block of territory ceded under the treaty to the United States. Article VIII provides that:

> Mexicans now established in territories previously belonging to Mexico, and which remain for the future within ... the United States ... shall be free to continue where they now reside, or to remove to the Mexican Republic.... Those who shall prefer to remain in said territories, may either retain the title and rights of Mexican citizens, or acquire those of citizens of the United States. But, they shall be under the obligation to make their election within one year from the date of the exchange of ratifications of this treaty; and those who shall remain in said territories, after the expiration of that year, without having declared their intention to retain the character of Mexicans, shall be considered to have elected to become citizens of the United States.

Article IX further provides that:

> The Mexicans who ... shall not preserve the character of citizens of the Mexican Republic ... shall be incorporated into the Union of the United States and be admitted, at the proper time (to be judged by the Congress of the United States) *to the enjoyment of all rights of citizens of the United States according to the principles of the Constitution.* (emphasis added)

Both articles of the Treaty of Guadalupe Hidalgo promised Mexican citizens in the surrendered territories the option of US citizenship and guaranteed those who exercised that option the same rights as all other US citizens. The liberality of the citizenship provisions for Mexican citizens provoked controversy, with some Americans expressing the view that Mexicans were unworthy of US citizenship.

Articles VIII and IX of the treaty resulted in some benefits for Mexican citizens. For example, although most racial minorities were treated as nonwhites in a time when US law generally limited naturalization to "white" immigrants, the court in one important case found that the Treaty of Guadalupe Hidalgo compelled the classification of Mexican immigrants as "white" for naturalization purposes. The court found that Article VIII compelled the conclusion that citizenship rights applied to "Mexicans (and the term includes all Mexicans, without discrimination as to color)."[2]

As summarized in chapter 2, the United States experienced great difficulty in honoring the promise of equal citizenship in Article IX of the Treaty of Guadalupe Hidalgo to the new US citizens of Mexican ancestry. For example, Anglos, with the help of the US government, invoked various legal and illegal mechanisms to strip persons of Mexican ancestry of their property rights. Similarly, the California Supreme Court rejected a challenge under the treaty to a California foreign miners tax directed at persons of Mexican ancestry.[3]

In the end, much of the Mexicans' land and property were stolen, rights were denied, language and culture suppressed, and opportunities for employment, education, and political representation thwarted. The US government ultimately failed to fully protect the rights guaranteed under the Treaty of Guadalupe Hidalgo to Mexican citizens who became US citizens.

■ The North American Free Trade Agreement

The 1990s saw a major change in the relationship between the United States and Mexico, as well as with Canada. The **North American Free Trade Agreement (NAFTA)** promoted free trade of goods and services between the United States, Canada, and Mexico and created a new relationship among the nations of North America.

NAFTA, however, did not permit labor migration between the three nations. Still, some supporters claimed that the agreement, by improving the Mexican economy over time, would dampen migration pressures from Mexico and in the long run decrease undocumented immigration. That has not proven to be the case. NAFTA in fact has been blamed for economic dislocations in Mexico that have *increased*, not *decreased*, migration to the United States.

Like the Treaty of Guadalupe Hidalgo, NAFTA's terms have a relatively limited direct impact on US immigration laws. The agreement primarily eases immigration restrictions for narrowly defined business and trade-related purposes. The signatories unquestionably did not intend the trade agreement to address the "big picture" labor migration questions among the United States, Mexico, and Canada.

The topic of immigration was excluded from NAFTA negotiations presumably because the United States feared the political, economic, and social consequences of increased immigration from Mexico. The administration under President George H. W. Bush probably concluded that any far-reaching treatment of migration issues in NAFTA would decrease the possibility of congressional approval of an agreement. The negotiations culminating in NAFTA followed by just a few years the tumultuous debate over the Immigration Reform and Control Act of 1986, which spanned much of the 1980s.[4]

To complicate matters, the national interests of the United States and Mexico tugged in diametrically different directions on immigration. Political exigencies in the United States demanded provisions limiting undocumented immigration from Mexico and bolstering border enforcement. Mexico, however, indirectly benefits from the migration of some of its citizens to the United States.

To further complicate matters, the Mexican government had expressed concern with human rights abuses of its citizens along the border by US authorities. Some in Mexico advocated the addition of provisions to NAFTA to protect expatriate Mexican workers and halt the many border enforcement measures that the US government had been adopting. Such provisions might well have been expected to raise the hackles of the United States.

In the end, NAFTA expressly recognizes each country's sovereign right to protect its domestic labor force and pursue its own immigration policies, thereby allowing each nation to take measures designed "to ensure border security."[5]

When it came time to seriously consider ratifying NAFTA, some politicians—most of them opponents of the treaty—linked it with immigration in two distinct, but related, ways. First, they claimed that the agreement should include express provisions restricting undocumented immigration from Mexico.

Second, they debated the indirect positive consequences of NAFTA on undocumented immigration from Mexico. Detractors claimed that NAFTA would increase legal and undocumented immigration to the United States. In contrast, supporters contended that NAFTA was the only long-term solution to undocumented immigration from Mexico. NAFTA would improve the Mexican economy, they argued, which in turn would decrease the pressures for migration.

Some politicians and interest groups claimed that an immigration side agreement, similar to those dealing with environmental and labor issues, to NAFTA should be a condition for congressional ratification. The proposed side agreement would strive to limit illegal immigration between the United States and Mexico. Because Mexico very much wanted NAFTA, the US government arguably could have exercised leverage to obtain concessions on immigration. The Mexican government, however, registered strong objections to any suggestion that it attempt to halt immigration of its citizens unlawfully to the United States. To do so, the Mexican government argued, would violate the Mexican Constitution by infringing the freedom of its citizens to travel.

Although it seems fair to say that a proposed immigration side agreement was given short shrift, there was considerable debate on the impact of NAFTA on undocumented immigration from Mexico to the United States. Some, including former President Gerald Ford, who along with former presidents Carter and Bush endorsed NAFTA, claimed that because undocumented immigrants come to this country for economic opportunity (i.e., jobs), the agreement would reduce undocumented immigration to the United States in the long run by fostering economic growth in Mexico. Others questioned that assertion, and argued that this "solution" would take many, many years to decrease undocumented immigration to the United States. Still others postulated that NAFTA might have a more subtle and speculative positive future effect on immigration. By improving the relations between the United States and Mexico, future cooperation on restricting undocumented immigration might be easier.

A consensus ultimately emerged that, even if NAFTA might decrease migration pressures in Mexico in the long run, increased migration pressures would exist to some degree for the foreseeable future. An increase in undocumented immigration in the near future was a possibility because of the potential displacement of small farmers in Mexico as a consequence of the elimination of crop subsidies under NAFTA. Others responded that the possible short-run migration pressures were overstated, and in any event, the trade agreement remained the only durable solution to undocumented immigration from Mexico.

■ A Brief History of the Inadmissibility Grounds under US Immigration Laws

In the first century of this nation's existence, several states sought to exclude the poor, as well as criminals and other "undesirables," from their territorial jurisdiction. When the federal government began comprehensively regulating immigration to the United States in the late 1800s, US immigration law from its inception sought to exclude the poor from our shores.

The United States also has a long history of restricting entry of, if not outright excluding, certain groups of racial minorities. Not coincidentally, the federalization of US immigration laws culminated with Congress's decision to exclude the poor, specifically targeting Chinese laborers, as well as criminals, prostitutes, and other noncitizens deemed to be unworthy of admission into the national community.

As their name—Chinese exclusion laws—unmistakably suggests, racial exclusions were part and parcel of the early forays of Congress into the realm of immigration regulation. The Chinese exclusion laws of the late 1800s were expressly race based, as well as class conscious. Congress later expanded the racial exclusions to apply to all persons of Asian ancestry, not only noncitizens from China.

In addition, Congress in 1924 added a national origins quota system, an elaborate system that tied immigration quotas to the nation's population demographics according to the 1890 census, which effectively denied admission to many southern and eastern Europeans—including many Jews—who were viewed as racially different from the desired Anglo Saxon norm. The discriminatory quota system remained central to US immigration laws until 1965.

US immigration laws have permitted race and class to play roles that are truly extraordinary in American law—almost always to the detriment of would-be immigrants. Why is this the case? Unlike mainstream constitutional law, in which the courts are charged with vindicating the rights of discrete and insular minorities, on immigration matters, the courts generally defer to the decisions of the legislative and executive branches of the US government, which are said to possess plenary power under the law over immigration. Through invocation of this doctrine, the courts permit "aliens" to be expressly disfavored under the law in ways that US citizens—including the poor and racial minorities—could never be.

Even though the Supreme Court fashioned the doctrine more than a century ago to bar review of the discriminatory Chinese exclusion laws, the plenary power doctrine remains the law of the land. The doctrine creates a wide gulf between ordinary constitutional law, which generally bans discrimination on the basis of race and class, and the constitutional law of immigration. And it permits noncitizens to be treated in ways that US citizens could never be.

The bottom line is that, under the Immigration and Nationality Act (INA), the proverbial deck is stacked against potential immigrants from the developing world. US immigration laws presume that "aliens" cannot enter the United States. Available immigrant visas are directed toward noncitizens with family members in this country and highly skilled workers. Various exclusions and other features of US immigration laws make it difficult for noncitizens with limited education and moderate means, even if eligible for an immigrant visa, to immigrate to the United States. Because of the plenary power doctrine, the courts let it all stand.

Changing racial sensibilities—and the civil rights movement of the 1960s—resulted in removal of the racial exclusions by Congress in 1965. However, the operation of the immigration laws continues to have starkly disparate impacts on groups of particular national origins. Features of the INA, such as the **public charge exclusion** discussed in this chapter, preclude many prospective immigrants from the developing world from lawfully immigrating to the United States.

Both race and class have historically operated in tandem under the immigration laws and in their enforcement. Examples like the Chinese exclusion laws in American history are legion.

The discriminatory treatment suffered by persons of Mexican ancestry (discussed extensively in chapter 2) was often based on both race and class. During the Great Depression, for example, state and local authorities, with federal support, arrested many persons of Mexican ancestry, mostly US citizens, in parks and other public places often used primarily by people of modest means; many subsequently were "repatriated" to Mexico to save jobs and public benefits for "true" Americans. The Bracero Program, which brought temporary, or guest, workers from Mexico to the United States from World War II through the mid-1960s, focused on bringing unskilled workers to this country to work in agriculture—only for the workers to be exploited as wage and labor protections under international agreements went largely unenforced. Operation Wetback in 1954 was a mass deportation campaign directed at workers of Mexican ancestry pursued at the same time the Bracero Program brought Mexican workers into the United States.

The remainder of this chapter outlines an important set of limitations on who can lawfully enter the United States. We identify the grounds on which, even if eligible for a visa, a noncitizen can be denied entry into the United

States under the INA. Then we further identify how the various inadmissibility grounds especially affect prospective immigrants from Mexico.

We pay special attention to the *public charge* exclusion, which allows for the denial of entry of most poor and working noncitizens into the United States and has long been a significant barrier to immigration from Mexico. This exclusion generally has disproportionate effects on potential migrants from developing nations populated by people of color. This chapter further discusses the rights available to noncitizens in proceedings in which they challenge their denial of admission into the United States.

■ The Inadmissibility Provisions of the Immigration and Nationality Act

No special treaty governs migration from Mexico to the United States, although there are generally applicable treaties that, among other things, govern the relief from deportation that the US government must provide to refugees and victims of torture. The rules of admission and inadmissibility broadly apply to nationals of all nations.

The INA's provisions, which apply to most citizens of Mexico who seek admission into this country, require a noncitizen to be eligible for a lawful permanent resident visa (an immigrant visa, or a green card) or a nonimmigrant (temporary) visa in order to enter the United States. Chapter 5 outlines the admissions criteria and procedure.

Even if a noncitizen is eligible for an immigrant visa, he or she may still be found by US immigration authorities to be excludable or inadmissible under US immigration laws. The INA includes a long laundry list of inadmissibility grounds—a "magic mirror, reflecting the fears and concerns of past Congresses," as the quote that begins this chapter states—that can result in an otherwise eligible immigrant being denied entry into the United States. The inadmissibility grounds are one way for Congress to seek some kind of "quality control" over noncitizens being admitted into the country.

Even though an applicant for admission may meet the requirements to qualify for a particular immigration category, for example, as the spouse of a US citizen or as a professional of extraordinary ability, the person may still be precluded from the issuance of an immigrant visa if he or she falls within any of the criteria of inadmissibility.

INA § 212, 8 USC § 1182, lists the grounds of inadmissibility. To enter the United States, a noncitizen will need to convince both the US

Department of State in applying for a visa and the immigration officers at the border when entering the United States that he or she is not subject to any grounds for inadmissibility (see chapter 5).

■ Rights of Persons Seeking Admission

Noncitizens seeking entry have a right to a hearing. At that hearing, the burden is on the noncitizen to show that he or she satisfies all the requirements for a visa and is not subject to any inadmissibility grounds. He or she can present evidence and can be represented by an attorney (at no cost to the government). An applicant for a temporary visa must also defeat the presumption that he or she seeks to remain indefinitely in the United States.

Noncitizens seeking admission into the United States have relatively few constitutional rights. However, there is one major exception for lawful permanent residents returning to the United States after a brief trip.

In 1982, the Supreme Court, in *Landon v. Plasencia*, held that a lawful permanent resident who was returning to the United States from a weekend trip to Mexico must have a hearing that comports with the Due Process Clause of the Fifth Amendment.[6] The Court restated the essence of the basic rule that "an alien seeking initial admission has no constitutional rights regarding his application, for the power to admit or exclude aliens is a sovereign prerogative." However, the Court went on to observe that "once an alien gains admission to our country and begins to develop the ties that go with permanent residence, his constitutional status changes accordingly. Our cases have frequently suggested that a continuously present resident alien is entitled to a fair hearing when threatened with deportation." Because Plasencia was absent from the United States for only a few days, the Court found that she was entitled to a hearing concerning her admission consistent with due process.

Currently, the INA provides a hearing to noncitizens who want to challenge their exclusion from the United States. In that hearing, they can present evidence challenging a finding of inadmissibility, but they bear the burden of proof. The grounds for inadmissibility reflect a list of criteria that Congress has enacted to promote compliance with the immigration laws and to exclude persons who are likely to be a danger to public health, safety, and security, or who are otherwise "undesirable" in the eyes of Congress. The list is a way of ensuring a certain minimum "quality" of immigrants into the United States. Historically, as applied, the inadmissibility grounds have made it difficult for poor and working people of color from the developing world to enter the country.

The INA Inadmissibility Grounds

Here is a brief summary of the major inadmissibility grounds of the INA.

IMMIGRATION CONTROL. A substantial number of inadmissibility grounds focus on violation of immigration controls, such as visa fraud, alien smuggling, and unlawful presence in the United States. In other words, violation of an immigration law itself can be grounds for inadmissibility. Immigration control grounds are a common ground invoked for denying admission of a noncitizen into the United States.

Under INA § 212(a)(6)(C), an "alien" who "by fraud or willfully misrepresenting a material fact, seeks to procure (or has sought to procure or has procured) a visa, other documentation, or admission into the United States" is inadmissible—for example, when a noncitizen seeks to enter the country based on fraudulent documents, borrowed or stolen papers, or similar forms of fraud.

Under INA § 212(a)(9), any "alien" who has been "unlawfully present" in the United States for more than 180 days but less than a year, and who voluntarily departed before any removal proceedings, is barred from admission for *three years*. Any alien who has been unlawfully present in the United States for a year or more and who is seeking readmission will be barred for *ten years*. Any person removed is subject to the ten-year bar if he or she was unlawfully present for more than 180 days.

The three- and ten-year bars have onerous impacts on prospective immigrants. Because some of the lines for immigration to this country are rather long—in some instances, many years, if not decades—some noncitizens are tempted to enter unlawfully to rejoin close family. If apprehended, they may be barred for many years from lawfully entering the United States.

Unlawful presence for purposes of the three- and ten-year bars includes those who have overstayed their visas as well as those who entered without proper inspection. Approximately 40 percent of all undocumented immigrants are visa overstays. This includes those who have entered the country lawfully but overstayed or otherwise violated the terms of their visas.

A more severe, permanent bar to admission applies to those who have been unlawfully present in the United States for an aggregate period of more than one year, depart, and then reenter or attempt to reenter the

United States without permission. These individuals cannot even apply for a waiver of this provision until *ten years* have elapsed since their last departure from the United States.

In general, any noncitizen who has been ordered removed from the United States when attempting to seek admission is inadmissible for five years from the date of such removal. A noncitizen who has been removed from the United States after having gained admission is inadmissible for ten years from the date of such removal. However, if the person has already been removed at least once in the past, or if the noncitizen was removed due to a criminal conviction for an **aggravated felony**, a crime deemed by Congress to be particularly serious, the person is inadmissible for twenty years.

Noncitizens who were previously removed, deported, or excluded from the United States and who reenter without permission are guilty of a crime under INA § 276. The federal government has vigorously prosecuted the crime of unlawful reentry, which is a felony, in the last few years.

In federal courts in the border regions, such as in San Diego and South Texas, illegal reentry prosecutions have contributed greatly to the caseload of the federal courts and created quite a lengthy backlog in the court dockets. Generally speaking, over the last decade, the prosecution of immigration crimes has increased dramatically while prosecution of other crimes, including white collar crimes like securities fraud, has been declining.

POLITICAL AND NATIONAL SECURITY. Under INA § 212(a)(3), activities considered threatening to the security of the United States can result in being denied admission into the United States. Those activities include espionage, sabotage, terrorist activity, and genocide. The preclusion also applies to those who were Nazis or members of Communist or totalitarian parties. The INA further allows for the exclusion of noncitizens whose entrance would have "serious adverse foreign policy consequences" for the United States.

Terrorist activity, an increasingly invoked national security ground for inadmissibility after September 11, 2001, is broadly defined in US immigration laws. It can include monetary contributions or any support, even if purely political (such as leafleting), for a group deemed to be a "terrorist organization" by the US government. The **USA PATRIOT Act** enacted in response to the events of September 11, 2001, added new grounds of inadmissibility for representatives of foreign terrorist organizations or any group that publicly endorses acts of terrorist activity, *and their spouses and children.*[7]

Because of heightened public fears after September 11, the United States has seen increased enforcement of the political and national security inadmissibility grounds in recent years, especially to deny entry to Arab and Muslim noncitizens.

CRIMINAL. There are few defenders of criminal noncitizens who seek to enter the United States, just as there are few defenders of noncitizens who commit crimes in the United States. Consequently, the criminal inadmissibility grounds under the INA are tough and have gotten harsher in recent years. They are ostensibly designed to protect the public from criminals.

Under INA § 212(a)(2)(A)(i)(I), an "alien" who has been convicted of, or who has admitted the commission of, a **crime involving moral turpitude** is inadmissible. Whether a crime involves "moral turpitude" depends on what must be proven for a conviction. The courts have established the basic rule that a crime involves moral turpitude if, from the statutory definition, the crime necessarily or "inherently" involves moral turpitude. Courts have ruled that crimes of moral turpitude include murder, voluntary manslaughter, aggravated assault, rape, kidnapping, theft, lewd conduct, bigamy, fraud, and other crimes having the intent to defraud as an element. On the other hand, courts have concluded that crimes such as joyriding and simple assault do not involve moral turpitude.

Noncitizens who have been convicted of two or more criminal offenses, regardless of whether moral turpitude or drugs were involved, are inadmissible under INA § 212(a)(2)(B) if the aggregate sentence to confinement actually imposed was five years or more.

Persons who have committed offenses relating to narcotics and marijuana are extremely disfavored under US immigration laws. This is part and parcel of the "war on drugs," which has been waged domestically in the United States for several decades.

Under INA § 212(a)(2)(A)(i)(II), "aliens" convicted of violating *any* law or regulation relating to a controlled substance are inadmissible. The statute also renders inadmissible "aliens" whom the US authorities "know[] or [have] reason to believe" are or have been drug traffickers. A mere arrest for a controlled substance offense, without a conviction, may form the basis for a reasonable belief that a noncitizen was a drug trafficker. Noncitizens who are determined to be drug addicts or abusers are also inadmissible.

Under INA § 212(a)(2)(D), noncitizens who are prostitutes or procurers, or entering the United States to engage in other unlawful commercialized

Criminal Aliens

Although this op-ed discusses removals, not noncitizens denied admission, it gives the reader an idea of how "criminal aliens" are generally disfavored under US immigration laws.

Bill Ong Hing, "Deported for Shoplifting?"

Would we deport Winona Ryder for shoplifting? Of course not. In fact, for her felony conviction, Ryder will pay restitution, engage in community service, and face no jail time. Yet, every day, the United States deports lawful immigrants and refugees who have been convicted of minor offenses such as shoplifting and writing bad checks. Yes, some have committed more serious crimes involving violence or narcotics, but all have been incarcerated, then deported on top of that.

The planned deportation of almost 1,400 Cambodian refugees back to a country with one of the world's worst human rights records should make us rethink our deportation laws. For years Cambodia would not accept deportable refugees, but last March, enticed by further economic aid from the United States, it signed a repatriation agreement. Since then, 36 Cambodian nationals have been sent back, while others await processing by US immigration officials. Those deported have been detained by the Cambodian government for weeks at a time awaiting further "processing," while they and their US families have been pressured with extortion demands. Money is requested for every little privilege, such as $50 for the use of towels.

The real tragedy of the deportation of Cambodian refugees is who they are. Most of those being deported have little connection to contemporary Cambodia, their only memories being of the cruelty and starvation under the Khmer Rouge and the "Killing Fields" massacre of more than 2 million of their countrymen. Some do not speak Khmer, and many do not read or write the language. Some were born in refugee camps in Thailand and have never set foot in Cambodia.

Others entered the United States as infants. Most have resided in the United States for more than 20 years and for all intents and purposes are Americans, having grown up here. Like it or not, they are products of the American environment.

Who are the Cambodian deportees? Lundy See of Philadelphia entered as a refugee at age 8; he was convicted of assault at 16 and served 14 months in prison. Sokha Sun of Seattle, who possessed a gun illegally, came to the United States as a three-week-old refugee. Borom Chea, who grew up near Sacramento, entered at the age of 3. At 17 he was convicted of robbery and served 7 1/2 years in state prison. Other Cambodian deportees, who wish to remain anonymous, include a young man whose offense was public urination; another was convicted of drunken driving; one was convicted of two petty thefts. A recent group of deportees who arrived in Phnom Penh included an 80-year-old man. Left behind are their spouses, children, parents, and friends. In years past, deportation relief might have been afforded to many of these people if certain hardships or rehabilitation could be established, but an overhaul of the immigration laws in 1996 closed this avenue for a second chance to most "alien criminals."

As a sovereign nation, we certainly have the technical authority to punish and remove these people from our country. But even though we have this power, how, when and on what basis should we exercise it? Are we really proud of deporting people who entered the country as infants to a land where they have no real ties? People who have served their criminal sentences? People who may have convincing evidence of rehabilitation? People who have stable families and communities ready to help get them back on their feet? Many of these deportees deserved a second chance, but our system provided them with no opportunity to present their cases.

Winona Ryder is lucky she did not enter the country as a toddler from a Thai refugee camp. If she had, she might be faced with an armed escort to Phnom Penh.

Source: Washington Post, Dec. 29, 2002, B7 ∎

vice, and who have engaged in prostitution or procuring within ten years of the application for admission, are inadmissible. The provision also applies to noncitizens coming to the United States to engage in loan sharking or gambling.

Because the public safety rationales are similar to those underlying the criminal inadmissibility grounds, the criminal deportation grounds are also aggressively enforced by US immigration authorities. Even though September 11, 2001, led to increased concern with national security, "criminal aliens" are the vast majority of the 200,000 or more noncitizens removed from the United States each year, with close to 90 percent regularly from Mexico and Central America.

PUBLIC HEALTH. Public health concerns animate certain inadmissibility grounds, which are subject to a noncitizen's screening upon entry into the United States. Health inadmissibility grounds can be divided into four categories: (1) communicable diseases; (2) failure to obtain vaccinations; (3) mental or physical disorders; and (4) drug addiction or abuse.

Under INA § 212(a)(1)(A)(i), an applicant for a visa who has a communicable disease is inadmissible. Tuberculosis and sexually transmitted disease, including gonorrhea and syphilis, are examples of diseases that subject a noncitizen to a finding of inadmissibility. A noncitizen testing positive for these illnesses can have the disease treated and cured and then be admissible.

Until the Obama administration changed the policy in 2009, a noncitizen with the virus that causes acquired immune deficiency syndrome (AIDS) was also inadmissible. Although individuals who are HIV-positive were inadmissible, they could under certain strict conditions qualify for a waiver. The HIV exclusion was controversial and is one of the few health grounds that, until 2008, was expressly mentioned in the INA. Contrary to the opinions of health professionals, Congress feared the spread of the virus in the United States as well as the possible medical costs of noncitizens who later develop AIDS.

Under INA § 212(a)(1)(A)(ii), an applicant is inadmissible for failing to present evidence of vaccination against preventable communicable diseases: mumps, measles, rubella, polio, tetanus and diphtheria toxoids, pertussis, influenza type B, and hepatitis B. This provision may be waived if the applicant obtains a vaccination, or if a civil surgeon or similar official certifies that the vaccination would not be medically appropriate, or if the vaccination would be contrary to the person's religious or moral beliefs.

Under INA § 212(a)(1)(A)(iii), applicants are inadmissible if they have a mental or physical disorder and related behavior that may threaten the property, welfare, and safety of themselves or others, or who have had such a disorder in the past that is likely to recur.

Alcoholism can serve as a basis for a finding of inadmissibility. A conviction for driving under the influence can serve as evidence of alcoholism. Under § 212(a)(1)(A)(iv), drug addicts and drug abusers are inadmissible. This inadmissibility criterion applies to current, not past, abuse or addiction.

ECONOMIC: THE PUBLIC CHARGE EXCLUSION. One of the most commonly raised substantive grounds of inadmissibility is under INA § 212(a)(4), which allows denial of entry to a prospective immigrant deemed likely to become a public charge. US Department of State and US Citizenship and Immigration Service officials have much discretion in determining whether an applicant is likely to become a public charge. Some of the factors generally considered are the age of the noncitizen and his or her ability and willingness to work, promise of a job, close relatives in the United States, and mental and physical health. One would expect that a healthy person in the prime of life ordinarily should not be considered likely to become a public charge.

The public charge exclusion has a long, if not illustrious, history in the United States. Despite the stated ideal that the nation openly embraces the

The "Huddled Masses"—A Myth?

Emma Lazarus wrote the sonnet "The New Colossus" in 1883. Its final lines were engraved on a bronze plaque placed on the pedestal of the Statue of Liberty in 1912:

> Give me your tired, your poor,
> Your huddled masses yearning to breathe free,
> The wretched refuse of your teeming shore.
> Send these, the homeless, tempest-tossed to me, I lift my
> lamp beside the golden door! ∎

"huddled masses" of the world, the United States has not been particularly open to poor and working-class people seeking admission into the country. Buried in the American psyche is the deep and enduring fear that unless strong defensive measures are put into place and aggressively enforced, poor immigrants will come in flocks to the United States, flood the poorhouses, and overconsume scarce public benefits that many Americans believe should be reserved for US citizens.

Responding to the fear of immigrant public benefit users, US immigration laws long have provided that, even if otherwise eligible for an immigrant or nonimmigrant (temporary) visa, "aliens" "likely at any time to become a public charge" cannot be admitted into the United States.[8] Over time, Congress has significantly tightened the public charge exclusion, and during the last decade, it has been enforced with increased vigor.

Because of similar concerns, federal, state (including California and Arizona), and local governments have limited public benefit eligibility for noncitizens, legal as well as undocumented immigrants. "Welfare reform" in 1996 achieved most of its monetary savings by denying benefit eligibility to legal immigrants.

Currently, consular officers must consider the following factors in applying the public charge exclusion to noncitizens seeking entry into the United States: the noncitizen's age, health, family status, assets, resources and financial status, and education and skills. Put differently, a prospective entrant must establish that they are and will continue to be a member of a particular socioeconomic class—most definitely not poor or likely to ever become poor—to lawfully migrate to the United States.

To this end, the law requires that each prospective immigrant secure a well-heeled sponsor willing to "agree[] to provide support to maintain the sponsored alien at an annual income that is not less than 125 percent of the Federal poverty line."[9] Sponsors must submit legally enforceable *affidavits of support*, which obligate the sponsor to reimburse the government if an immigrant somehow manages to secure public benefits.

The US government routinely invokes the public charge exclusion as a ground to deny immigrant and nonimmigrant (temporary) visas to the United States to noncitizens from the developing world. For well over a century, the exclusion in one form or another has made it especially difficult for poor and working people from Asia, Africa, and Latin America to travel lawfully—even for a short visit—to the United States.

In 1996, Congress toughened the public charge exclusion, including significant tightening of the affidavit of support provisions to, among other things, expressly make the affidavits legally enforceable in courts of law, which had not previously been the case. The unmistakable intent was to make it more difficult for noncitizens of modest means to migrate to the United States. The very same year, Congress stripped lawful immigrant residents—including those who paid taxes—of eligibility for several major federal public benefit programs.[10]

As the existence of the public charge exclusion suggests, the fear that immigrants may overconsume scarce public benefits remains prevalent. Consider California's watershed Proposition 187, a law passed overwhelmingly by the Golden State's voters in 1994, which would have denied almost all public benefits, including an elementary and secondary school education, to undocumented immigrants.[11] Deep-seated anti-Mexican animus and concern with the socioeconomic class of today's immigrants, combined with legitimate concerns surrounding immigration control and immigrant benefit receipt, contributed to overwhelming voter support for the measure.

Although a court prevented the bulk of the initiative from ever taking effect, the passage of Proposition 187 unquestionably signaled to the US Congress the widespread discomfort among many Americans with immigration, specifically public benefit receipt by undocumented immigrants. Soon after, Congress passed welfare reform in 1996, which achieved the bulk of its fiscal savings by denying legal immigrants access to many federal benefit programs. Congress also increased funding for greatly heightened enforcement measures along the US–Mexico border. Like many of the inadmissability grounds, these measures had disparate impacts on prospective immigrants from Mexico.

RACIAL AND CLASS IMPACTS OF THE CURRENT INADMISSABILITY RULES. With this background in mind, we can look at the specific inadmissibility rules that adversely affect legal migration from Mexico. As seen with the public charge exclusion, the enforcement of the inadmissibility grounds have race, class, and national origin impacts. Indeed, there may be no better body of American law to illustrate the close nexus between race and class than US immigration law and enforcement.

At bottom, the provisions of US immigration laws on admissibility and inadmissibility and their enforcement have historically operated—and continue to operate—to prevent many poor and working-class people of color from migrating to, and to punish those living in, the United States.

For much of US history, express racial exclusions, such as the Chinese exclusion laws that Congress later extended to migration from all of Asia, were endemic to US immigration laws. Unlike in the past, express racial exclusions can fortunately no longer be found in US immigration laws.

A by-product of the civil rights movement, the **Immigration Act of 1965** abolished the discriminatory national origins quota system that had remained a bulwark of US immigration laws since 1924 and had set quotas by country based on population in the late nineteenth century (before the large migration from southern and eastern Europe).[12] As a consequence of the change in the law, the nation saw a dramatic shift in the racial demographics of immigration, with a sharp increase in migration from Asia.

Although Congress eliminated the racial exclusions from the immigration laws, economic litmus tests, arbitrary annual limits on the number of immigrants per country, and other provisions of the current US immigration laws that limit entry into the United States all have racially disparate impacts on the stream of immigrants to the United States. Everything else being equal, people from the developing world—predominantly "people of color," as that category is popularly understood in the United States— find it much more difficult under US immigration laws to gain admission to this country than similarly situated noncitizens from the developed (and predominantly white) world. Nonetheless, because of the consistently high demand among people in the developing world to migrate to the United States, people of color consistently dominate the stream of immigrants to this country.

Although racial exclusions are something of the past, the express—and aggressive—exclusion of the poor through the public charge exclusion remains a fundamental function of modern US immigration law and its enforcement. In sharp contrast, domestic laws generally cannot—constitutionally at least—discriminate on their face against poor and working people, such as by regulating their right to domestic travel. The express discrimination against poor and working-class noncitizens by US immigration laws has disparate national origin and racial impacts.

In fact, race and class permeate modern US immigration law and enforcement. This in part results from the critical roles both race and class play in the formation and maintenance of the American national identity, which ultimately rests at the core of a nation's immigration laws. Immigration law helps determine who is allowed access to the United States and who, once they are here, possesses full membership in US society (and thus who is truly American). The exclusion of poor and working people of color from the group of immigrants eligible for admission into the United States reveals how we as a nation see ourselves as well as our aspirations.

A significant component of undocumented immigrants are poor and working-class people. The majority of immigrants in modern times are people of color. Immigrants as a group find themselves marginalized in US society as a result of their immigration status, with undocumented status more stigmatizing and subordinating than lawful status (but with lawful immigrants afforded fewer legal and social advantages than US citizens). Noncitizens are generally subordinated in American social life based on, among other characteristics, race, class, and immigration status.

Besides the public charge exclusion, other features of US immigration laws restrict the admission of noncitizens and have disparate racial impacts.

THE WESTERN HEMISPHERE AND PER COUNTRY CEILINGS. Congress passed the Immigration Act of 1965 in the wake of the **Civil Rights Act of 1964,** not only abolishing the national origins quota system but also barring racial considerations from expressly entering into immigrant visa decisions and imposing for the first time a ceiling of 120,000 on migration from the Western Hemisphere. Immigration from the Western Hemisphere had not previously been restricted through quotas. This limitation was part of a congressional compromise by those who wanted to remove discriminatory quotas and those who feared—and sought to avoid—a drastic upswing in Latin American immigration.

Put differently, Congress in 1965 coupled more generous treatment of those outside the Western Hemisphere with less generous treatment of Latin Americans. The blue ribbon Select Commission on Immigration and Refugee Policy summarized the unseemly history:

> The United States was ... far from free of prejudice ... and one part of the 1965 law reflected change in policy that was in part due to anti-foreign sentiments. *Prejudice against dark-skinned people ... remained strong. In the years after World War II, as the proportion of Spanish-speaking residents increased, much of the lingering nativism in the United States was directed against those from Mexico and Central and South America....* Giving in to ... pressures as a price to be paid for abolishing the national

origins system, Congress put into the 1965 amendments a ceiling [on Western Hemisphere immigration] to close the last remaining open door of US policy.[13]

The abolition of the national origins quota system in 1965 thus removed blatant racially based exclusions but nonetheless failed to cleanse all remnants of racism from US immigration laws. Various characteristics of modern immigration laws, although facially neutral, disparately impact—some might say discriminate against—noncitizens of color from developing nations, including Mexico.

Later, the Western Hemisphere ceiling was eliminated and per-country ceilings were applied to each nation in the hemisphere, an across-the-board annual numerical limit of approximately 26,000 immigrants from each nation. Per-country ceilings in US immigration law today still generally limit immigration from any one country in a year.[14] Certain categories of immigrants, such as noncitizen spouses of US citizens, are exempt from this ceiling. The limits apply uniformly, however great the demand of a particular country's citizens to come to the United States. Although facially neutral, the ceilings in operation have both class and nationality (and thus racial) impacts.

Countries that have much less demand among their citizens for immigrating to the United States, such as Iceland, Denmark, and Sweden, enjoy the same annual ceilings as countries like Mexico, the Philippines, India, and China, all nations whose demand among their citizens to migrate to this country greatly exceeds their maximum annual ceiling. Even with important exceptions to the ceilings—for immediate relatives, for example—the per-country limits create long lines of prospective immigrants from certain countries and significantly shorter, or no, lines for similarly situated people from almost all other nations for certain immigrant visas.

Here is one example of the disparate impacts of the per-country ceilings on one group of prospective immigrants from Mexico. In June 2009, the State Department was processing first-preference immigrant visas for sons and daughters of US citizens filed in *November 2002*, except for Mexico, whose visas had been filed in *October 1992*; Mexican natives had to wait a *decade longer* than similarly situated noncitizens from other nations.[15] Mexico is one of only a handful of nations—all of them developing nations populated by people of color—that are adversely affected in disproportionate ways by the per-country ceilings.

It is worth highlighting that, as this example illustrates, some prospective immigrants may be forced to wait many years—indeed decades—to immigrate lawfully to the United States. Many prospective immigrants find such long waits to be unrealistic and undoubtedly are attracted to circumvent the immigration laws through undocumented immigration. Can you imagine waiting nearly seventeen years or more to rejoin your parents in another country? Is it realistic to expect anyone to wait that long?

And these are the fortunate noncitizens. For many without family members in this country and who are not skilled professionals, there is *no line* to wait in at all to come lawfully to the United States. The standard claim that undocumented immigrants should "wait in line" to immigrate lawfully makes little sense for those who have no legal avenues for admission. Their only choice is to come to, or remain in, the United States unlawfully.

Given the lower average annual incomes in the developing world, including Mexico compared with those in this country, and the relative economic opportunity in the United States, the per-country ceilings have class and racial impacts. Many low- and medium-skilled workers of color from those nations seek to immigrate to the United States to pursue superior economic opportunities. Thousands of prospective immigrants from nations with demand much greater than the fixed annual ceilings—developing nations populated by people of color—encounter much longer lines for admission than similarly situated prospective immigrants from other nations. Citizens of Mexico are one of the nationality groups most adversely affected.

LIMITED EMPLOYMENT VISAS.   Immigrants with family visas constitute the greatest number who come to the United States each year. The lack of legal avenues for employment-related immigration, especially for low- and moderately skilled workers, greatly contributes to undocumented immigration, especially from Mexico. The employment visas, which are relatively few and often have long lines, are generally limited to professionals and highly skilled workers.

If a noncitizen is not eligible for an immigrant visa, he or she is not eligible for entering the United States. There is an enduring concern from many quarters about the limited number and type of employment visas available—especially for low- and medium-skilled workers—under US immigration laws. A frequently voiced criticism is that the numerical and other requirements for immigrant visas based on employment skills are not adequately calibrated to US labor needs.

Importantly, employment visas under the INA are much more plentiful for skilled workers than for unskilled ones. "One critique of the entire [American] immigration system is the fact that low-skilled workers, as a practical matter, do not have an avenue for lawful immigration to the United States, either temporarily or permanently."[16]

Consequently, many low- and moderately skilled workers cannot lawfully migrate to the United States unless they are eligible for family visas (and then they still must overcome the public charge exclusion). As a result, many enter and remain in the country in violation of US immigration laws. To make matters worse, for the undocumented immigrants who circumvent the immigration laws, they often find themselves working in the secondary labor market for low wages in poor conditions.

Even skilled workers often find it difficult to secure visas for which they are lawfully eligible in a timely manner. The complexities and delays of the US Department of Labor process of certification for many employment visas has been the subject of sustained criticism from business leaders and organizations such as the US Chamber of Commerce. Microsoft CEO Bill Gates regularly testifies before Congress about the difficulties employers experience in lawfully seeking to bring skilled noncitizen workers to the United States.

In short, the bulk of the employment visas under US immigration laws are for highly skilled workers and investors. Professional athletes, for example, regularly—and relatively easily—migrate to the United States. This disproportionately affects low- and moderately skilled workers from the developing world, who are generally not eligible for employment visas but nonetheless desire to come for jobs in this country.

The lack of lawful avenues for workers to migrate not only helps to explain the continuing flow of undocumented immigrants to the United States, but also illuminates the persistent complaints by business leaders about the difficulties of bringing skilled workers to this country as well as advocacy for guest worker programs that would allow unskilled labor to lawfully enter the country. The fact that 60 percent of the undocumented immigrants are from Mexico reflects the impact of the lack of employment visas for many prospective immigrants from that country.

■ Racial Impacts of the Inadmissibility Rules

Express bars on the admission of certain races, such as the Chinese exclusion laws and the national origins quota system disfavoring immigration from southern and eastern Europe, mar this nation's otherwise proud immigration history. Racial exclusions have evolved into new and different devices that have racially disparate impacts on prospective immigrants to the United States. Consequently, race remains a significant issue in the operation and enforcement of US immigration laws.

Many devices, combined with the class-based exclusions, disproportionately exclude people of color from immigrating to the United States. The public charge exclusion and per-country ceilings, for example, have racial, as well as class, impacts. The limited opportunities for unskilled noncitizens to secure employment visas, which tends to disproportionately impact people from the developing world (many of whom are people of color), do as well.

Moreover, race-based enforcement is endemic to modern US immigration laws. People of color dominate the populations of both legal and undocumented immigrants. At the same time, people of color are disparately affected by the various inadmissibility grounds in US immigration laws and frequently experience roadblocks to their lawful admission. Not coincidentally, people of color are disproportionately represented among the noncitizens deported from the United States.[17]

■ Concluding Thoughts

The race and class biases in US immigration laws are deeply interrelated. These laws include several inadmissible grounds that directly affect migrants from Mexico.

Importantly, the public charge exclusion and per-country ceilings have significant impacts on poor and working persons from Mexico, even those who might otherwise be eligible for a visa. The lack of employment visas—and the denial of entry to any noncitizen without a visa—for low- and medium-skilled workers makes it difficult for these workers to come to the United States lawfully. These features of US immigration law contribute to pressures for undocumented migration from Mexico to the United States and no doubt contribute to the sizeable undocumented Mexican immigrant population in the country.

More liberal admissions and more limited exclusion and inadmissibility grounds would help reduce the pressures for undocumented immigration. Reform of the immigration laws is necessary to allow more workers into the United States and to reduce the current incentives in the system to circumvent the law.

■ Discussion Questions

1. The US immigration laws apply in the same ways to noncitizens of Zambia as to those from Mexico. Should there be special immigration rules governing Mexico and the United States given the historic relationship, lengthy shared land border, and long history of migration between the two neighboring nations? What might a possible treaty between the two countries governing migration provide?

2. Inscribed on the Statue of Liberty, the famous poem of Emma Lazarus declares that the United States embraces the "huddled masses" of the world. Given that credo, why has US immigration law consistently sought to restrict the number of poor and working immigrants coming to the United States? Explain your reasoning. Through such devices as the public charge exclusion, per-country ceilings, and the lack of avenues for legal immigration for low- and medium-skilled workers, do US immigration laws keep the "huddled masses" from entering and remaining in the United States?

3. Should the United States eliminate the public charge exclusion and other features of its immigration laws that have disparate racial and socioeconomic impacts on immigrants and prospective immigrants from the developing world, especially Mexico? Explain your reasoning. Why is it politically popular to erect barriers to the poor and to racial minorities from migrating to the United States and to deny public benefits to immigrants, especially "illegal aliens," in the United States?

4. What should the admission rules be for permanent immigrants and temporary visitors under US immigration laws? Should the law have any rules of inadmissibility for noncitizens? Why not allow more liberal immigration policies and perhaps even open borders? See Jason L. Riley, *Let Them In: The Case for Open Borders* (New York: Gotham Books, 2008). Explain your reasoning.

5. Race- and class-based immigration enforcement is a central characteristic of the operation of US immigration laws. Should the consideration of race be eliminated from immigration enforcement? Class? If so, how? Explain your reasoning. (We consider these questions in detail in chapter 9.)

■ Suggested Readings

Acuña, Rodolfo. 2007. *Occupied America: A History of Chicanos,* 6th ed. New York: Pearson Longman.

Balderrama, Francisco E., and Raymond Rodriguez. 2006. *Decade of Betrayal: Mexican Repatriation in the 1930s.* Rev. ed. Albuquerque: University of New Mexico Press.

Johnson, Kevin R. 2004. *The "Huddled Masses" Myth: Immigration and Civil Rights.* Philadelphia: Temple University Press.

Salyer, Lucy E. 1995. *Laws Harsh as Tigers: Chinese Immigrants and the Shaping of Modern Immigration Law.* Chapel Hill: University of North Carolina Press.

Trujillo, Bernard. 2000. "Immigrant Visa Distribution: The Case of Mexico." *Wisconsin Law Review* 2000, no. 3: 713.

———. 2010. "Mexican Families and United States Immigration Reform." *Fordham Urban Law Journal* 38, no. 1: 415.

■ Notes

Epigraphs: *Landon v. Plasencia*, 459 US 21, 32 (1982), emphasis added; *Lennon v. INS*, 527 F.2d 187, 189 (2d Cir. 1975).

1. Treaty of Guadalupe Hidalgo, aka Treaty of Peace, Friendship, Limits, and Settlement, Feb. 2, 1848, United States–Mexico, 9 Stat. 922, TS No. 207, 9 Bevans 791; North American Free Trade Agreement, United States–Canada–Mexico, Dec. 17, 1992, 32 I.L.M. 296 (1993).

2. *In re* Rodriguez, 81 F. 337, 352 (W.D. Tex. 1897).

3. *People v. Naglee*, 1 Cal. 232, 248–51 (1850).

4. Pub. L. No. 99–603, 100 Stat. 3359 (1986).

5. NAFTA, Article 1601.

6. *Landon v. Plasencia,* 459 US 21 (1982).

7. Pub. L. No. 107–56, 115 Stat. 272 (2001).

8. INA § 212(a)(4), 8 USC § 1182(a)(4). The INA further provides that the receipt of public benefits within five years of entry into the United States by a noncitizen may result in the immigrant's deportation. See INA § 207(a)(5), 8 USC. § 1227(a)(5).

9. INA § 213A(a)(1), 8 USC § 1183A(a)(1).

10. See the Personal Responsibility and Work Opportunity Reconciliation Act of 1996, Pub. L. No. 104–193, 110 Stat. 2105. Congress later restored certain benefits to lawful immigrants. See Noncitizen Benefit Clarification and Other Technical

Amendments Act of 1998, Pub. L. No. 105–306, 112 Stat. 2926. Undocumented immigrants are generally ineligible for all major federal public benefit programs.

11. A court invalidated most of Proposition 187 as an unconstitutional intrusion on the federal power over immigration. See *League of United Latin Am. Citizens v. Wilson*, 908 F. Supp. 755 (C.D. Cal. 1995). Arizona later adopted a measure similar in important respects to Proposition 187, which the courts refused to disturb. See *Friendly House v. Napolitano*, 419 F.3d 930 (9th Cir. 2005).

12. Pub. L. 89–236, 79 Stat. 911 (1965).

13. US Select Commission on Immigration and Refugee Policy, *Staff Report: US Immigration Policy and the National Interest* 208 (1981), emphasis added; footnote omitted.

14. INA § 203(a)(3), 8 USC § 1153(a)(3).

15. See US Department of State, *Visa Bulletin for June 2009* (2009), available at www.travel.state.gov/visa/bulletin/bulletin_4497.html.

16. Enid Trucios-Haynes, "Civil Rights, Latinos, and Immigration: Cybercascades and Other Distortions in the Immigration Reform Debate," *Brandeis Law Journal* 44 (2006): 637, 643.

17. See US Department of Homeland Security, *Yearbook of Immigration Statistics* (2007), table 39, showing that approximately two-thirds of all persons deported from the United States were from Mexico; www.dhs.gov/xlibrary/assets/statistics/year book/2007/ois_2007_yearbook.pdf.

7

Removal

A lot of the guys I work with did nothing but the most complex cases—taking down multigenerational crime families, international crime, drug trafficking syndicates—you know, big fish. Now these folks are dealing with these improper entry and illegal reentry [immigration] cases. It's demoralizing for them, and us.

—unnamed senior federal prosecutor working on the US border

How is US immigration law used to throw people out of the country? The United States can deport (lawyers use the formal term *remove*) all sorts of immigrants, from those who have crossed into this country a few minutes ago, to those who have been living and working in the United States for decades. This chapter examines how immigration law is used to remove tens of thousands of noncitizens every year.

We examine the ways in which an individual may be removed, moving from the least formal to the most formal procedures. We start by looking at **voluntary return**, an administrative device that is frequently used but involves little process. We then study *expedited removal*, a low-process mechanism designed to hasten the removal of some kinds of noncitizens.

Next, we consider the higher-process mechanisms of removal and the substantive grounds (such as committing a crime) that authorize removal. We also examine the two most common forms of relief from removal provided by the Immigration and Nationality Act (INA): (1) *voluntary departure*, which allows an otherwise deportable noncitizen to depart the country without being formally removed; and (2) *cancellation of removal*, which not only halts deportation but even gives the noncitizen a green card. Finally, we will look at a recent trend in immigration enforcement, dubbed **Operation Streamline**, which uses federal criminal law to enhance the punishment for unlawful crossers and continues to blur the distinction between immigration as administrative law and immigration as criminal law.

■ Voluntary Return

One of the most common ways of removing people from the United States receives slight attention in the INA but has developed as a necessary mechanism for Border Patrol officers to manage the flow of crossers.[1]

Voluntary return is a quick, nonjudicial process offered to undocumented border crossers who lack criminal backgrounds and are caught unlawfully crossing the southern border. This process consists of Border Patrol detecting and apprehending the undocumented immigrant, processing the immigrant at the closest Border Patrol station, and then transporting the crosser back to the Mexican border for release.

Border Patrol officers are trained to handle the influx of undocumented immigrants in the most expeditious and least costly way possible. Once a border crosser is apprehended, the Border Patrol checks for criminal histories in IDENT. IDENT is an automated biometric identification system that digitally scans the immigrant's right and left index fingers and categorizes the immigrant depending on criminal and immigration history. The IDENT system stores names and biographical information. If the undocumented immigrant has a criminal record, removal proceedings are initiated.

If the immigrant does not have a criminal record, voluntary return is an option with virtually no stigma attached. Voluntary return takes significantly less time and paperwork than initiating formal removal proceedings, which is required for noncitizens with criminal records. The amount of time it takes to process an undocumented immigrant for voluntary return depends on the experience of the Border Patrol officer and how quickly he or she can obtain and input the personal data into IDENT.

Border Patrol agents are trained to offer captured crossers a sort of Hobson's choice. The immigrants (typically Mexican immigrants caught crossing the southern border of the United States into Arizona, California, or Texas) are given a choice between jail time (an increasingly credible threat since the advent of Operation Streamline) and voluntary (and immediate) return. The officer informs the undocumented crosser that the alternative to prosecution is to voluntarily return to Mexico, after supplying some personal information. Most often, the immigrant chooses to voluntarily return to Mexico.

The cost of return is borne by the US government. Voluntary return does not trigger the five- or ten-year bars for readmission that would keep out people who were "unlawfully present" in the United States for a period under the inadmissibility rules. The Border Patrol typically allows up to thirty voluntary returns to a single crosser before initiating more formal removal proceedings.

Voluntary *return* is completed at or within miles of the border and is not to be confused with voluntary *departure*, which is determined and requested in removal proceedings.

◼ Expedited Removal

Working our way up from *no-process* removal (voluntary return), we now turn to *low-process* removal, the process instituted by congressional reforms to US immigration laws in 1996 known as *expedited removal*. The expedited removal process was established to address the perceived problem that some noncitizens who had very weak claims to enter the United States were getting "too much process" before being removed. At the time expedited removal was enacted, as well as today, some noncitizens present false documents to border officers or otherwise misrepresent themselves in an effort to gain admission to the United States. Expedited removal was designed to skim off applicants with the weakest claims and remove them quickly at low cost in terms of process and lawyering.

Before 1996, immigration officials had no authority to remove a noncitizen at the border for improper documentation; that authority was reserved to immigration judges. The public perceived that noncitizens were using legal technicalities to delay their inevitable deportation. Policy makers considered it unfair to give undocumented entrants the same access to counsel and formal removal proceedings as people who had been lawfully admitted. Now, border officials return some noncitizens to their home country without giving them a hearing before an immigration judge. During the expedited removal process, noncitizens may be kept in detention. Anyone removed in this way is also subject to the five- or ten-year bars for admission.

Built into expedited removal is a safeguard to avoid turning away legitimate refugees (i.e., noncitizens fleeing political and related persecution). We would expect some to arrive in the United States without adequate immigration documents. To identify these individuals, border officials are required to determine whether the person held a "credible fear" of persecution associated with return to his or her home country. If a person expresses such fear to a border official, he or she is referred to an asylum officer for a "credible fear" interview. Persons not speaking English are provided with an interpreter. Finally, if a person placed in expedited removal makes a claim of status as a US citizen, lawful permanent resident, asylee, or refugee, they have access to administrative and judicial review.

Since the events of September 11, 2001, undocumented immigration rightly or wrongly has been viewed as a serious threat to national security. Consequently, expedited removal, considered a valuable tool for border enforcement, has been expanded in several ways since then. For example, immigration agents currently can apprehend and remove individuals not only at the border but up to one hundred miles from a port of entry and up to fourteen days after entry. It is now more common for asylum seekers to be detained during evaluation of their claims until it is determined whether or not they should be removed.

Border officials refer aliens who express fear to an asylum officer from Citizen and Immigration Services (CIS), who then makes a determination of credible fear. If the asylum officer determines that the person has a credible fear, the case is referred to an immigration judge for potential

Expedited Removal at Work

Immigration procedure requires Department of Homeland Security personnel to ask a series of "protection questions" to determine if a noncitizen has a "credible fear" of persecution if returned to their home country. The questions are:

1. Why did you leave your home country or country of last residence?

2. Do you have any fear or concern about being returned to your home country or being removed from the United States?

3. Would you be harmed if you were returned to your home country or country of last residence?

4. Do you have any questions or is there anything else you would like to add?[1]

1. Congressional Research Service, *Immigration Policy on Expedited Removal of Aliens*, http://opencrs.com/document/RL33109/2006-01-18, updated January 18, 2006, at CRS-4 n19. ∎

asylum. If the officer finds that the person does not have a credible fear, the entrant may request review of the asylum officer's findings by an immigration judge. The system allows for review of immigration judges' findings by the Board of Immigration Appeals (BIA).

The Department of Homeland Security (DHS) reported 106,200 expedited removals in 2007, making up about 33 percent of all removals that year.[2] Mexican citizens composed almost 61 percent of all expedited removals in 2007 and 65 percent of removals overall. Removals have steadily increased since 2001; there were 70 percent more removals in 2007 than in 2001.[3]

The great majority of noncitizens subject to expedited removal voluntarily withdraw their applications rather than be subject to actual removal or even to continue pursuing a credible fear determination. In 2003, of 177,040 noncitizens subject to expedited removal, 72.5 percent withdrew their applications, 24.5 percent were removed, and 3.0 percent progressed to the credible fear interview. Of those referred to CIS for a credible fear determination, more than 93 percent were approved.[4]

Expedited removal has been a lightning rod for criticism. A study of the expedited removal process conducted soon after it was initiated indicated that most individuals who successfully advanced claims for asylum based on the credible fear interview were educated English-speaking males with family contacts in the United States and Canada.[5] The study concluded that women, the poor, and those without English fluency had difficulty prevailing in the credible fear interview process. This may be because officials are not consistently applying the appropriate criteria, or that certain individuals are less capable of understanding and expressing their right to asylum, or both.

The Center for Human Rights and International Justice also evaluated a government report on expedited removal and determined that many of its methods for reporting efficiency and effectiveness did not accurately reflect what was actually happening during expedited removal interviews and proceedings.[6] Data presented in the report were largely self-reported and may therefore not be sufficiently reliable, as would be a study that includes on-site observation as part of the research. For example, the data indicate that "almost all persons who gave up their claims of fear were ordered removed, rather than being permitted to withdraw their applications," which subjected those individuals to a five-year bar on their return to the United States.

Stories of individual experiences with the expedited removal process include those of US citizens who were detained in error and non-English-speaking asylum seekers who were denied interpreter assistance with the credible fear interview. Some critics maintain that the procedural system fails to meet the needs of unaccompanied children swept up in the expedited removal process, particularly minors from Mexico. Children are less likely to request available resources when officially entered into immigration and removal proceedings.

The US Commission on International Religious Freedom (USCIRF) has prepared several reports on expedited removal and submitted its recommendations to the DHS.[7] The commission was directed to examine the effect of expedited removal, specifically whether immigration officials were improperly encouraging noncitizens to withdraw their applications, incorrectly failing to refer noncitizens for credible fear determinations, incorrectly removing noncitizens to countries where they may face persecution, or improperly or under inappropriate conditions detaining aliens.[8]

In its study, USCIRF was able to observe actual inspections at ports of entry and found serious flaws overall in the expedited removal process. Although the policy and procedures for expedited removal and credible fear determinations are clear, the USCIRF found that the policy is not consistently followed. For example, in 15 percent of observed cases in which the noncitizen expressed a fear of removal, a referral to the interview was not given. The study also found discrepancies between processes at different ports of entry. For example, San Antonio released 94 percent of asylum seekers from detention pending their hearing, but New Jersey released fewer than 4 percent.[9] USCIRF also expressed concern about expanding expedited removal without addressing previously identified flaws in the process.[10]

USCIRF continues to exchange information with the DHS and advocate for improving the quality of the expedited removal program. Recommendations under consideration are the creation of an Office for Refugees and Asylum Seekers to address and coordinate asylum issues, improvement of detention facilities, new parole policies, and better oversight of the expedited removal process.

Although expedited removal serves an important policy goal, studies have identified flaws in the process.

■ "Regular Removal": Substantive Grounds

After our examination of the extraordinary, deliberately low-process forms of removal, we now consider removal as it is regularly conceived of in the INA.

Lawful permanent residents may lose that lawful status by violating the law or the terms of their residency agreement.[11] In effect, noncitizen residents are under closer observation than their US citizen counterparts and are vulnerable to removal if they engage in certain activities, including some activities that would be perfectly lawful if performed by a US citizen.

There is a long list of conduct by the noncitizen that may trigger removal, including matters involving a perceived threat to national security. For the purposes of this chapter, we focus on the grounds for removal that involve criminal activity, the most frequently invoked grounds today. If lawful permanent residents engage in a criminal activity specified in the INA, they will not only face criminal charges and penalties but also could lose their lawful immigration status and be removed. Immigrants who commit crimes are subject to consequences that typically far exceed the criminal penalties involved.

Deportation for crimes has a long history. In 1875, the beginning of federal immigration regulation, criminal activity rendered applicants inadmissible to the United States. Starting in 1917, crimes were made a grounds for deporting immigrants who had been lawfully admitted.

Immigration reforms enacted by Congress in 1996 greatly expanded the criminal grounds for removal. Under these amendments, a multitude of additional crimes subjected a noncitizen to removal. For example, an aggravated felony will result in the deportability of a noncitizen. When Congress introduced the Anti-Drug Abuse Act of 1988 as part of the government's "war on drugs" initiative, aggravated felonies included only murder, firearms trafficking, and drug trafficking. Later, the definition of aggravated felonies was expanded to include certain crimes of fraud or deceit and a number of other offenses. Several crimes that are classified as misdemeanors under state law may nonetheless fit the definition of aggravated felonies for federal immigration purposes.

In addition to the increase in crimes warranting removal, the 1996 reforms also resulted in an increase in the number of noncitizens removed and in the number of detainees awaiting removal proceedings. The federal government has begun to pursue criminal deportations much more aggressively; the removal of criminal aliens reached record levels in the years following the passage of the 1996 amendments.[12]

The following types of criminal conduct and convictions may result in removal: (1) certain criminal acts that do not result in a conviction;

(2) aggravated felonies as defined in the INA; (3) drug convictions; and (4) crimes of "moral turpitude."

Specific deportable offenses include firearm offenses, domestic violence, participation in document fraud or the smuggling of noncitizens into the country, noncitizen voting offenses, marriage fraud to gain admission to the United States, and becoming a public charge within the first five years of entry.

It might surprise a reader new to immigration policy that noncitizens can be deported without a criminal conviction. Yet a person can be deported if immigration officials conclude that the person was engaged in smuggling other noncitizens into the United States, offenses related to national security, violation of civil domestic protection orders, or drug abuse or addiction.

In general, the criminal grounds for removal listed within the INA can be grouped into three broad categories: (1) crimes involving moral turpitude; (2) controlled substance offenses; and (3) aggravated felonies.

Crimes of "moral turpitude" are a common category of deportation. The INA authorizes the redeportation of noncitizens who are convicted of one crime involving moral turpitude within five years of entry, for which a sentence of one year may be imposed. A *conviction* for federal immigration purposes means: (1) a judge or jury has found the person guilty or the person has entered a plea of guilty or *nolo contendere* [also known as "no contest"] or has admitted sufficient facts to warrant a finding of guilt, and (2) the judge has ordered some form of punishment, penalty, or restraint on the person's liberty to be imposed.

There is a tremendous variation in what constitutes a crime of moral turpitude. It has been defined as a crime that "shocks the public conscience as being inherently base, vile, and depraved, contrary to accepted rules of morality."[13] The tests employed to determine a crime of moral turpitude often rest on the intent element and seek to identify crimes of moral laxity, bad character, or violence. Ultimately, crimes of moral turpitude can have tremendous consequences for noncitizens.

A second group of deportable offenses involves controlled substances and drug trafficking. Included within the realm of deportability for controlled substances are second convictions for simple drug possession.[14] Even if not technically an aggravated felony under the criminal code, these sections allow a noncitizen to be deported for any controlled substance offenses, with the exception of a single offense for 30 grams or less of marijuana.

It makes no difference whether the offense is a felony or a misdemeanor under the criminal code.

Third, an aggravated felony under the INA often includes crimes that are not necessarily always "aggravated" or a "felony" under the criminal law. For example, movie star Winona Ryder's conviction a few years ago for shoplifting in Beverly Hills would have subjected a noncitizen to detention and removal as an aggravated felon.[15] Lucky for Ryder that she is a US citizen. Aggravated felony has been the most frequently expanded criminal deportation category for federal immigration purposes in recent years.

A noncitizen convicted of an aggravated felony at any time after admission is deportable. INA § 101(a)(43) contains an ever-growing list of aggravated felonies. Congress continues to add crimes to this list every year, and today most felonies under the criminal system are aggravated felonies for immigration purposes. Today, the aggravated felony category basically includes any crime of violence or one for which the term of imprisonment is at least one year.[16] To make matters worse, each time Congress adds crimes to the list, the effect is *retroactive*. Thus, if a noncitizen pleads guilty to a crime that was not on the aggravated felony list, the fact that it was later added by Congress allows the person to be treated as an aggravated felon for immigration purposes.

There is a strong message to take from the treatment of criminal grounds for removability—every noncitizen must be extremely careful. Participation in some of the same acts as their US citizen counterparts may cause a noncitizen to be deported.

Relief from Removal

Cancellation of Removal

If employment officials detect a removable offense, the noncitizen may receive a Notice to Appear (NTA), which is the beginning of formal removal proceedings. The immigrant who has received an NTA may contest removability before the immigration judge. Alternatively, the immigrant may concede removability and apply for discretionary relief. This relief may take two forms: (1) *cancellation of removal*, which, if granted, will result in the applicant receiving a green card, and (2) *voluntary departure*, which allows for the immigrant to self-deport, without triggering the five- or ten-year bars to readmission into the United States.

Cancellation can be sought by both permanent and nonpermanent residents. There is a cap of 4,000 cancellations per fiscal year.[17] Also, although an immigrant might demonstrate eligibility for cancellation, the grant of cancellation is entirely within the discretion of the immigration court.

Becoming eligible for cancellation is easier for lawful permanent residents (LPRs) than it is for the non-LPRs. Eligibility requirements for cancellation of removal for LPRs include being lawfully admitted into the US as a permanent resident no less than five years before, having resided in the United States continually for seven years after being lawfully admitted, and having no past convictions of any aggravated felony.[18]

A non-LPR has a much higher standard to meet to be eligible for cancellation. The non-LPR must have been physically present in the United States for the ten years immediately preceding the application for cancellation, have good moral character during that time, have no convictions of certain crimes, and show that there will be an exceptional and extremely unusual hardship to US citizens or a lawful permanent resident spouse, parent, or child.[19]

The final element, "exceptional and extremely unusual hardship," is extraordinarily difficult to fulfill. Only a spouse, child, or parent who is either a US citizen or a lawful permanent resident will be considered when determining exceptional and extremely unusual hardship. Some factors to this are advanced age or illness requiring the immigrant to care for the relative or having a child who will have to move with the parent and who is entirely acculturated into the United States.[20]

Voluntary Departure

Voluntary departure is a discretionary grant of relief once the noncitizen has been put into formal removal proceedings. It is in the best interest of immigrants to request voluntary departure early in the proceedings if they are not eligible for any other forms of relief. Immigrants who are granted voluntary departure are required to pay their own way back to their home country and prove that they have the means and intent to return.

Not every immigrant may request voluntary departure. Since 1996, it has become more difficult to meet the eligibility requirements for this form of relief. Immigrants who are aggravated felons or national security threats are not eligible for voluntary departure.

At the commencement of removal proceedings, with the issuance of the NTA, the immigrant may contact the federal official and request voluntary departure. If granted, the immigrant may receive up to 120 days to depart. Typically, the departing immigrant must post a bond of five hundred dollars.

Immigrants may also request that the immigration court grant them voluntary departure. Although an immigrant may be statutorily eligible, it is at the discretion of the immigration court to grant voluntary departure. In addition, the immigration court's decision on the length of time to depart is not reviewable.

If the request is made before the master calendar hearing, the immigration court has discretion to grant the immigrant up to 120 days to depart. If the immigrant decides to request voluntary departure at this point, four requirements must be met: the noncitizen must (1) withdraw all requests for relief; (2) concede removability; (3) waive his or her right to any and all appeals; and (4) present all travel documents, including a passport, to the deporting authorities.

The immigrant may also ask for voluntary departure at the end of removal proceedings. This far along in the proceedings, only the immigration court has the authority to grant voluntary departure. The eligibility requirements at this stage are harder to meet than at earlier stages in the proceedings. To grant voluntary departure at the conclusion of proceedings, the immigration court must find that the immigrant was present in the United States for at least one year preceding the NTA issuance, has been a person of good moral character for the five years immediately preceding the application, is not an aggravated felon, has not engaged in terrorist activity, and has the means and intent to depart the United States. The immigration court has the authority to grant up to sixty days to depart. Furthermore, the immigrant is required to post a bond no less than five hundred dollars.

When immigrants are granted voluntary departure, they receive a "Bag and Baggage" letter informing them of the time and place they are to report to the point of entry (e.g., an international airport) for departure. The penalties for failing to depart under an order of voluntary departure are harsh, including a fine not less than three thousand dollars and a bar of ten years.

■ Operation Streamline: The Use of Criminal Law to Enforce US Immigration Laws

For many years, immigration from Mexico has been a top priority for policy makers, the media, and US citizens. This issue has sparked debates, protests, proposals for legislative reform, and calls to better secure the border between Mexico and the United States. In this new political climate, frustration with the policy some call "catch and release," in which most undocumented migrants are merely sent back across the border, has mounted. As a result, in December 2005, the DHS initiated and funded a new task force dubbed Operation Streamline.

Under this zero tolerance program, undocumented immigrants are charged with criminal misdemeanors and prosecuted under existing laws in mass trials. During the mass trials, a large number of shackled undocumented immigrants are brought before a federal judge and, in general, plead guilty and are convicted. The sentence for this type of misdemeanor is typically two weeks in jail but may be up to six months for repeat offenders.[21] Following the completion of their sentence, undocumented migrants are ordered removed. Moreover, as a direct result of the conviction, each immigrant convicted under the program is barred from reentering the United States for five years. Ultimately, the purpose of these stricter penalties is to decrease the number of immigrants attempting to cross illegally, as immigrants will fear going to jail if they are caught.

Initially, the program targeted undocumented immigrants in the Del Rio sector, which represents two hundred miles of border near Eagle Pass, Texas. However, in December 2006, the program was extended to the Border Patrol sector of Yuma, Arizona. Today, the program has been established in high-traffic sectors, including Del Rio and Laredo, Texas, as well as Yuma and Tucson, Arizona. In total, Operation Streamline now applies to nearly five hundred miles, or one-fourth of the US–Mexico border.

The number of apprehensions in the Yuma sector fell from 118,459 in 2006 to 37,992 following Operation Streamline's implementation in 2007. Likewise, apprehensions are down nearly 70 percent in the Del Rio sector. Moreover, apprehensions fell 22 percent in the Laredo sector during the last quarter of 2008. Former DHS secretary Michael Chertoff described the success of Operation Streamline as follows: "Individuals who are caught at certain designated high-traffic, high-risk zones are prosecuted and if convicted are jailed. This has an unbelievable return effect. In Yuma sector, over . . . October through December [2007] the Department of Justice prosecuted over 1,200 cases. And as a consequence, apprehension rates dropped nearly [seventy] percent."[22]

Other federal officials also note that the program and other measures have contributed to a 20 percent drop in apprehensions at the US–Mexico border in 2007, down to 857,000. However, some of the decline may be due to reduced migration resulting from the dramatic downturn in the US economy.

Operation Streamline has greatly increased the number of immigration prosecutions, even though the number of border apprehensions are falling. The resources of the federal courts and prisons from Texas to California are inundated with immigration-related trials. Some judges in this region hear between 1,000 and 1,200 cases per year, twice that of federal judges in other areas of the country. In fact, five of the country's ninety-four districts—Southern California, New Mexico, Arizona, West Texas, and South Texas—hear approximately 75 percent of all criminal cases heard in federal district courts throughout the country.

Critics of Operation Streamline contend that the increased number of cases unnecessarily burdens the judicial system, deprives lawyers and judges of adequate time to properly hear cases, and denies defendants a fair trial. Moreover, Operation Streamline has saddled prosecutors in their ability to use discretion in choosing the cases to pursue.

■ Concluding Thoughts

The United States has many means at its disposal for deporting immigrants, from the very low-process means of voluntary return to the high-process mechanisms of formal removal. Congress has enacted substantive criteria for separating the "good" migrant from the "bad" migrant, and the administrative agencies that regulate immigration have adopted many procedures for execution of these criteria.

Some removal mechanisms give the immigrant certain procedural rights, while many other removal mechanisms focus on getting the immigrant out of the country as quickly and as cheaply as possible.

■ Discussion Questions

1. Are the flaws in the expedited removal process outweighed by the speed and efficiency with which fraudulent entrants are removed? Is there room for more process and the opportunity for lawyers to represent noncitizens in the expedited removal process?

2. How do you feel about the informal process of voluntary return? Is it an ineffective "catch and release" concession to lawbreaking? Or is it a necessary administrative remedy? Is it possible to formally remove every undocumented crosser?

3. Should the federal criminal law be employed to deter violation of US immigration laws? Are immigration violations properly considered administrative violations or criminal violations? Does the state regulate immigration via its police power or via administrative power?

■ Suggested Readings

Bogan, Brad. "Operation Streamline Coming to Laredo." *Fifth Circuit Blog*, October 26, 2007, available at http://circuit5.blogspot.com/2007/10/operation-streamline-coming-to-laredo.html.

Center for Human Rights and International Justice. "The Expedited Removal Study: Report on the First Three Years of Implementation of Expedited Removal." *Notre Dame Journal of Law, Ethics and Public Policy* 15 (2001): 1.

Dominguez, Ivan. 2009. "Cold ICE Brings Heat, But Not Light, to Immigration Debate." *Champion*, Feb. 2009, 53.

Komisaruk, Katya, and Tim Maloney. 2003. *Beat the Heat: How to Handle Encounters with Law Enforcement*. Oakland, CA: AK Press.

Reimer, Norman L. 2008. "Operation Streamline is Operation Heartbreak." *Champion*, April 2008, 51.

■ Notes

Epigraph: Quoted in the *New York Times*, January 12, 2009.

1. See INA § 235(a)(4), 8 USC § 1225(a)(4).

2. DHS Office of Immigration Statistics, *Immigration Enforcement Actions: 2007,* December 2008 Annual Report, www.dhs.gov/immigrationstatistics.

3. Ibid. The 2001 figure is 189,026; in 2006, 280,974; and in 2007, 319,382.

4. Congressional Research Service, CRS-8 and CRS-9.

5. See T. Alexander Aleinikoff, *Expedited Removal Study* (Washington, D.C.: Carnegie Endowment for International Peace, 1998).

6. See Center for Human Rights and International Justice, *The Expedited Removal Study: Evaluation of the GAO's Second Report on Expedited Removal* (San Francisco: University of California, Center for Human Rights and International Justice, 2000).

7. "USCIRF Disappointed that DHS Action on Expedited Removal Process Falls Short," uscirf.gov, Press Release Jan. 9, 2009.

8. USCIRF, *Asylum Seekers in Expedited Removal*, Feb. 8, 2005, p. 2.

9. USCIRF Report Card 2 Years Later, at 5.

10. USCIRF, *Asylum Seekers in Expedited Removal*, 2.

11. See INA § 237(a), 8 USC § 1227(a).

12. Human Rights Watch, "National Statistics on Deportation for Crimes," in *Forced Apart: Families Separated and Immigrants Harmed by United States Deportation Policy* (2007), available at www.hrw.org/reports/2007/us0707/6.htm.

13. *Hamdan v. INS*, 98 F.3d 183, 186 (5th Cir. 1996); see *Jordan v. DeGeorge*, 341 US 223 (1951), finding that conspiring to defraud on taxes was a "crime of moral turpitude."

14. *United States v. Garcia-Olemdo*, 112 F.3d 399, 400–01 (9th Cir. 1997).

15. Kevin R. Johnson, *Opening the Floodgates: Why America Needs to Rethink Its Border and Immigration Laws* (New York: New York University Press, 2007), 157.

16. See *United States v. Guzman-Bera*, 216 F.3d 1314 (11th Cir. 2000), requiring a court to impose a sentence of a year rather than the statute merely authorizing a sentence of a year.

17. INA § 240A(e)(1), 8 USC § 1229b(e)(1).

18. INA § 240A(a), 8 USC § 1229b(a).

19. INA § 240A(b)(1), 8 USC § 1229b(b)(1).

20. See *In re* Kao and Lin, 23 I. & N. Dec 45 (BIA 2001).

21. Persons who enter the United States without inspection are charged under INA § 275, 8 USC. § 1325, and placed into detention facilities to await trial.

22. "Remarks by Homeland Security Secretary Michael Chertoff and Attorney General Mukasey at a Briefing on Immigration Enforcement and Border Security Efforts" (Feb. 22, 2008), available at www.dhs.gov/xnews/releases/pr_1203722713615.shtm.

8

Regulating the Migration of Labor

I have met many, many farm workers and friends who love justice and who are willing to sacrifice for what is right. They have a quality about them that reminds me of the beatitudes. They are living examples that Jesus' promise is true: they have been hungry and thirsty for righteousness and they have been satisfied. They are determined, patient people who believe in life and who give strength to others. They have given me more love and hope and strength than they will ever know.

—César Chávez

It is among the oldest of migration stories: one leaves home and family and moves to a new country in order to work. The labor market of the United States attracts many migrants. The regulation of migrant labor is an important part of American migration history. How does US law regulate the attraction of migrant labor? How does law integrate migrant laborers into the American economic, legal, and social community?

This chapter begins by reviewing some demographic characteristics of the US workforce. We look at Latinas and Latinos generally in the workforce and then examine foreign-born US workers, with special attention paid to those born in Latin America and especially Mexico. We then review basic data about undocumented foreign nationals (UFNs) in the workforce. Next, we examine how US immigration law regulates labor migration to the United States, looking especially at the H-2A nonimmigrant visa program for agricultural workers and at the Immigration Reform and Control Act of 1986. Finally, we look at how bodies of law other than immigration law regulates migrants in the workplace.

■ Demographics of the Laboring Migrant Population

We are interested in the profiles of three different (but potentially interconnected) groups in the US labor force: (1) the Latina/o worker (both foreign born and native born); (2) the foreign-born worker; and (3) the undocumented foreign national worker.

We are initially interested in the laboring Latina/o, whether native or foreign born. An overarching goal of this book is to explore the substantial continuity between the Mexican aspiring to migrate and the Mexican American who was born in the United States. As such, we are interested in data describing the characteristics of the Latina/o labor force in the United States.

Table 8.1 shows the fourth-quarter changes from 2007 to 2008 in the native-born and foreign-born Latina/o workforce. There is a notable continuity among native-born and foreign-born Latinas/os in the services and retail sectors. Discontinuities are sharpest in hospitality and construction (more foreign born than native born) and education and public administration (more native born than foreign born).

We turn next to natives and foreign born more generally, with secondary specification by ethnicity. Figure 8.1 shows the rate of participation in the workforce, by gender and education level of native-born US citizens, foreign-born workers from outside Mexico and Central America, and workers born in Mexico or Central America.

Among men, we see substantial variations among those whose educational level is high school or less. At this educational level, foreign-born, especially Mexican- and Central American–born, participate more than natives in the workforce. The meaningful variations among the ethnic groups diminish as the educational level increases. Among women, the ethnic variation increases as the amount of education grows.

We can also study the foreign-born participation in the labor force, relative to the native population. Table 8.2 shows that workers born in Mexico are more fully employed than workers from any other group, and that the jobs are largely in agriculture, construction, and services.

Table 8.3 provides more information about foreign-born Latinas/os, showing labor force participation broken down by period of arrival. We see that Latinas/os who entered in the 1980s are participating in the labor force at a very high rate (around 76 percent); those who entered in the 1990s participate at 73 percent; and those who entered in the 2000s are participating at around 70 percent.

We can turn now to UFN population. Continuing the focus on labor-force participation, we see from figure 8.2 (using slightly older data than the earlier figures) that the participation rate of UFN males is recorded at

Table 8.1 Employment of Latinas/os, by industry, fourth quarters 2007 and 2008 (nonseasonally adjusted, ages 16 and older, numbers in thousands)

INDUSTRY	NATIVE BORN (2007)	NATIVE BORN (2008)	CHANGE 2007 TO 2008	FOREIGN BORN (2007)	FOREIGN BORN (2008)	CHANGE 2007 TO 2008
Agriculture, forestry, fishing, and mining	116	155	39	422	403	−18
Construction	726	666	−60	2,153	1,870	−283
Manufacturing—durable goods	439	472	32	888	795	−93
Manufacturing—nondurable goods	364	324	−39	729	724	−5
Wholesale and retail trade	1,534	1,585	51	1,224	1,222	−2
Transportation and warehousing	491	535	44	531	498	−33
Utilities	81	100	19	32	56	24
Publishing, broadcasting, communications, and information services	216	208	−8	103	104	1
Finance, insurance, and real estate	682	604	−79	390	353	−36
Professional and other business services	1,054	1,008	−47	1,287	1,348	61
Educational services	796	806	10	348	400	52
Hospitals and other health services	848	968	121	548	545	−2
Social services	266	258	−8	194	191	−2
Arts and entertainment	166	164	−2	159	116	−43
Eating, drinking, and lodging services	738	755	17	1,370	1,408	39
Repair and maintenance services	143	147	4	227	235	8
Personal and laundry services/private household services	165	190	25	401	429	28
Public administration	480	506	27	127	139	12
Total	9,304	9,451	147	11,131	10,839	−292

Note: Data for 2007 have been adjusted to account for the effects of annual revisions to the CPS. All numbers and percentages are rounded after shares or year-to-year changes have been computed.

Source: Pew Hispanic Center tabulations of Current Population Survey data.

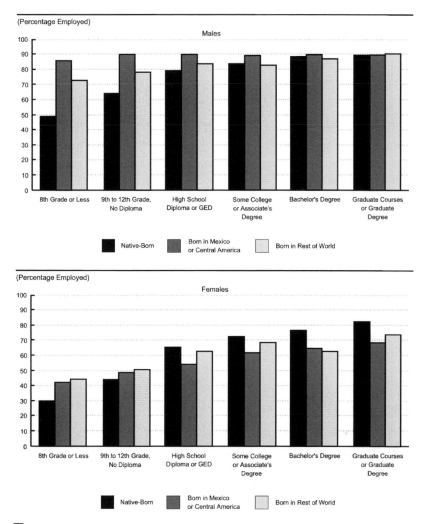

(Percentage Employed)

Males

(Percentage Employed)

Females

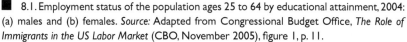

■ 8.1. Employment status of the population ages 25 to 64 by educational attainment, 2004: (a) males and (b) females. *Source:* Adapted from Congressional Budget Office, *The Role of Immigrants in the US Labor Market* (CBO, November 2005), figure 1, p. 11.

a whopping 94 percent, above the rates of native workers and workers who lawfully migrated. The UFNs who enter, enter to work.

We see that UFN men are nearly fully employed in the labor market, more than other immigrants and more than natives. That trend is reversed among women, with women UFNs less engaged in the workforce than native women or other immigrant women.

Table 8.2 Employment by industry and occupation in the United States, by nativity and Mexican birth, 2008 (in thousands unless otherwise indicated)

	US BORN*	FOREIGN BORN ALL COUNTRIES	OTHER THAN MEXICO	MEXICO
Employment status[†]				
Employed	122,555	23,616	16,014	7,602
Unemployed	6,899	1,496	828	668
Not in labor force	68,640	11,620	8,172	3,448
Unemployment rate (% of labor force)	5.3	6.0	4.9	8.1
Labor force participation (%)	65	68	67	71
Industries[‡]				
Construction, agriculture, and mining	10,476	3,446	1,304	2,142
Manufacturing	12,988	3,030	1,880	1,150
Trade and transportation	24,606	4,109	3,016	1,092
Information, finance, and other services	74,485	13,031	9,814	3,217
Occupations[‡]				
Management, professional, and related occupations	45,974	6,427	5,855	572
Services	18,992	5,367	3,254	2,113
Sales and office support	31,972	4,069	3,242	828
Construction, extraction, and farming	6,714	3,188	1,096	2,091
Maintenance, production, transportation, and material moving	18,902	4,565	2,567	1,997

Note: Based on civilian noninstitutional population.

*"US born" includes persons born in the United States, Puerto Rico, or other US territories as well as those born elsewhere to parents who are US citizens.

[†]Civilians ages 16 and older

[‡]Currently employed civilians ages 16 and older

Source: Pew Hispanic Center tabulations of augmented March 2008 Current Population Survey adjusted for undercount.

Figure 8.3 gives us a window into market sectors where UFNs work. We see that UFN workers have huge representation in private households (landscaping, domestic services, etc.) and significant representation in several other sectors, including farmwork, construction, services, and hospitality. UFNs are concentrated in job sectors characterized by lower

Table 8.3 Labor market status of foreign-born Latinas/os, by period of arrival, fourth quarters, 2007 and 2008 (nonseasonally adjusted, ages 16 and older, numbers in thousands)

	2007, FOURTH QUARTER	2008, FOURTH QUARTER	CHANGE 2007 TO 2008
Before 1980			
Population	2,944	2,984	40
Labor force	1,702	1,688	−13
Labor force participation rate (%)	57.8	56.6	−1.2
Employment	1,630	1,590	−40
Employment rate (%)	55.4	53.3	−2.1
Unemployment	71	99	27
Unemployment rate (%)	4.2	5.9	1.7
1980 to 1989			
Population	3,866	3,664	−203
Labor force	3,000	2,807	−193
Labor force participation rate (%)	77.6	76.6	−1.0
Employment	2,856	2,593	−263
Employment rate (%)	73.9	70.8	−3.1
Unemployment	143	214	70
Unemployment rate (%)	4.8	7.6	2.8
1990 to 1999			
Population	5,451	5,337	−114
Labor force	3,981	3,937	−44
Labor force participation rate (%)	73.0	73.8	0.7
Employment	3,762	3,593	−169
Employment rate (%)	69.0	67.3	−1.7
Unemployment	219	345	125
Unemployment rate (%)	5.5	8.7	3.2
2000 or later			
Population	4,220	4,759	540
Labor force	3,046	3,352	306
Labor force participation rate (%)	72.2	70.4	−1.8
Employment	2,883	3,063	181
Employment rate (%)	68.3	64.4	−4.0
Unemployment	163	289	125
Unemployment rate (%)	5.4	8.6	3.3

Notes: Data for 2007 have been adjusted to account for the effects of annual revisions to the Current Population Survey. All numbers and percentages are rounded after shares or year-to-year changes have been computed.

Source: Pew Hispanic Center tabulations of Current Population Survey Data.

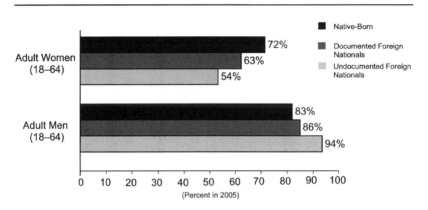

8.2. Labor force participation rate by gender, nativity, and status: March 2005. *Source:* Jeffrey A. Passel, *The Size and Characteristics of the Unauthorized Migrant Population in the US.* Estimates based on the March 2005 Current Population Survey (March 7, 2006). Used by permission.

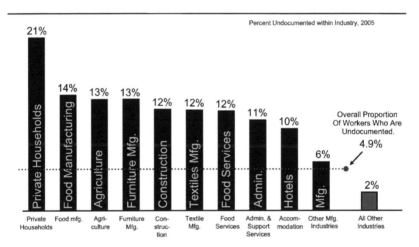

8.3. Proportion of undocumented foreign national workers for selected industries: March 2005. *Source:* Jeffrey Passel, *The Size and Characteristics of the Unauthorized Migrant Population in the US* (Pew Hispanic Center, March 7, 2005). Pew Hispanic Center tabulations of augmented March 2005 Current Population Survey, adjusted for omissions. Used by permission.

wages and riskier work environments.[1] One in five low-wage workers is an immigrant.[2] Finally, table 8.4 gives a finer breakdown of the UFN share of specific occupations.

We see that UFNs make up 36 percent of all insulation workers, 29 percent of all roofers and miscellaneous agricultural workers, 27 percent of all butchers, and 28 percent of all drywall installers.

Table 8.4 Undocumented foreign national share of selected specific occupations: March 2005 (in thousands)

DETAILED OCCUPATION	TOTAL WORKERS	UNDOCUMENTED WORKERS	
		NUMBER	SHARE (%)
Total civilian labor force (with an occupation)	148,615	7,255	4.9
Insulation workers	56	20	36
Miscellaneous agricultural workers	839	247	29
Roofers	325	93	29
Drywall installers, ceiling tile installers, and tapers	285	79	28
Helpers, construction trades	145	40	27
Butchers and other meat, poultry, and fish processing workers	322	87	27
Pressers, textile, garment, and related materials	83	21	26
Grounds maintenance workers	1,204	299	25
Construction laborers	1,614	400	25
Brickmasons, blockmasons, and stonemasons	198	49	25
Dishwashers	367	85	23
Helpers: production workers	64	15	23
Maids and housekeeping	1,531	342	22
Graders and sorters of agricultural products	74	16	22
Painters, construction, and maintenance	768	167	22
Cement masons, concrete finishers, and terrazzo workers	141	29	21
Computer hardware engineers	54	11	20
Packaging and filling machine operators and tenders	367	75	20
Packers and packagers, hand	548	111	20
Cleaners of vehicles and equipment	427	85	20
Carpet, floor, and tile installers and finishers	330	66	20
Cooks	2,218	436	20
Parking lot attendants	64	12	19
Upholsterers	72	13	18
Sewing machine operators	292	51	18
Food preparation workers	758	128	17
Laundry and dry-cleaning workers	206	30	15

Source: Pew Hispanic Center tabulations of augmented March 2005 Current Population Survey, adjusted for omissions. Occupations shown have at least 50,000 workers, and unauthorized share at least three times the national share (4.9%)

Based on the demographic portrait, we can conclude that immigration supplies crucial labor in many low-wage sectors that might otherwise go underserved in the US economy.

Finally, a point about the relative youth of the foreign born, and especially the UFN worker. Figure 8.4a shows the age ranges of UFNs. Figure 8.4b gives the same data for lawful migrants. while figure 8.4c gives data for the US-born population.

It is striking to view these data end-to-end. They show the youth of the foreign born—especially the UFN—relative to the native. Significantly, the foreign-born population bulges in precisely the same age-range (mid-20s to mid-40s) where the native workforce is scarce. The in-flow of immigrant labor thus may have implications for the future sustainability of programs such as Social Security, which depend on contributions

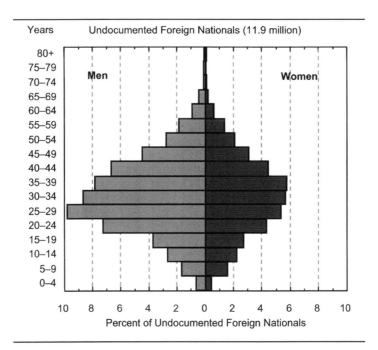

■ 8.4. Latinas/os by age and sex, 2008: (a) undocumented foreign nationals, (b) documented foreign nationals, and (c) US natives. *Source:* Adapted from Jeffrey S. Passel and D'Vera Cohn, *A Portrait of Unauthorized Immigrants in the United States* (Pew Hispanic Center, April 14, 2009), figures 7, 8, and 9, pp. 4–5. Used by permission.

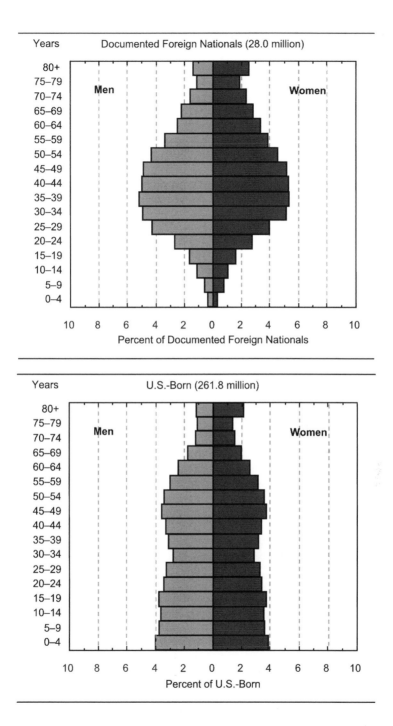

from current workers to assure payments to those who have left the workforce.

■ Regulating Labor Migration through the Immigration Laws

In chapter 5, we reviewed how US immigration law regulates the inflow of primarily high-skilled, high-wage labor migrants through the employment-based visa categories and the nonimmigrant visa system. In this chapter, we focus specifically on how US immigration law regulates the immigrant supply to the low-wage job sectors. In this regard, we focus on two major aspects of US immigration laws: the H-2A NIV program for seasonal agricultural workers, and the employment regulation established by the Immigration Reform and Control Act of 1986 (IRCA).

Nonimmigrant Visas under H-2A

We have reviewed demographic evidence demonstrating the importance of immigration for supplying low-wage labor to the United States in important sectors like agriculture, construction, and services. We now show that immigration law provides these workers very limited lawful means of accessing the US labor market.

The primary lawful way of entering the United States to engage in low-wage labor is through the H-2A program, which are nonimmigrant visas available to seasonal agricultural workers (SAWs). The program gives visas that allow the holder to enter the United States temporarily to perform seasonal work in the agricultural sector. While there is no numerical "cap" on the number of visas, administrative difficulty and other reasons have kept the annual number issued to between thirty thousand and forty thousand. This is an extremely low number, especially considering that California alone requires over nine hundred thousand seasonal agricultural laborers per year.[3]

The H2-A program is also prone to abuse by employers. H2-A visas are valid for only one employer, yet most farmers require employees for only a relatively brief harvesting period. The result has been that the "employer," which is the entity that petitions the migrant worker into the country via the H2-A program, is typically a large firm acting as a middleman, contracting the laborer out to various agricultural entities over the course of the season. These large contractors usually transport the workers from job to job and provide them—often substandard—housing. As such, the laborer becomes dependent on the contracting firm in ways that give the firm much leverage over the workers' lives and employment choices.

All told, the H2-A program results in a radical undersupply of lawful low-wage workers in agricultural and other sectors of the US economy.

Another important regulator of incoming migrant labor is IRCA, which attempted to address the labor migration phenomenon with a two-pronged attack. First, the act recognized that many people lived in the United States without proper documentation. IRCA gave *amnesty* and lawful permanent resident status to undocumented immigrants who met certain requirements.

Second, IRCA sought to eliminate the so-called jobs magnet. The act authorized sanctions on employers who employ persons lacking the proper documents to work. To this end, IRCA requires that every prospective employee fill out the I-9 form, which presents documentation that the applicant is eligible to work.

Over time, it became clear that employers were in very little danger of actual sanction. Businesses developed practices to protect themselves from potential liability under IRCA, and the government helped matters along by enforcing sanctions against employers with extreme infrequency. Needless to say, IRCA failed to end the flow of undocumented workers into the United States. After the amnesty, the undocumented immigrant population grew to the point that, today, approximately 12 million undocumented immigrants reside here.

The posture of US law regarding the undocumented worker thus developed into a deliberate ambivalence, giving lip service to the proposition that a worker could not enter or work except through lawful channels, all the while keeping those lawful channels astonishingly narrow. In the meantime, the US labor market aggressively courted the entry and deployment of these workers into the low-wage sectors of the workforce. These dynamics of market and law have resulted in a surging population of undocumented workers.[4]

■ Regulating Labor Migration through Law Other than Immigration Law

We now turn to other sources of American law that affect the experience of the immigrant laborer in the workplace. These are laws, such as labor laws, workers' compensation, and unemployment insurance, that are designed to protect workers in the US labor market.

American labor law tradition recognizes the right of US workers to organize into unions and participate in collective bargaining with an employer for wages, benefits, and other conditions of employment. American unions and the rights of labor were at their strongest in the first half of the twentieth century, when manufacturing industries made up a large part of the national economy and thousands of blue-collar workers were employed in the automotive, steel, textile, and oil and coal industries.

The rights of American workers were enhanced as a result of extensive civil rights legislation in the second half of the twentieth century. These laws gave workers the right to sue employers who treat workers unfairly on the basis of race, national origin, color, gender, age, or disability. Laws also guaranteed workers certain rights, such as safe working conditions, accommodations for medical disabilities, and leaves of absence to care for sick or disabled family members.

The US government provides financial and medical benefits to workers after they reach a certain age and have worked a number of years, as well as to workers who are injured on the job and lose working capacity, and even to people who have never worked as a result of a disability. These benefits are provided by law to those who meet certain eligibility requirements.

Here is an all-important question: Should an undocumented worker be able to enjoy the same protections and benefits as other US workers? It could be considered unfair to deny undocumented foreign national workers such rights. American labor traditions value fairness to workers regardless of their nationality. In addition, does denying undocumented foreign national workers the protection of US labor or civil rights laws give employers an incentive to hire these workers, knowing they will not be held liable for mistreating them? On the other hand, many Americans are concerned about the fairness of providing rights and benefits to workers who disregard immigration laws. Giving these expensive benefits to the undocumented immigrants is seen as unfair to legally documented workers, who contribute taxes (as do many undocumented immigrants) into these compensation systems.

When US labor law gives a protection or benefit to all workers, but US immigration law would deny that same protection or benefit, which law should control? Since the Supreme Court decided the case of *Hoffman Plastic Compounds, Inc., v. NLRB*, the general view is that US labor law fails to fully protect the rights of undocumented workers.[5] (See the sidebar.) However, some questions about this area of the law have not been conclusively settled by the US Supreme Court. As a result, cases brought by undocumented foreign nationals seeking benefits have succeeded in lower-level courts in some states.

National labor laws prohibit employers from interfering with their employees' right to organize into a union. Under the law, they may not fire a worker for union-organizing activity. The law gives the worker a right to file a complaint for unfair termination with the **National Labor Relations Board (NLRB)**. The board has the responsibility to investigate the complaint and conduct hearings. If the NLRB finds that the employer did unlawfully fire the worker, it can order the employer to rehire the worker and give the worker backpay for the time he or she was unemployed.

However, current US immigration law prohibits an employer from knowingly hiring a worker who is not authorized to work in the United States. In *Hoffman Plastics*, a UFN worker from Mexico was one of four people fired for union-organizing activity. After a hearing, the NLRB ordered the employer to offer all four workers reinstatement and backpay. One worker's status as an undocumented foreign national was then discovered, and the employer objected that this order would cause it to violate US immigration law. Reinstatement was out of the question, but the validity of the backpay order was unclear. The order was challenged in the courts until the Supreme Court rendered a final decision: the worker was not entitled to backpay.

Under *Hoffman Plastics*, the authority of the NLRB to protect workers is limited by the more comprehensive immigration law. While the board may still order an employer to stop interfering with lawful union-organizing activity and order that employer to rehire and give backpay to a worker it has unlawfully discharged, only workers with legal documentation status are eligible for such relief.

Note that *Hoffman Plastics* involves an official *order* of the NLRB. That term has special legal status as a final action of the board. A recent decision of the US Court of Appeals for the Ninth Circuit (*NLRB v. C&C Roofing Supply, Inc.*) held that an employer may legally pay undocumented workers an amount of money—liquidated damages—that represents the value of actual reinstatement without violating immigration laws.[6] Like *Hoffman Plastics*, this case involved undocumented workers who were illegally fired in retaliation for union activity. But this employer settled

Hoffman Plastic Compounds, Inc., v. National Labor Relations Board, 535 US 137 (2002)

Facts

Hoffman Plastic Compounds, Inc., hired Jose Castro on the basis of documents appearing to verify his authorization to work in the United States. After Castro engaged in union-organizing activities, Hoffman laid him off. The National Labor Relations Board (NLRB) found that the lay-off violated the National Labor Relations Act (NLRA) and ordered back-pay for Castro. At a hearing, Castro testified that he was born in Mexico, that he had never been legally admitted to, or authorized to work in, this country, and that he had gained employment with Hoffman only after tendering a birth certificate that was not his. The administrative law judge found that the Immigration Reform and Control Act of 1986 (IRCA), which makes it unlawful for employers to knowingly hire undocumented workers or for employees to use fraudulent documents to establish employment eligibility, precluded Castro's award. In reversing, the NLRB noted that the most effective way to further the immigration policies embodied in IRCA is to provide the NLRA's protections and remedies to undocumented workers in the same manner as to other employees. The court of appeals enforced the board's order.

Question Presented

Does the NLRB have the discretion to award backpay to an undocumented employee who was not legally authorized to work in the United States?

Ruling

No. In a 5–4 opinion delivered by Chief Justice William H. Rehnquist, the Supreme Court held that such relief is foreclosed by federal immigration policy, as expressed by Congress in IRCA. The Court reasoned that allowing the board to award backpay to undocumented workers ran counter to explicit statutory prohibitions critical to federal immigration policy, and that however broad the board's discretion to fashion remedies when dealing only with the NLRA, it was not so unbounded as to authorize the award. "Congress has expressly made it criminally punishable for an alien to obtain employment with false documents. There is no reason to think that Congress nonetheless intended to permit backpay where but for an employer's unfair labor practices, an alien-employee would have remained in the United States illegally, and continued to work illegally, all the while successfully evading apprehension by immigration authorities," wrote Chief Justice Rehnquist.

Justice Stephen Breyer dissented, joined by Justices John Paul Stevens, David Souter, and Ruth Bader Ginsburg.

Source: The Oyez Project, at www.oyez.org/cases/2000-2001/2001_00_1595. The Oyez Project is a multimedia archive devoted to the Supreme Court of the United States and its work. It aims to be a complete and authoritative source for all audio recorded in the Court since the installation of a recording system in October 1955. ■

the dispute with the NLRB voluntarily through a written settlement agreement. The court found that a provision for liquidated damages was acceptable under state and federal immigration laws even though actual reinstatement was not.

In the US court system, if the facts of a case exactly match the facts of another one that has already been decided, the rule of the first case will apply. After *Hoffman Plastics*, any undocumented foreign national worker fired for unionizing activity should not expect to receive an award of backpay even if the employer is ordered to do so by the NLRB. Despite the Supreme Court's ruling in *Hoffman Plastics*, some undocumented foreign national workers have won financial settlements from their employers in other cases. Like *C&C Roofing*, which involved liquidated damages instead of backpay, these cases are different enough from *Hoffman Plastics* that the rule against backpay on an order from the NLRB does not apply.

First, workers who are injured on the job have been allowed to claim benefits under the federal workers' compensation program, as their noncitizenship status does not negate the applicability of their legal worker's compensation benefits. Undocumented foreign workers may be considered "covered employees" for purposes of these laws.[7] UFN claims have included temporary as well as disability compensation but have been terminated in at least one case when the employer discovered the worker's status as a UFN.[8]

Second, workers who are injured on the job have been awarded settlements in civil cases against employers brought under state labor laws. Remember that in the United States, only federal laws such as the NLRA apply to people in all fifty states. States have the right to issue their own laws. New York business law may differ from that in Texas. California personal injury law may not be the same as personal injury law in Illinois. Courts in both New Hampshire and New York have recognized the right of UFN workers to sue in state court for lost wages even though those wages would be precluded if only the immigration laws were applied.[9] For example, several personal injury cases involved workers injured on construction sites that were not fully compliant with state safety laws.[10]

Courts have also found that employers may be required to pay even undocumented workers wages under terms of the federal Fair Labor Standards Act (FLSA) and related state labor laws. The principle in these cases is that if an employer hires a UFN worker, he or she may not use the person's undocumented status as a reason for refusing to pay. Courts in these cases have held that IRCA does not preempt the state laws or the FLSA (see chapter 10 for a discussion of **federal preemption** of state and local laws designed to regulate immigration); while hiring a UFN may be illegal under the law, an employer is still required to honor his labor contracts.[11]

The Supreme Court could reconsider the question of backpay if it arises in a case brought under Title VII of the Civil Rights Act of 1964. Although *Hoffman Plastics* established that backpay ordered by the NLRB is precluded by federal immigration laws, backpay is also a remedy under the Civil Rights Act for cases of discrimination. Currently, courts are undecided about whether *Hoffman Plastics* should be interpreted to apply to civil rights cases. In *Rivera v. NIBCO, Inc.*, the court indicated that in this type of case, backpay might be allowable: "We seriously doubt that *Hoffman* is as broadly applicable as NIBCO contends, and specifically believe it unlikely that it applies in Title VII cases. The NLRA and Title VII are different statutes in numerous respects. Congress gave them distinct remedial schemes and vested their enforcement agencies with different powers. For purposes of this opinion, we note at least three significant differences between the two statutes."[12]

However, in *Escobar v. Spartan Security Service*, the court denied back-pay to an employee who had brought a suit under Title VII complaining of sexual harassment by his employer.[13]

In 2005, the Supreme Court declined further review of the issues decided by the lower court in *Rivera v. NIBCO, Inc.*, which means that the question of whether immigration laws will preclude claims for backpay under Title VII as it does for orders of the NLRB remains unsettled.

Other important benefits are unavailable to undocumented workers. For example, the Federal Unemployment Tax Act mandates that "compensation shall not be payable on the basis of services performed by an alien unless such alien is an individual who was lawfully admitted for permanent residence at the time such services were performed, was lawfully present for purposes of performing such services, or was permanently residing in the United States under color of law at the time such services were performed."[14]

Is the undocumented worker exploitable because of lack of access to legal protections? UFN workers face a constant risk of discovery and removal, as well as prosecution for falsely presenting documentation to obtain work. Some US laws that protect all workers against unsafe work sites and unfair employers have been interpreted to not exclude UFN workers. However, some of the financial benefits enjoyed by documented workers have been denied to the UFN worker under federal labor and immigration laws. It may only be through close attention to the details of state personal injury and labor laws, or possibly through some courts' interpretation of civil rights legislation, that UFN workers may receive similar benefits.

■ Concluding Thoughts

This chapter has considered data concerning the position of the migrant worker in the United States. We have seen that immigrants, particularly those from Mexico and elsewhere in Latin America, come to the United States to work. We have also seen that these workers are younger than the native population, thus supplementing the American labor market in important ways.

US legal culture cultivates an ambivalance toward migrant labor. On the one hand, the law stresses that only those who lawfully enter may lawfully work. Yet the law holds open very few avenues to entry relative to the market demand.

■ Discussion Questions

1. Some observers criticize US immigration laws for failing to regulate migrant labor. What would be some more effective ways of regulating the flow of migrant labor to and from the United States?

2. Why do you think undocumented foreign national workers come to the United States to work? Do wages alone attract foreign workers? Do you think workers know about American civil rights laws that prohibit discrimination on the basis of race, gender, national origin, or disability? Do they have an expectation that safety in American workplaces is enforced by the government? Do you think that foreign workers expect to be able to join a union or help organize fellow workers?

3. What should undocumented workers do if they are, for example, sexually harassed on the job? Should they be able to report the employer to government officials without risking deportation from the United States? Explain your reasoning.

4. Should undocumented foreign national workers pay taxes into government benefit programs like Social Security and Medicare? If so, should they be eligible for benefits?

■ Suggested Readings

Cameron, Christopher David Ruiz. 2003. "Borderline Decisions: Hoffman Plastic Compounds, The New Bracero Program, and the Supreme Court's Role in Making Federal Labor Policy." *UCLA Law Review* 51: 1.

Correales, Robert I. 2003. "Did *Hoffman Plastic Compounds, Inc.*, Produce Disposable Workers?" *Berkeley La Raza Law Journal* 14: 103.

Durand, Jorge. 2004. *Crossing the Border: Research from the Mexican Migration Project*. New York: Russell Sage Foundation.

García, Ruben J. 2003. "Ghost Workers in an Interconnected World: Going Beyond the Dichotomies of Domestic Immigration and Labor Laws." *University of Michigan Journal of Law Reform* 36: 737.

Harvard Law Review Association. 2005. "Developments in the Law: Jobs and Borders." *Harvard Law Review* 118: 2171.

Massey, Douglas S., Jorge Durand, and Nolan J. Malone. 2002. *Beyond Smoke and Mirrors: Mexican Immigration in an Era of Economic Integration*. New York: Russell Sage Foundation.

Trujillo, Bernard. 2010. "Mexican Families and US Immigration Reform," *Fordham Urban Law Journal* 38: 415.

■ Notes

1. AFL-CIO, *Immigrant Workers at Risk: The Urgent Need for Improved Workplace Safety and Health Policies and Programs* (Aug. 2005), available at www.aflcio.org/aboutus/laborday/upload/immigrant_risk.pdf.

2. Randy Capps, Michael Fix, Jeffrey S. Passel, Jason Ost, Dan Perez-Lopez, *A Profile of the Low-Wage Immigrant Workforce* (Urban Institute, Nov. 2003).

3. Don M. Mitchell, "The Geography of Injustice: Borders and the Continuing Immiseration of California Agricultural Labor in the Era of Free Trade," *Richmond Journal of Global and Business Law* 2 (2001): 145, 156.

4. See Bernard Trujillo, "Mexican Families and US Immigration Reform," *Fordham Urban Law Journal* 38 (2010): 415, 425–28.

5. 535 US 137 (2002).

6. *NLRB v. C&C Roofing Supply, Inc.*, 569 F.3d 1096, 1099 (9th Cir. 2009).

7. See *Design Kitchen and Baths v. Lagos*, 388 Md. 718, 882 A.2d 817 (Md. 2005); *Correa v. Waymouth Farms, Inc.*, 664 N.W.2d 324 (Minn. 2003); *Reinforced Earth Co. v. W.C.A.B. (Astudillo)*, 570 Pa. 464, 810 A.2d 99 (Pa. 2002).

8. See *Sanchez v. Eagle Alloy Inc.*, 254 Mich. App. 651, 658 N.W.2d 510 (Mich. App. 2003), *appeal granted*, 469 Mich. 955, 671 N.W.2d 874 (Mich. 2003), *vacated*, 471 Mich. 851, 684 N.W.2d 342 (2004), holding that undocumented immigrants' use of false documents to obtain employment constituted "commission of crime," warranting suspension of benefits from the date on which employer discovered the immigrant's employment status.

9. See *Rosa v. Partners in Progress, Inc.*, 152 N.H. 6, 868 A.2d 994 (N.H. 2005). An undocumented immigrant generally "may not recover lost United States earnings, because such earnings may be realized only if that illegal alien engages in unlawful employment." Ibid. at 868, 1000. However, "given the strict requirements of IRCA and the compensation and deterrence principles of tort law, a rule holding a person responsible for an 'illegal alien's' employment liable for lost United States earnings when that person knew or should have known of an 'illegal alien's' status will not undermine the policy goals of IRCA." Ibid. at 1001.

10. See, for example, *Balbuena v. IDR Realty LLC*, 6 N.Y.3d 338, 812 N.Y.S.2d 416 (N.Y. 2006), holding that the IRCA did not expressly preempt state laws regarding permissible scope of recovery in personal injury actions predicated on state labor laws; *Madeira v. Affordable Housing Foundation, Inc.*, 315 F.Supp.2d 504, 507 (S.D.N.Y. 2004), holding that noncitizenship status does not prevent defendant from recovering compensatory damages for his violation of New York labor law, and *Hoffman Plastics* does not prevent the state from enforcing the state's wage payment laws on behalf of

undocumented immigrants: "The fact is, undocumented aliens do obtain work in the United States. Recognizing this incontrovertible fact, New York's public policy does not bar compensation in the form of back pay for undocumented workers who are injured in the manner of the instant plaintiff."

11. See *Coma Corp. v. Kansas Dept. of Labor*, 283 Kan. 625, 154 P.3d 1080 (Kan. 2007). But see *Bastas v. Board of Review*, Dept. of Labor and Ind., 155 N.J. Super. 312, 315, 382 A.2d 923 (1978), holding that undocumented immigrants may not receive unemployment benefits.

12. 364 F.3d 1057, 1067 (9th Cir. 2004).

13. 281 F. Supp.2d 895 (S.D. Tex. 2003).

14. Internal Revenue Code § 3304(a)(14)(A).

9

US-Mexico Border Enforcement

We have lost control of our borders.
—Attorney General William French Smith

The likelihood that any given person of Mexican ancestry is an alien is high enough to make Mexican appearance a relevant factor, but standing alone it does not justify stopping all Mexican Americans to ask if they are aliens.
—*United States v. Brignoni-Ponce*

This chapter touches on an issue that is unquestionably relevant today to the continuing debate over US immigration law and policy. Over the last decade, the US government has greatly increased border enforcement operations, especially along the nation's southern border with Mexico. The result has been thousands of deaths along the US–Mexico border and, surprisingly enough, a doubling of the undocumented immigrant population in the United States.

Moreover, border enforcement operations have had other negative collateral consequences. They have led to more networks of human smugglers, who charge immigrants thousands of dollars for passage to the United States. And the beat goes on. Immigration enforcement increased dramatically after the tragic events of September 11, 2001 (which are discussed in chapter 11), and even more enforcement remains a popular choice among many politicians and US citizens.

Unfortunately, US government enforces the laws in ways that have unquestionably disparate racial impacts. This can be seen with the common problem of racial profiling in immigration enforcement, which has been sanctioned by the US Supreme Court, as well as the fact that those arrested in immigration raids are of particular racial backgrounds. Enforcement of the immigration laws has been directed at Mexican and Central American nationals. This is no doubt because the modern immigration "problem" is primarily perceived to be "illegal aliens" from Mexico.

■ Demons of Our Time: Mexican Immigrants

As the pattern of immigration enforcement suggests, Mexican and other Latina/o immigrants—especially undocumented immigrants—are among the most disfavored immigrants of modern times. Their current demonization fits into a long history of discrimination against immigrants from Mexico as well as, more generally, all persons of Mexican ancestry in the United States. This discrimination unfortunately has often directly affected US citizens of Mexican descent as well as immigrants from Mexico.

As outlined in chapter 2, discrimination against persons of Mexican ancestry has a long history, particularly in the US–Mexico border region. From the days of the US–Mexican War, which ended in 1848, to more recent times, with such things as the "repatriation" of persons of Mexican ancestry during the Great Depression, the mass deportation campaign known as Operation Wetback in 1954, and Proposition 187 in 1994, there has been an anti-Mexican undercurrent to US immigration law and its enforcement in the United States. This undercurrent continues to this day, with some recent examples being the anti-immigrant, anti-Mexican agitation seen in the last few years that has fueled the enactment of a flood of state and local immigration legislation.

Anti-Mexican sentiment, often combined with class-based bias, has long been common to American social life and specifically to US immigration laws. Persons of Mexican ancestry are often stereotyped as nothing other than peasants who undercut the wage scale of "American" workers because they will work for "inhuman" wages, which they presumably can do because they are less than human.

The modern debates over the ever-expanding fence along the US–Mexico border and immigration enforcement generally, the proliferation of state and local immigration enforcement measures, and the fear that some Americans express over the "Hispanization" of the United States reveal both anti-Mexican and anti-immigrant sentiment as well as legitimate concerns with lawful immigration and immigration controls. The difficulty of disentangling lawful from unlawful motivations for supporting such controls does not change the fact that invidious motives to some degree influence both the enactment and the enforcement of US immigration law and policy.

Public concern is often expressed with the magnitude of the flow of immigrants from Mexico. Chapter 1 provides data about the numbers of immigrants from Mexico who come annually to the United States. Some people contend that the United States is being inundated—"flooded" is the word frequently used—with poor Mexican immigrants. The "flood" of migrants, in the view of some, is effectively ruining the United States economically, politically, and socially. Related to the fear of the destruction of America as we know it is the alleged failure of immigrants to assimilate into US society, which is also an oft-expressed concern with today's immigrants.

The conventional wisdom has been that federal power over immigration is exclusive, with little room for state and local immigration enforcement and immigrant regulation. Nonetheless, in the last few years, several state and local governments, frustrated with the failure of Congress to enact comprehensive immigration reform and uneasy with the real and imagined changes brought by new immigrants to their communities, have adopted measures that purport to address undocumented immigration and immigrants. Race and class have unquestionably influenced the passage of these measures, with the response in part due to the increase in the Latina/o population in the United States.

Without question, today's immigrant demons are Mexican. Arab and Muslim noncitizens constitute another group of immigrants who have been subject to aggressive immigration enforcement in recent years, especially after the tragic events of September 11, 2001. After September 11, the concern with fighting terrorism came to dominate immigration law and enforcement and the national debate over immigration reform.

■ Racial Profiling in Immigration Enforcement

Given that Mexican immigrants are the disfavored immigrants of this day and time, it is no surprise that US immigration enforcement targets them. But, before we delve into that issue, some background is in order.

A few years ago, policy makers and the courts began a long overdue reconsideration of racial profiling, the formal and informal targeting of African Americans, Latinas/os, and other racial minorities for police stops on account of their race. The rationale for profiling is the alleged statistical probabilities that certain racial groups are more likely to be involved in criminal activity. Presidents Bill Clinton and George W. Bush decried racial profiling in law enforcement. Many state and local law enforcement agencies have been investigated for engaging in this unlawful practice.

Importantly, racial profiling in criminal law enforcement violates the US Constitution. Police, for example, cannot lawfully stop a person solely because of the color of his or her skin. The Fourth Amendment provides that "The right of the people to be secure in their persons, houses, papers, and effects, against unreasonable searches and seizures, shall not be violated, and no Warrants shall issue, but upon probable cause, supported by Oath or affirmation, and particularly describing the place to be searched, and the persons or things to be seized."

Alleged criminal propensities of African American and Latino men cannot justify a police stop under the Fourth Amendment. Despite acknowledging the unlawfulness of the practice, policy makers face the nagging problem of how to enforce the law and to end the use of race in routine police stops. The Fourth Amendment also limits the power of the federal government to engage in traffic stops to enforce the immigration laws.

However, racial profiling is part and parcel of immigration enforcement in the United States. Not surprisingly, immigration officers regularly— and often quite candidly and openly—profile persons of Mexican ancestry as potential "illegal aliens."

Two major Supreme Court decisions, *United States v. Brignoni-Ponce* and *Martinez-Fuerte v. United States*, expressly state that "Mexican appearance" can be considered by immigration enforcement officers.[1] *Brignoni-Ponce* found that "Mexican appearance" could be one of many factors in justifying an immigration stop, and in *Martinez-Fuerte*, the Court ruled that immigration officers could direct persons of "Mexican appearance" to secondary inspection at immigration enforcement checkpoints.

Today, as a consequence of these decisions allowing the consideration of "Mexican appearance," we regularly hear reports of racial profiling in border enforcement, with many Latinas/os, US citizens as well as lawful immigrants, often adversely affected. Racial profiling in immigration enforcement disproportionately burdens persons from Mexico and Central America, the vast majority of whom are US citizens or lawful immigrants.

The harmful effects of racial profiling range from embarrassment and humiliation of the persons stopped to the undermining of the civil rights of all Latinas/os—citizens and noncitizens alike—in US society. Each year close to 90 percent of the persons deported from the country are from Mexico and Central America, when significantly less of the overall undocumented population is Latina/o. Race-based immigration enforcement helps reinforce and perpetuate the erroneous—yet enduring—stereotype that *all* Latinas/os in the United States are "foreigners."

The Supreme Court Approves Racial Profiling

Given that the decision has so greatly influenced immigration enforcement in the United States, the Supreme Court's 1975 decision in *United States v. Brignoni-Ponce* warrants careful consideration. The Court held that an immigration stop by the Border Patrol violated the Fourth Amendment because Border Patrol officers relied exclusively on "the apparent Mexican ancestry" of the occupants of an automobile. So far, so good. The Court further stated, however, in the quote that prefaces this chapter that "*the likelihood that any given person of Mexican ancestry is an alien is high enough to make Mexican appearance a relevant factor*" in an immigration stop. This statement from *Brignoni-Ponce* has greatly influenced immigration enforcement in the United States over the last thirty-plus years.

In *Brignoni-Ponce*, the Court authorized the Border Patrol to rely on the "Mexican appearance" of automobile occupants even if no individual, much less one who "appears Mexican," has been specifically identified as having violated the immigration laws. In support of its reasoning, the Court relied on the US government's assertion that 85 percent—an inflated estimate contrary to the available evidence—of the undocumented immigrants in the United States come from Mexico. According to the best estimates, however, Mexican citizens make up only about 50–60 percent of the undocumented population.

In any event, rather than focus on the percentage of undocumented persons of Mexican ancestry in the country, the Supreme Court in *Brignoni-Ponce* should have considered the percentage of the entire Latina/o population in the United States comprising US citizens and lawful immigrants. This represents the population—"persons who are of Mexican appearance"—subject to the dignitary injuries caused by racial profiling in immigration enforcement.

The large population of persons of "Mexican appearance" lawfully in the United States but nonetheless subject to race-based immigration stops has grown substantially over more than three decades since the Court decided *Brignoni-Ponce*. In 2000, nearly 30 million people of Hispanic ancestry, over 12.5 percent of the total US population, lived in the United States. A crude estimate from these figures reveals that the vast majority

United States v. Brignoni-Ponce 422 US 873 (1975)

On the evening of March 11, 1973, two Border Patrol officers parked at the checkpoint perpendicular to Interstate Highway 5, a major north–south thoroughfare miles north of San Diego and the US–Mexico border, watching northbound traffic. They pursued an automobile driven by Felix Humberto Brignoni-Ponce, a US citizen of Puerto Rican ancestry, saying later that their only reason for the stop was that the automobile's three occupants appeared to be of "Mexican" descent. The officers established that two passengers, one from Mexico and one from Guatemala, lacked proper US immigration documentation. All three were arrested. The driver, Brignoni-Ponce, was later charged with the crime of transporting undocumented immigrants.

Brignoni-Ponce moved to suppress the testimony of and about the passengers, claiming that the evidence was the fruit of a stop and seizure in violation of the Fourth Amendment. Border Patrol agent Terrance J. Brady offered the following straightforward justification for the stop of Brignoni-Ponce's vehicle:

Q. Did these people in the car appear to be of Mexican descent to you?
A. Yes, sir.
Q. And that, if there was any, appeared to be the reason that you stopped them?
A. Yes, sir.

Judge Turrentine denied the suppression motion.

After a trial, a jury found Brignoni-Ponce guilty. The court sentenced him to four years in prison.

Brignoni-Ponce appealed to the US Court of Appeals for the Ninth Circuit. The court of appeals held that Mexican appearance of the automobile occupants alone was insufficient to justify a stop and that the district court should have granted the motion to suppress.

The US government sought review in the US Supreme Court. Justice Louis Powell delivered the Supreme Court's decision in *United States v. Brignoni-Ponce*. The Court reasoned that "Mexican appearance" failed to furnish "reasonable grounds to believe that the three occupants were aliens." However, the Court elaborated that "Mexican appearance" can still be one relevant factor considered by a Border Patrol officer in making a stop: "The likelihood that any given person of Mexican ancestry is an alien is high enough to make Mexican appearance a relevant factor, but standing alone it does not justify stopping all Mexican Americans to ask if they are aliens."

At first glance, *United States v. Brignoni-Ponce* might be seen as a victory for immigrants. That is technically true; the Court found that the immigration stop violated the Fourth Amendment, and Brignoni-Ponce's criminal conviction was reversed. However, the Court made it clear that immigration officers enjoy wide discretion in making stops and offered its own laundry list of factors that might be considered, including:

- the "characteristic appearance of persons who live in Mexico, relying on such factors as the mode of dress and haircut";
- the "characteristics of the area in which they encounter a vehicle";
- the "proximity to the border";
- the "usual patterns of traffic on the particular road";
- "previous experience with alien traffic";
- "information about recent illegal border crossings in the area";
- the "driver's behavior" and "erratic driving";
- "obvious attempts to evade officers";
- "aspects of the vehicle," such as "certain station wagons, with large compartments for fold-down seats or spare tires" or appearing "heavily loaded";
- "an extraordinary number of passengers, or the officers['] ... observ[ations of] persons trying to hide"; and
- the "facts in light of [the officer's] experience in detecting illegal entry and smuggling."

The broad discretion afforded to border enforcement officers in *United States v. Brignoni-Ponce* contributed to future racial profiling in immigration enforcement. To this day, many Latina/o citizens claim that they are profiled based on their "Mexican appearance" by immigration officers. ■

(in the neighborhood of 80 percent) of the Latinas/os in the United States are lawful immigrants or citizens.

The magnitude of the negative impacts of racial profiling in immigration enforcement promises to expand as the Latina/o population increases. The Bureau of the Census has projected that, by 2050, Hispanics will constitute nearly 25 percent of the US population.[2] Given the millions of Latinas/os who lawfully live in the United States, "Mexican appearance" holds limited probative value in determining whether a person lacks proper immigration documentation.

The Rationale for Profiling

In affording broad discretion to the Border Patrol, the Supreme Court in *United States v. Brignoni-Ponce* appeared to be swayed by the US government's claimed need for flexibility in border enforcement. This "need" is based on the unproven fact that undocumented immigrants impose great social, economic, and other costs on US society. The Court emphasized that

> the Government makes a convincing demonstration that the public interest demands effective measures to prevent the illegal entry of aliens at the Mexican border. Estimates of the number of illegal immigrants in the United States vary widely. A conservative estimate in 1972 produced a figure of about one million, but the [Immigration and Naturalization Service] now suggests there may be as many as 10 or 12 million aliens illegally in the country. *Whatever the number, these aliens create significant economic and social problems, competing with citizens and legal resident aliens for jobs, and generating extra demand for social services.* The aliens themselves are vulnerable to exploitation because they cannot complain of substandard working conditions without risking deportation.... The Mexican border is almost 2,000 miles long, and even a vastly reinforced Border Patrol would find it impossible to prevent illegal border crossings. Many aliens cross the Mexican border on foot, miles away from patrolled areas, and they purchase transportation from the border to inland cities, where they find jobs and elude authorities. Others gain entry on valid temporary border-crossing permits, but then violate the conditions of the entry. Most of these aliens leave the border area in private vehicles, often assisted by professional "alien smugglers." The Border Patrol's traffic-checking operations are designed to prevent this inland movement. They succeed in apprehending some illegal entrants and smugglers,

and they deter the movement of others by threatening apprehension and increasing the cost of illegal transportation. (emphasis added)

Despite the Court's unqualified pronouncement that undocumented "aliens create significant economic and social problems," the question of whether the costs of undocumented immigration outweigh its benefits remains hotly disputed in the academic literature to this day. Research studies, on balance, suggest that the aggregate economic benefits of immigration generally outweigh any costs.[3]

Chief Justice Warren Burger concurred in the judgment in *Brignoni-Ponce* but lamented that

as the Fourth Amendment now has been interpreted by the Court it seems that the Immigration and Naturalization Service is powerless to stop the tide of illegal aliens—and dangerous drugs—that daily and freely crosses our 2,000-mile southern boundary. Perhaps these decisions will be seen in perspective as but another example of a society seemingly impotent to deal with massive lawlessness. In that sense history may view us as prisoners of our own traditional and appropriate concern for individual rights, unable—or unwilling—to apply the concept of rea- sonableness explicit in the Fourth Amendment in order to develop a rational accommodation between those rights and the literal safety of the country.[4]

In an extraordinary twist, Chief Justice Burger further noted, "In the *Baca* case [*United States v. Baca*, 368 F. Supp. 398, 402–403 (S.D. Cal. 1973)], Judge Turrentine conducted a thorough review of the entire problem and the present Government response." Appended to Chief Justice Burger's opinion is an excerpt from Judge Turrentine's opinion in *Baca* describ- ing the "illegal alien problem" and "the law enforcement response."[5] The appendix included a lengthy excerpt from the *Baca* decision on "The Ille- gal Alien Problem" and "The Law Enforcement Problem," which viewed migration from Mexico as a monumental problem for the United States that is basically out of control.

The Undocumented Immigrant "Profile"

With the leeway afforded by *Brignoni-Ponce*, immigration officers rou- tinely employ crude undocumented immigrant profiles, with race as the touchstone in the United States border region and far beyond. Immigration and Customs Enforcement (ICE) officers often rely on a person's "Hispanic appearance" as an important factor in making a stop.

In one lawsuit in which plaintiffs alleged that the INS engaged in a pattern and practice of exclusively race-based stops, officials of the INS testified that an officer might properly rely on, along with Hispanic appearance, a "hungry look" and a person appearing "dirty, unkempt," or wearing "work clothing."[6] Plaintiffs in many other lawsuits allege that the immigration authorities rely almost exclusively on race in making immigration stops. Importantly, charges of race-based immigration enforcement are made far from the southern border of the United States and in every region of the United States, from the Midwest to the Pacific Northwest to the South.

Illegal alien profiles, with Hispanic appearance as their touchstone, usually rely at least in part on the stereotype that Latinas/os are foreigners of suspect immigration status and therefore are presumptively subject to an immigration stop. The popular stereotype flies in the face of the current estimates that roughly 40 percent of the undocumented immigrants in the United States are not from Mexico, and that a majority of Latinas/os are in fact US citizens and lawful immigrants.

By emphasizing that a Border Patrol officer may consider race in deciding whether to conduct an immigration stop and bestowing immigration officers with vast discretion, the Supreme Court in *United States v. Brignoni-Ponce* opened the door to Border Patrol reliance on race combined with little more than a hunch that a brown person is undocumented. As a study of immigration enforcement a few years after the Court decided *Brignoni-Ponce* concluded, immigration "officers can easily strengthen their reasonable suspicion for an interrogation *after they have begun talking to an individual. . . . It is easy to come up with the necessary articulable facts after the fact*," which is commonly known within the Border Patrol as "*canned p.c.* [probable cause]."[7]

Moreover, the study found that officers may believe they can identify an undocumented person to a near certainty when, in fact, they err more often than not. The "totality of the circumstances" approach of *Brignoni-Ponce* appears to have been tailor made for authorizing stops based on "Mexican appearance," with the officers after the fact concocting a legally defensible rationale for the stop based on that "suspicious" appearance combined with a multitude of seemingly neutral facts.

The great discretion afforded immigration enforcement officers may easily be abused. One federal judge observed critically that the US government had articulated "virtually anything and everything" as justifying a stop in the border region, which suggests that something else, such as the race of automobile occupants, is primarily at work:

> The vehicle was suspiciously dirty and muddy, or the vehicle was suspiciously squeaky-clean; the driver was suspiciously dirty, shabbily dressed and unkempt, or the driver was too clean; the vehicle was suspiciously traveling fast, or was traveling suspiciously slow (or even was traveling suspiciously at precisely the legal speed limit); the [old car, new car, big car, station wagon, camper, oilfield service truck, SUV, van] is the kind of vehicle typically used for smuggling aliens or drugs; the driver would not make eye contact with the agent, or the driver made eye contact too readily; the driver appeared nervous (or the driver even appeared too cool, calm, and collected); the time of day [early morning, mid-morning, late afternoon, early evening, late evening, middle of the night] is when "they" tend to smuggle contraband or aliens; the vehicle was riding suspiciously low (overloaded), or suspiciously high (equipped with heavy duty shocks and springs); the passengers were slumped suspiciously in their seats, presumably to avoid detection, or the passengers were sitting suspiciously ramrod-erect; the vehicle suspiciously slowed when being overtaken by the patrol car traveling at a high rate of speed with its high-beam lights on, or the vehicle suspiciously maintained its same speed and direction despite being overtaken by a patrol car traveling at a high speed with its high-beam lights on; and on and on ad nauseam.[8]

Courts rarely find that immigration stops fail to satisfy the Supreme Court's minimal requirements. Although civil remedies exist for race-based immigration enforcement, the evidentiary requirements in proving such claims are difficult to satisfy and serve as formidable barriers to suit.

The deficiencies in existing law authorizing the immigration authorities to consider race in immigration stops require changes in the law. The "Hispanic appearance" classification is dramatically overbroad and includes US citizens and lawful immigrants as well as undocumented ones.

The Dignitary Harms of Racial Profiling

Race-based law enforcement stops are based on probabilities, not individualized suspicion. Reliance on group probabilities as the justification for stopping an individual runs afoul of fundamental principles of human dignity at the core of the Equal Protection Clause of the **Fourteenth**

Amendment of the US Constitution. Resulting harms, including but not limited to emotional turmoil, humiliation, embarrassment, and physical abuse, regularly fall on innocent racial minorities, particularly Latinas/os, including US citizens and lawful immigrants.

That ICE targets persons of "Hispanic appearance" almost invariably contributes to the fact that close to 90 percent of the removed persons from the country are of Mexican and Latin American descent, even though they constitute closer to one-half of the total undocumented population in the United States. Similarly, race-based enforcement reportedly has led to the unlawful arrest, and sometimes even wrongful deportation of, US citizens of Mexican ancestry. It may well contribute to the increased violence against undocumented immigrants and other persons of Mexican ancestry in the US–Mexico border region.

The pattern and practice of racial profiling in immigration enforcement deeply harms the Latina/o community as a whole, not simply the individuals subject to immigration stops. Targeting one group stigmatizes persons of "Hispanic appearance" and undercuts Latinas/os' claim to full membership and equal citizenship in US society. Racial profiling further marginalizes Latinas/os by subjecting the community to concrete harms not suffered by Anglos. This singles out Latinas/os as a group for immigration inquiries and reinforces their perceived second-class status in the United States.

Ultimately, the Supreme Court's endorsement in *United States v. Brignoni-Ponce* of the use of "Mexican appearance" in immigration enforcement, along with the vast discretion afforded immigration enforcement officers, in effect authorizes blatant civil rights violations. Under current law, US citizens of Latin American ancestry and lawful Latina/o immigrants may be subjected to immigration stops primarily because of their physical appearance. Racial profiling in immigration enforcement thus is based on and reinforces the perception that persons of Latin American ancestry, citizens and noncitizens alike, are "foreigners" in the United States.

■ Modern Immigration Enforcement

As discussed above, Mexican American citizens, as well as lawful immigrants, often contend that immigration enforcement officers engage in racial profiling in the enforcement of US immigration laws. Similarly, their communities (despite having large US citizen components) are presumed generally to be composed of "foreigners" subject to immigration enforcement.

The increasingly rigorous enforcement of the nation's southern border with Mexico compared with the relatively lax enforcement of the northern border with Canada is often pointed to as evidence of racism at work. In addition, as discussed later in this chapter, immigration raids consistently result in disparate racial impacts with large numbers of undocumented (and relatively unskilled) immigrants of color, especially from Mexico and Central America, arrested.

In myriad ways, the Supreme Court's decision in *United States v. Brignoni-Ponce* has greatly shaped immigration enforcement in the United States over the past thirty-plus years. Unfortunately, the Court has not revisited the use of race in immigration stops since 1975.

Subsequent Supreme Court cases have built on the considerable discretion given Border Patrol officers by the Supreme Court in *Brignoni-Ponce*. In *United States v. Cortez*, the Court relied on *Brignoni-Ponce* to engage in a fact-intensive analysis upholding the validity of an immigration stop under the Fourth Amendment and refused to disturb criminal convictions for transporting undocumented immigrants. Chief Justice Warren Burger, writing for the Court, emphasized that "this case portrays at once the enormous difficulties of patrolling a 2,000-mile open border and the patient skills needed by those charged with halting illegal entry into this country."[9]

After the Court decided a flurry of border enforcement cases in the 1970s and 1980s, there were not many subsequent decisions of much consequence for several years. In *United States v. Arvizu*, the Supreme Court in 2002 held that the Border Patrol had reasonable suspicion for an immigration stop near the US–Mexico border in southern Arizona. The court of appeals had held that most of the factors identified by the district court, including the driver's slowing down, failure to acknowledge the officer, and the raised position of the children's knees, as justifying the stop "carried little or no weight in the reasonable-suspicion analysis." In a unanimous opinion written by Chief Justice William Rehnquist, the Court reversed this decision: "We have said repeatedly that [courts] must look at the 'totality of the circumstances' of each case to see whether the detaining officer has 'a particularized and objective basis' for suspecting legal wrongdoing." The Court held that the court of appeals' "rejection of seven of the listed factors in isolation from each other does not take into account the 'totality of the circumstances' as our cases have understood that phrase." The Court found that, in the case before it, the facts "taken together ... sufficed to form a particularized and objective basis for [the stop], making the stop reasonable within the meaning of the Fourth Amendment."[10]

One lower court reconsidered the reliance on race in immigration enforcement. In *United States v. Montero-Camargo*, the US Court of Appeals for the Ninth Circuit found that the Court's statement in *Brignoni-Ponce* that "Mexican appearance" could be one factor in an immigration stop was outdated and held that the Border Patrol cannot lawfully consider "Hispanic appearance" in deciding to make a stop.[11] The court based its holding on the fact that many lawful immigrants and citizens of Latin American ancestry live in the United States, and thus "Hispanic appearance" was a weak indication of unlawful immigration status. It also relied on the fact that in applying the Equal Protection Clause of the Fourteenth Amendment, the Supreme Court in recent years had repeatedly emphasized that all racial classifications—even those in affirmative action programs designed to promote diversity of student bodies at public universities—are constitutionally suspect.

To this day, many lower courts regularly rely on *United States v. Brignoni-Ponce* in determining whether an immigration stop was supported by reasonable suspicion. Lower courts often employ a laundry list of factors offered by the Court in determining whether there is reasonable suspicion to stop a motor vehicle for violation of the immigration laws. Many cases involve challenges to the constitutionality of stops by the Border Patrol; the officers often admit to relying upon "Hispanic appearance," an expansion from the "Mexican appearance" that the Supreme Court authorized in *United States v. Brignoni-Ponce*. Presumably, this expansion resulted from increased migration from Central America, with Central Americans (as well as other Latin Americans) often confused with "Mexicans."

Ultimately, *Brignoni-Ponce* opened the floodgates for immigration agents to rely on race in ways that would be impermissible for other law enforcement officers. Part of the deep dissatisfaction among many Latinas/os with US immigration law almost inevitably results from the racial profiling endemic in its enforcement by the US government. Unfortunately, the Supreme Court in *Brignoni-Ponce* arguably increased reliance on race in immigration stops by allowing immigration officers great discretion in making stops and deferentially reviewing the "totality of the circumstances" offered by the officers for justifying the stop. This approach remains central to the Supreme Court's review of immigration stops to this day.

A long history of discrimination against persons of Mexican ancestry, particularly in the US–Mexico border region, may help explain why the impacts on Mexican Americans of immigration enforcement's consideration of "Mexican appearance" have been undervalued, if not ignored outright, by the public and policy makers. From the days of the US–Mexican War to more recent times, there has long been an anti-Mexican undercurrent to the debate about immigration law and its enforcement in the United States. This undercurrent continues to this day, with some recent examples being the anti-immigrant, anti-Mexican agitation seen in local cities and municipalities culminating in the passage of a plethora of anti-immigrant measures in just the last few years.

As discussed previously (see chapter 1), the Supreme Court has consistently considered undocumented immigration from Mexico to be a serious law enforcement problem that justifies aggressive action. The perception remains to this day. As Congress debated comprehensive immigration reform in 2006–07, for example, the focus remained almost myopically on Mexican migration, with increased enforcement measures often proposed.

Immigration Raids

The disparate impacts on Latinas/os can also be seen in other areas of immigration enforcement other than the roving patrols in the US–Mexico border region. In its waning years, the Bush administration increasingly employed immigration raids in the interior of the United States as part of an effort to demonstrate the federal government's commitment to aggressive immigration enforcement at a time when the US Congress was considering immigration reform. The US government specifically conducted immigration raids with increased rigor at work sites across the United States.

For example, the May 2008 raid at a meat-processing plant in **Postville, Iowa** (discussed later in this chapter), constituted one of the largest raids on undocumented workers at a single site in US history. Almost all the noncitizens arrested in the raids were from Guatemala and Mexico. The US government did not simply seek to deport the undocumented workers but, in a dramatic change from past practice, pursued questionable criminal prosecutions of the workers on immigration and related crimes. The employer was also prosecuted. Rather than simply facing deportation, the arrested noncitizens faced criminal charges and incarceration as well as deportation.

Racial and Class Impacts of Modern Border Enforcement

Similar to the enforcement of the inadmissibility grounds discussed in chapter 6, Congress's near-myopic focus on increased border enforcement—and undocumented immigrants who enter without inspection—has both class and racial impacts. Noncitizens who enter without inspection are more likely to be poor and working people from the developing world than visa overstays who have sufficient resources to avoid the public charge exclusion and who at least initially lawfully enter the United States. This salient fact goes all but ignored by immigration policy makers and proponents of greater border enforcement, such as those who support extending the fence along the border between the United States and Mexico.

Moreover, noncitizens excluded and deported from the United States tend to be poor and working people, with US immigration laws exuding class-based biases that negatively affect people of color from the developing world. To make matters worse, for those immigrants able to come and remain in this country, the exploitation of working-class undocumented immigrants continues virtually unabated. Unfortunately, undocumented workers enjoy precious few protections under the law.

Labor Market Impacts of Modern Border Enforcement

As a result of the operation of US immigration laws, the undocumented immigrants who successfully make it to this country participate in a labor force that in many respects resembles a racial caste system. Dual labor markets exist with undocumented workers—predominantly people of color—participating in one market without legal protections while US citizens and legal immigrants enjoy protections of the law in a separate labor market. A well-known example is the plight of farm workers, including many from Mexico, who often suffer severe exploitation in the fields, where labor protections are rarely enforced.

The truth of the matter is that wage, labor, and other protections are but a faraway dream for many undocumented workers in the United States. Put differently, there is a Jim Crow quality to the labor markets in the United States today.

To make matters worse, sporadic workplace immigration enforcement by the US government has terrified immigrant (and minority citizen) communities and forced them deeper underground. In 2007–08, the US government ramped up the number of immigration raids of workplaces, which negatively impacted many undocumented immigrants from

Mexico and Central America as well as their families (including US citizen children). This is consistent with this nation's harsh treatment of Central Americans in the 1980s and 1990s; the US government generally classified the vast majority of Central Americans fleeing civil war as "economic migrants" and thus ineligible for relief from deportation under the asylum provisions of US immigration laws, which provide relief only to persons fleeing actual or possible persecution.

Death at the Border

In the 1990s, the US government dramatically heightened immigration enforcement by massing forces along its southern border with Mexico, including high profile operations adopted with much fanfare. These measures have resulted in a human toll that is nothing short of horrific. A week rarely goes by without press reports of undocumented Mexican immigrants who have died on the long, treacherous journey to the United States. The title of one October 2002 *New York Times* article tells it all: "Skeletons Tell Tale of Gamble by Immigrants."[12]

Unfortunately, many poor migrants die horrible deaths in the desert seeking nothing more than to make a better life for themselves and their families in the United States. The vast majority of the attempted border crossers in no way can be characterized as dangers to the national security, public safety, or otherwise injurious to the nation. They are simply ordinary people seeking economic opportunities in the proverbial "land of opportunity."

Military-style operations on the Southwest border, such as **Operation Gatekeeper** in San Diego and Operation Hold the Line in El Paso, have channeled immigrants away from large urban areas and into remote, desolate locations, where thousands have died agonizing deaths from heat, cold, exposure, and dehydration. To add to the danger, at various times US military forces have patrolled the border. In one infamous incident in 1997, US Marines mistakenly shot and killed a teenage goat herder (and US citizen), Esequiel Hernandez Jr.

Despite the rising death toll, the US government continues to pursue enforcement operations with vigor. Indeed, Congress consistently enacts proposals designed to bolster border enforcement, including extension of the border fence along the US–Mexican border.

The deaths cannot be the least bit surprising to the US government. Indeed, Operation Gatekeeper demonstrates the US government's

The Killing of a Goat Herder

On May 20, 1997, Esequiel Hernandez, Jr.... was herding his family's goats 100 yards from his home on the US–Mexican border in Redford, Texas, as he did every day. Six days before, he had turned 18 years old.

Unknown to Esequiel or any of the other residents of Redford, a group of four Marines led by 22-year old Corporal Clemente Banuelos had been encamped just outside the small village along the Rio Grande River for three days. After watering his small flock of goats in the river, Esequiel started on his way back home when the Marines began stalking him from a distance of 200 yards.

The four camouflaged Marines were outfitted with state-of-the-art surveillance equipment and weapons. Esequiel carried an antique .22 caliber rifle—a pre-World War I, single shot rifle to keep wild dogs and rattlesnakes away from his goats. The autopsy showed that Esequiel was facing away from the Marines when he was shot. He probably never knew the Marines were watching him from 200 yards away.

Thus it was that a 22 year-old United States Marine shot and killed an innocent 18 year-old boy [and a US citizen by birth] tending his family's goats. This outrageous act was the inevitable consequence of a drug prohibition policy gone mad. Esequiel Hernandez was killed not by drugs but by military officers of the US government.

Source: DPFT: Drug Policy Forum of Texas, available at www.dpft.org/hernandez/gallery/index.htm ■

indifference to the human tragedy resulting from its aggressive border enforcement policy. In the words of one informed commentator, "The real tragedy of [Operation] Gatekeeper ... is the direct link ... to the staggering rise in the number of deaths among border crossers. [The US government] has forced these crossers to attempt entry in areas plagued by extreme weather conditions and rugged terrain that *[the US government] knows to present mortal danger.*"[13]

In planning Operation Gatekeeper, the US government knew that its strategy would risk the lives of migrants but nonetheless proceeded with implementation of the new enforcement measure. As another observer concludes, "Operation Gatekeeper, as an enforcement immigration policy financed and politically supported by the US government, flagrantly violates international human rights *because this policy was deliberately formulated to maximize the physical risks of Mexican migrant workers, thereby ensuring that hundreds of them would die."*[14]

The deaths are not the only human rights abuses in the US–Mexico border region. US immigration authorities—from the old Border Patrol to the modern ICE—have long had a reputation for committing human rights abuses against immigrants and US citizens of Mexican ancestry. Originally created to police the US–Mexican border, the Border Patrol has historically been plagued by reports of brutality, shootings, beatings, and killings.[15] Amnesty International, American Friends Service Committee, Human Rights Watch, and many other groups have all issued reports documenting human rights abuses by the Border Patrol and its border operations.[16]

For years, many migrants have depended on smugglers for passage into the United States. Since the new border operations went into effect, heightened immigration restrictions and bolstered immigration enforcement have caused a sharp increase in the fees charged by smugglers. Smuggling fees increased from a few hundred dollars in the 1990s to several thousand dollars today. It now is much more expensive for an undocumented immigrant to come to the United States than before the new border operations went into effect in the 1990s.

To pay for the trip through smugglers, some migrants are forced to become indebted to their smugglers and to work off the debts through forced labor, which thus takes the exploitation of undocumented workers to new and frightening levels. Failure to work off the debts may result in brutal consequences.

In sum, human trafficking through the smuggling of migrants for profit and deaths of immigrants (almost all Mexicans) on the US–Mexico border, which have both increased since the early 1990s due to heightened border enforcement measures, tend to disproportionately affect poor and working noncitizens of color—those forced to take great risks to try to come to the United States because they lack legal ways of entering the country.

But a migrant's ability to pay is not the only cost of human trafficking. The journey itself is replete with hazards. Among the many risks faced by migrants is the possibility of being abandoned. In May 2003, nineteen migrants, including a five-year-old child, died of asphyxiation, heat exposure, and dehydration in the back of a smuggler's truck in South Texas. The smuggler had fled, leaving the migrants to die. One of the dead "had worked five years in the United States before he returned to Mexico to fetch his children, hoping to provide them comforts he could not give them in Mexico."[17]

Today, because of the money to be made in this black market, criminal syndicates thrive in trafficking human beings. These syndicates resemble the criminal networks that emerged in response to the federal government's efforts during Prohibition's unsuccessful ban on commerce in alcohol early in the twentieth century. Criminal elements grew and have asserted control over a new, lucrative industry.

But it gets worse. Some undocumented immigrants have been enslaved by smugglers. Reports of slavery have increased dramatically in the last few years. One 2005 report concluded as follows:

> Our research identified 57 forced labor operations in almost a dozen cities in California between 1998 and 2003, involving more than 500 individuals from 18 countries....Victims labored in several economic sectors including prostitution and sex services (47.4 percent), domestic service (33.3 percent), mail order brides (5.3 percent), sweatshops (5.3 percent), and agriculture (1.8 percent).... Victims of forced labor often suffer severe hardships and deprivations. Their captors often subject them to beatings, threats, and other forms of physical and psychological abuse. They live in conditions of deprivation and despair. Their captors may threaten their families. Perpetrators exert near total control over victims, creating a situation of dependency. Victims come to believe they cannot leave....They are terrified of their captors but also fear law enforcement, a fear often based on bad experiences with police and other government officials in their countries of origin.[18]

Today, in no small part due to the operation of US immigration laws, cases of involuntary servitude regularly make the news.

The US–Mexico border region is filled with other risks as well. Vigilante groups, such as those known as the **Minutemen**, patrol the borders and at times threaten undocumented immigrants with violence. Undoubtedly feeling encouraged by the tough immigration laws and border enforcement efforts, along with the harsh anti-immigrant rhetoric of some political leaders, these vigilantes frequently claim that they are simply doing what the federal government has failed to do—enforce the immigration laws.

In 2005, the Minuteman Project, which garnered considerable press attention, patrolled the US–Mexico border in search of undocumented immigrants. Its members in effect engaged in armed hunting expeditions for migrants. They received vocal public support from a former member of the US Congress, Tom Tancredo, and longtime anti-immigrant advocate Pat Buchanan. The Minutemen frequently express deep antipathy for Mexican immigrants, "illegal aliens," and groups that support them.

To make matters worse, criminals frequently prey on unlawful entrants seeking to evade border inspection. Robberies, murders, and rapes of immigrants are all too common. The new isolated routes to which US border operations today funnel migrants expose them to more danger from criminal elements. Common crime poses a serious danger to border crossers.

Despite the high human toll, increased border enforcement has proven to be woefully ineffective. Its self-defeating nature is demonstrated by its counterintuitive consequences. Contrary to expectations, migrants who come to the United States under the current regime are more likely to remain permanently in the country than in the past. Understandably, undocumented immigrants who have successfully survived the journey to the United States do not want to again risk running the gauntlet of dangerous border controls and literally place their lives on the line for a second time. Consequently, the undocumented immigrant population in the country has *increased* from an estimated 5–7 million since the various border operations were put into place in the 1990s to approximately 12 million today.

This bears repeating. The undocumented population in the United States has increased despite the unprecedented border enforcement initiatives adopted over the last two decades and record-breaking budgets devoted to border enforcement, efforts that have cost hundreds of millions of dollars and resulted in the deaths of thousands of people. The undocumented immigrant population has also risen despite the unprecedented efforts to tighten border enforcement after September 11, 2001.

Ultimately, the border buildup has failed as a matter of policy *and* has had serious—indeed tragic—moral costs. Years of bona fide reform efforts, blue ribbon commissions, increased training, creation of civilian oversight boards, and civil rights lawsuits have failed to ameliorate the incredibly high human costs of border enforcement. Proposals for incremental reform strategies, including those made by the Select Commission on Immigration and Refugee Policy in the 1980s and the US Commission on Immigration Reform in the 1990s, have failed to change much. In fact, immigration enforcement measures arguably have become less fair and effective, as well as more arbitrary and capricious, in recent years, with tough immigration reforms in 1996 and 2005 as well as numerous immigration policy changes after September 11, 2001. They are unquestionably more deadly.

Unfortunately, the fact that mostly poor persons of Mexican ancestry are being killed along the US–Mexico border has muted the public outcry over the thousands of deaths. Indeed, the ever-rising death count has failed to trigger much of a reaction at all from the American public. Current border enforcement policies, however, in the future might well be equated with other unsavory and embarrassing chapters in US history, such as Jim Crow, the era of Chinese exclusion, the Japanese internment, and the previous mass deportation campaigns directed at persons of Mexican ancestry.

Indeed, we are confident that history will look back on the harsh border enforcement measures of the twentieth century, as well as the "war on terror," with deep regret and shame. This is especially the case with the military-style operations that have resulted in thousands of unnecessary deaths. Despite the death toll, these operations have failed to have much meaningful impact on reducing the undocumented immigrant population in the United States. At most, they have minimally decreased migration so that the undocumented population is not quite as high as it would have been absent the measures. However, migrants continue to embark on the arduous journey to the United States.

In sum, through the major border operations, the US government has redirected the flow of undocumented immigrants away from public view and into more dangerous locales. The movement of migrants in search of jobs, however, has continued virtually unabated. To make matters worse, such aggressive government actions have encouraged vigilantes to join in the unsavory hunt for human prey in the form of undocumented immigrants at the border, thereby increasing the risk of horrible, sometimes deadly, confrontations.

Detention as a Form of Modern Immigration Enforcement

The US government has long employed detention as an immigration enforcement device. Its use has escalated over time. In the 1970s and 1980s, for example, Central Americans, Cubans, and Haitians who claimed to be fleeing political persecution in their native countries were all held in detention while their claims were processed. The US government later adopted a policy of keeping unaccompanied minors, including many from Mexico, in detention as well.

Beginning in earnest in 1996, the US Congress greatly increased the use of detention of noncitizens as an immigration enforcement device. In immigration reform that year, Congress mandated detention of noncitizens facing removal because of conviction of certain crimes pending their deportation. At times, some noncitizens subject to deportation were detained indefinitely when their native country refused to accept their return.

Detention of immigrants has long been criticized. The detention of immigrants by the US government has been characterized as the "American Gulag." The conditions of detention, including the poor quality of the health care, have been the subject of attention and controversy. Many of the immigration detention facilities were not constructed with long-term detention in mind. In addition, many of the detention facilities are run by private enterprises that some contend have treated the detainees inhumanely. A popular 2008 movie *The Visitor* portrayed the travails of an unwitting immigrant—and those trying to help him—subject to detention and ultimate removal. Many of the facilities are in isolated locations, such as Oakdale, Louisiana; Florence, Arizona; and El Centro, California, where friends, families, and attorneys find it difficult to visit.

Postville, Iowa, Immigration Raids (2008)

While Congress debated comprehensive immigration reform beginning in late 2006, the Bush administration increasingly employed immigration raids in the interior of the United States in an effort to demonstrate the federal government's commitment to immigration enforcement. These raids have had racial and class impacts on particular subgroups of immigrant workers, namely low-skilled Latina/o immigrants.

Immigration raids are not an entirely new strategy of immigration enforcement, nor are their racial and class impacts. At various times in US history, the US government has employed raids—Operation Wetback in 1954 is a most famous example—as an immigration enforcement device, with undocumented Mexican immigrants a tried-and-true target of the raids. However, in the last few years, the US government has conducted immigration raids in increasing numbers—and with greater aggressiveness—at work sites across the United States.

The May 2008 raid in Postville, Iowa, constituted one of the largest raids on undocumented workers at a single site in US history. In the raid's aftermath, the US government did not simply seek to deport undocumented immigrants but pursued criminal prosecutions against them for immigration and related crimes. The new strategy, which devastated a rural community in America's heartland, proved to be most controversial.

With a massive show of force of helicopters, buses, and vans, immigration officers surrounded the Agriprocessors plant, the nation's largest kosher slaughterhouse and meat-packing plant and the economic lifeblood of Postville. Officers arrested suspected undocumented immigrants and detained them at the National Cattle Congress grounds, a cattle fairground seventy-five miles from Postville.[19]

According to press accounts, immigration authorities arrested 290 Guatemalan, 93 Mexican, 4 Ukrainian, and 2 Israeli workers.[20] Shackled and chained, the workers appeared in court and listened to interpreted court appearances through headsets. An observer of the mass legal proceedings commented,

> Those arrested appeared to be uniformly no more than 5 ft. tall, mostly illiterate Guatemalan peasants with Mayan last names, some being relatives, ... some in tears; others with faces of worry, fear, and embarrassment. They all spoke Spanish, a few rather laboriously [They presumably were native speakers of indigenous languages.]....Aside from their Guatemalan or Mexican nationality ... they too were Native Americans, in shackles. They stood out in stark racial contrast with the rest of us as they started their slow penguin march across the makeshift court.[21]

As the Postville raid suggests, recent immigration raids have had particularly negative impacts on Guatemalan immigrants. One of the largest workplace raids before Postville occurred in March 2007 in New Bedford, Massachusetts, with more than 360 workers arrested, the majority of whom were natives of Guatemala.

More than three hundred of those arrested in the Postville raid faced not only removal from the United States, but criminal charges for identity theft and related crimes. Most of the Guatemalans could not read or write, and many failed to understand that they were charged with *criminal* offenses, which would make it difficult, if not impossible, for them to ever immigrate lawfully to the United States, rather than simply facing deportation from the country. Court-appointed attorneys had little time to meet with the detained immigrant workers.

The rapid pace of the proceedings and the aggressive prosecution of criminal charges represented new strategies of the federal government in enforcing US immigration laws. Previously, the US government after a workplace raid ordinarily sought to swiftly deport the noncitizens arrested, not pursue criminal immigration-related crimes as in Postville. Many of the undocumented workers accepted plea bargains, with the hopes of faster release and quick deportation.

Months after the raids, the furor continued over the US government's Postville strategy and the harsh treatment of the immigrant workers. The title of one *New York Times* editorial—"The Shame of Postville"—pretty much summed it all up.[22]

The Postville immigration raids were directed at—and unquestionably impacted—unskilled Latina/o immigrant workers, who are among the most vulnerable persons in US society. Even if one defended the immigration-control goals of government, it is difficult to persuasively contend that the raid did not have distinctively racial and class impacts. To this point, the United States unfortunately has failed to address the root cause of undocumented immigration, that is, the more general problem with US immigration laws being out of sync with the nation's labor needs. Chapter 12 discusses this possibility.

■ Concluding Thoughts

Whether called "illegal aliens" or worse, Mexican immigrant are the demons of modern times. With that understanding, border enforcement in the United States in the twentieth century focused increasingly on the US–Mexico border and immigrants from Mexico. Although the events of September 11, 2001, raised concerns about border enforcement in general, the nation soon returned to a near-myopic focus on its southern border with Mexico. In no small part, this focus results from the general public concern with the migration of persons from Mexico and Latin America to the United States. The concern, in turn, has resulted in border and general immigration enforcement that consistently targets persons of Mexican ancestry.

Unfortunately, US immigration laws have a long history of discrimination against persons of Mexican ancestry—US citizens, lawful immigrants, and undocumented immigrants. That history, combined with the public's general fear of Mexican migration, has contributed to race-based immigration enforcement by the US government. The US Supreme Court has facilitated this type of enforcement through decisions sanctioning the reliance on "Mexican appearance" in immigration enforcement. Racial profiling in border enforcement and workplace raids plague the Mexican-ancestry community, as well as Latinas/os generally, in the United States. Often racial animus is obscured by the claim that "we are only anti–illegal immigrant," not anti-Mexican or anti-immigrant.

■ Discussion Questions

1. Is the current system of immigration enforcement in the United States working effectively and efficiently? Explain in detail why or why not. Does the presence of approximately 12 million undocumented immigrants in the United States strongly suggest a problem with the current immigration laws and their enforcement? Some observers have equated the enforcement of US immigration laws with the enforcement of the Prohibition-era anti-alcohol laws—frequently violated by otherwise law-abiding persons, extremely diffi-cult to enforce, and resulting in many negative collateral consequences (such as increased crime, smuggling, violence, a caseload crisis in the federal courts, and the like). Do you agree or disagree and why? What is the best way to improve the enforcement of the current US immigration laws?

2. Articulate and define specifically "Mexican appearance" and "Arab" or "Muslim" appearance. Are these inherently and inescapably vague descriptors what we as a society should want its law enforcement officers to rely on in making a stop of a person for a suspected violation of the immigration laws, terrorism, or general criminal activity? Explain your reasoning.

3. Over at least the last fifteen years, the United States has unfortunately experienced thousands of deaths of Mexican citizens along its southern bor-der with Mexico. Are the deaths an inevitable consequence of the effective enforcement of US immigration laws? Can we do anything to enforce the immigration laws and avoid the deaths? How will the history books look back on the deaths of migrants a century from now?

4. Should the United States continue to employ immigration raids to enforce the immigration laws? Why or why not? Are the impacts on families (including US citizen children), communities, businesses, and immigrants too severe to

justify the use of raids that have an extremely limited impact on reducing the overall undocumented population?

5. Is it necessary to reform US immigration laws to better fit with the nation's labor needs if we truly want to improve the enforcement of the immigration laws? See Kevin R. Johnson, *Opening the Floodgates: Why America Needs to Rethink Its Border and Immigration Laws* (New York: New York University Press, 2007).

■ Suggested Readings

Dow, Mark. 2004. *American Gulag: Inside US Immigration Prisons*. Berkeley: University of California Press.

Dunn, Timothy J. 1996. *The Militarization of the US–Mexican Border, 1978–1992: Low Intensity Conflict Doctrine Comes Home*. Austin: CMAS Books, University of Texas at Austin.

Johnson, Kevin R. 2000. "The Case Against Racial Profiling in Immigration Enforcement." *Washington University Law Quarterly* 78: 675.

Massey, Douglas S., Jorge Durand, and Nolan J. Malone. 2002. *Beyond Smoke and Mirrors: Mexican Immigration in an Era of Economic Integration*. New York: Russell Sage Foundation.

Mirandé, Alfredo. 1987. *Gringo Justice*. Notre Dame, Ind.: University of Notre Dame Press.

Nevins, Joseph. 2002. *Operation Gatekeeper: The Rise of the "Illegal Alien" and Making of the US–Mexico Boundary*. New York: Routledge.

Urrea, Luis A. 2004. *The Devil's Highway: A True Story*. New York: Little, Brown.

■ Notes

Epigraphs: Testimony of Attorney General William French Smith, *Immigration Reform and Control Act of 1983: Hearings on H.R. 1510 Before the Subcommittee on Immigration, Refugees, and International Law of the House Committee of the Judiciary*, 98th Cong., 1st sess. (1983), 1; *United States v. Brignoni-Ponce* 422 US 873, 886–87 (1975).

1. *United States v. Brignoni-Ponce*, 422 US 873 (1975); *Martinez-Fuerte v. United States*, 428 US 543 (1976).

2. US Bureau of the Census, *Current Population Reports—Population Projections of the United States by Age, Sex, Race, and Hispanic Origin: 1995 to 2050* (1996), table J, at 13.

3. See Kevin R. Johnson, *Opening the Floodgates: Why America Needs to Rethink Its Border and Immigration Laws* ((New York: New York University Press, 2007), 131–67.

4. *United States v. Ortiz*, 422 US 891, 899 (1975), Burger, C.J., concurring in the judgment; emphasis added. This concurrence in Ortiz also applied to *Brignoni-Ponce*.

5. Ibid., 422 US at 899 n.1, emphasis added.

6. *Nicacio v. INS*, 797 F.2d 700, 704 (9th Cir. 1985).

7. Edwin Harwood, "Arrests without Warrant: The Legal and Organizational Environment of Immigration Law Enforcement," *UC Davis Law Review* 17 (1984): 505, emphasis added.

8. *United States v. Zapata-Ibarra*, 223 F.3d 281, 282–83 (5th Cir. 2000), Weiner, J., dissenting; footnotes omitted, *cert. denied*, 531 US 972 (2000).

9. *United States v. Cortez*, 449 US 411, 416–17, 420–22 (1981).

10. *United States v. Arvizu*, 534 US 266, 272 (2002).

11. *United States v. Montero-Camargo*, 208 F.3d 1122 (9th Cir.) (en banc), *cert. denied sub nom.*, 531 US 889 (2000).

12. John W. Fountain with Jim Yardley, "Skeletons Tell Tale of Gamble by Immigrants," *New York Times*, Oct. 16, 2002, A1; see, e.g., Simon Romero and David Barboza, "Trapped in Heat in Texas Truck, 18 People Die," *New York Times*, May 15, 2003, A1.

13. Bill Ong Hing, "The Dark Side of Operation Gatekeeper," *U.C. Davis Journal of International Law and Policy* 7 (2001): 121, 135, emphasis added; footnote omitted.

14. Jorge A. Vargas, "US Border Patrol Abuses, Undocumented Mexican Workers, and International Human Rights," *San Diego International Law Journal* 2 (2001): 1, 69, emphasis added.

15. See generally Juan Ramon García, *Operation Wetback: The Mass Deportation of Mexican Undocumented Workers In 1954* (Westport, Conn.: Greenwood Press, 1980), analyzing the mass removal campaign; Alfredo Mirandé, *Gringo Justice* (Notre Dame, Ind.: University of Notre Dame Press, 1987), documenting history of human rights abuses by the Border Patrol and Immigration and Naturalization Service.

16. See, e.g., Border Network for Human Rights, the Border Action Network, and the U.S.–Mexico Border and Immigration Task Force, *US–Mexico Border Policy Report, Effective Border Policy: Security, Responsibility and Human Rights at the US-Mexico Border* (Washington, D.C., Nov. 2008); No More Deaths/No Más Muertes, *Crossing the Line: Human Rights Abuses of Migrants in Short-Term Custody on the Arizona/Sonora Border* (Tucson, Ariz., Sept. 2008); International Federation for Human Rights, *Walls, Abuses, and Deaths at the Borders* (Paris, France, Mar. 2008); Raquel Rubio-Goldsmith, M. Melissa McCormick, Daniel Martinez, and Inez Magdalena Duarte, *The "Funnel Effect" and Recovered Bodies of Unauthorized Migrants Processed by the Pima County Office of the Medical Examiner, 1990–2005*. Report Submitted to the Pima County Board of Supervisors. (Tucson, Ariz.: Binational Migration Institute, Mexican American Studies and Research Center, University of Arizona, Oct. 2006).

17. Elliot Spagat, "BC-Immigrants Killed," *Inland Valley Daily Bulletin* (Ontario, CA), July 9, 2005.

18. Human Rights Center, *Freedom Denied: Forced Labor in California* (Berkeley: University of California, 2005), 1.

19. See Erik Camayd-Freixas, "Interpreting After the Largest ICE Raid in US History: A Personal Account," *New York Times*, July 14, 2008.

20. See Spencer S. Hsu, "Immigration Raid Jars a Small Town," *Washington Post*, May 18, 2008, A1.

21. Camayd-Freixas, "Interpreting."

22. "The Shame of Postville," *New York Times*, July 13, 2008, WK11.

10

State and Local Regulation
of Immigration

Individuals may form communities, but it is institutions alone that can create a nation.
—Benjamin Disraeli, 1866

We discuss in chapter 3 that the federal government has the power to regulate immigration. Yet many other communities in the United States have exhibited an interest in regulating immigration and immigrants. These communities include state and local governments (including counties and municipalities), and even private associations (such as condominium associations and clubs). What happens when immigration regulation by nonfederal communities conflicts with federal regulation?

This chapter will examine how federal law interacts with state and local efforts to regulate immigration. First, we will examine how US constitutional law, through the **Supremacy Clause**, preempts certain nonfederal immigration laws. We also consider California's Proposition 187, a well-known example of a state's attempt to regulate immigration that a federal court struck down as unconstitutional. Next, we will consider how some states and localities attempt to regulate immigration by denying or conditioning the distribution of some public benefits, such as public education or welfare benefits. Finally, we will look at a recent spate of state and local initiatives aimed at undocumented workers, and how these local efforts are faring in federal courts.

■ Federal Preemption of State and Local Efforts to Regulate Immigration

Article 6, clause 2 of the Constitution of the United States is known as the Supremacy Clause. Its language proclaims that the federal Constitution and federal constitutional law are the "supreme Law of the Land." In practice, this language means that any regulation enacted by the federal government pursuant to its constitutional authority may preempt any state or local regulation of the same subject matter. Not wanting "too many cooks in the kitchen," the US Constitution identifies federal law as the boss in case of conflict.

One of the leading cases on **federal preemption** of state legislative initiatives regulating immigration is the US Supreme Court decision in *DeCanas v. Bica*, which held that the power to regulate immigration "is unquestionably exclusively a federal power."[1] Although this decision contains clear language declaring the power to regulate immigration as exclusively federal, it also makes it clear that not all nonfederal laws that affect immigration are preempted. The Court distinguished between regulating immigration, which is "essentially a determination of who should or should not be admitted into the country," and statutes, such as those regulating employment, that have some effect on immigrants. The Court held that just because immigrants are the subject of a state statute does not mean that the state statute is a regulation of immigration. Thus, according to the Supreme Court, states are constitutionally prohibited from regulating the conditions of legal entrance and residency in the United States, but states may enact statutes that affect immigrants.

More generally, the preemption doctrine does not entirely prohibit states and localities from passing laws pertaining to immigration. However, the doctrine does prohibit states and localities from going beyond federal law by framing their own classification system for immigrants or altering federal enforcement policies.

■ Proposition 187

In November 1994, California voters by a 2–1 margin passed Proposition 187, an initiative that would have denied public benefits, such as health care, education, and welfare, to undocumented immigrants. Under Proposition 187, law enforcement, teachers, and social service and health care workers would have had to verify a person's immigration status. If these workers determined that the person was undocumented, they would have been required to report the person to authorities and deny him or her social service, health care, and educational benefits. Many people regard Proposition 187 as one of the high-water marks of anti-immigrant sentiment in recent US history.

Immediately after the voters passed Proposition 187, several civil rights organizations, including the American Civil Liberties Union (ACLU), Mexican-American Legal Defense and Education Fund (MALDEF), and League of United Latin American Citizens (LULAC), filed lawsuits challenging the lawfulness of the initiative. A federal district court immediately enjoined Proposition 187 from taking effect and eventually ruled that most of Proposition 187 was an unconstitutional attempt by the government of California to regulate immigration, contrary to the Supremacy Clause and preemption doctrine.[2]

In 1998, while an appeal of the district court's decision was pending, Gray Davis, a Democrat, was elected governor of California. Governor Davis ultimately chose to drop the appeal. Preemption doctrine thus kept Proposition 187 from ever going into effect.

■ Public Benefits and Immigration

Even before Proposition 187, state and local governments had frequently attempted to regulate immigration by enacting statutes that conditioned immigrant access to public education or public benefits, or imposed fines on employers who employed undocumented immigrants, even though immigration can be regulated only by the federal government.

Until 1971, the US Supreme Court upheld most statutes that limited the opportunities of lawful permanent residents to engage in certain activities. In *Graham v. Richardson*, the Court reviewed provisions of state welfare laws that conditioned welfare benefits on US citizenship and imposed durational residency requirements on noncitizens.[3] The question was whether these statutes violated the Equal Protection Clause of the Fourteenth Amendment to the US Constitution, which provides that no state shall "deny to any person within its jurisdiction the equal protection of the laws."

In *Graham v. Richardson*, Carmen Richardson, a sixty-four-year-old Arizona resident, became permanently and totally disabled. She met all the requirements for state-administered federal assistance benefits. However, Arizona law required an individual to be a US citizen or to have resided in the United States for fifteen years in order to receive welfare benefits. Because Richardson did not meet the residency requirement, she was denied benefits. Richardson brought an action claiming that the Arizona statute violated the Equal Protection Clause, the constitutional right to travel, conflicted with the federal Social Security Act, and was preempted by federal law.

Graham v. Richardson also involved two other noncitizens. Beryl Jervis and Elsie Mary Jane Leger, lawfully admitted residents, applied for public assistance from the state of Pennsylvania after suffering from illnesses that required them to give up their employment. The women were denied benefits under Pennsylvania law because it required an individual to be a US citizen to receive public welfare benefits. The women brought a claim challenging the denial of benefits.

The Supreme Court concluded that a state's desire to preserve limited welfare benefits for its own citizens was not a sufficient reason to make noncitizens ineligible for public assistance. The Court added that a state's efforts to decrease welfare costs does not justify invidious discrimination against noncitizens. The Supreme Court thus held that a state statute that denies welfare benefits to resident immigrants and to immigrants who have not resided in the United States for a specified number of years violates the Equal Protection Clause.

In *Mathews v. Diaz*, the Supreme Court considered the constitutionality of alienage distinctions imposed by the federal government.[4] The question in *Mathews* was whether Congress may condition immigrants' eligibility for participation in a federal medical insurance program on continuous residence in the United States for a five-year period and admission for permanent residence. In *Mathews*, three Cuban refugees had applied for a federal supplemental medical insurance program. The law grants eligibility to resident citizens who are sixty-five years old or older, but denies eligibility to comparable immigrants unless they have been admitted as a legal permanent resident (LPR) for permanent residence and have also resided in the United States for five continuous years. At the time of application, only one of the applicants was an LPR, and none of them had resided in the United States for five continuous years.

The Supreme Court scrutinized the federal statutory conditions under the Due Process Clause of the Fifth Amendment and, invoking the plenary power doctrine (see chapter 3), found that the conditions were constitutional—Congress may treat different classes differently. The Court, however, stressed the breadth of the Fifth Amendment's reach, stating that there are "literally millions of aliens within the jurisdiction of the United States," and extended the due process protections of the Fifth Amendment to nonciti-zens whose presence in this country is "unlawful, involuntary, or transitory."[5]

Among the most important public benefits we consider is public edu-cation. In *Plyler v. Doe*, the US Supreme Court considered a Texas law that would have withheld funds to local school districts that educated the children of undocumented foreign nationals and authorized local school districts to deny enrollment to children who could not pay.[6] The school-children challenged the statute, claiming that it violated the Equal Protec-tion Clause of the Fourteenth Amendment of the US Constitution.

The Supreme Court held that the Texas statute violated the Equal Pro-tection Clause because undocumented foreign nationals and their children are people "in the ordinary sense of the term" and therefore are afforded the Fourteenth Amendment protections. Additionally, the Court struck down the law because it severely disadvantaged undocumented children by denying them an education, and because Texas could not prove that the regulation was needed to serve a compelling state interest.

In recent years, there has been great controversy over whether states can charge in-state fees for public colleges and universities to undocumented students who are residents of the state. Decisions on public university fees are generally in the power of the states. However, some anti-immigrant activists contend that charging undocumented immigrants the same fees as other residents conflicts with federal immigration law. On several occa-sions, Congress has considered **Development, Relief and Education for Alien Minors (DREAM) Acts,** which, among other things, would make clear that federal law permits undocumented residents to be charged the same university fees as other residents.

■ Recent Local Initiatives and the Federal Responses

In the last few years, there has been tremendous activity at the state and local levels concerning the regulation of immigration. This frenzy of legis-lative activity has been caused in part by the failure of the federal govern-ment to enact comprehensive immigration reform but also by demographic changes brought by migration to the states and localities that formerly had not had many Latina/o immigrants. These recent state and local immigra-tion initiatives fall into two broad classifications: (1) nonfederal enforce-ment of federal immigration law; and (2) restricting access of immigrants to goods, services, and employment.

Cooperation of Federal, State, and Local Officers in Enforcing Federal Immigration Law

The Immigration and Nationality Act (INA) § 287(g), 8 USC. § 1357(g), authorizes agreements between federal, state, and local governments to cooperate in the enforcement of US immigration laws. These coenforcement regimes are governed by **memoranda of agreement (MOAs)** executed between the federal government and the relevant state or local agency. The MOA is like a contract between federal immigration officials and local agents. These MOAs amount to a federal deputization of a local or state law enforcement office, allowing the latter to enforce federal immigration law.

To date, there have been dozens of MOAs. Table 10.1 lists some of the state and local law enforcement agencies that, as this book goes to press, have executed MOAs with Immigration and Customs Enforcement (ICE) of the Department of Homeland Security (DHS). More than 840 state and local officers have been trained and certified to enforce federal immigration law through MOAs executed pursuant to INA § 287(g).

More recently, MOAs have been signed by the Houston (Texas), Florence (Arizona), and Mesa (Arizona) police departments, among others. The particular MOA signed by ICE and the local law enforcement agency typically defines the scope and limitations of what the local agents are permitted to do. The MOA also establishes a structure for supervising the local agents. A MOA must be signed by the ICE assistant secretary and the governor, a senior political entity, or the head of the local agency before trained local officers are authorized to enforce US immigration law.

On July 10, 2009, the DHS secretary, Janet Napolitano, announced efforts to standardize the various MOAs and focus the efforts of federally deputized local law enforcement to the investigation of the more serious violent crimes and drug offenses.

Once a MOA becomes effective, a local officer has several powers. The local officer has the power and authority to interrogate any person believed to be a foreign national as to his or her right to be or remain in the United States. The local officer, under the MOA, may also process for immigration violations those individuals who are convicted of state or federal felonies. As of July 2009, however, the local jurisdiction must agree to pursue the criminal charges that prompted the immigrant's detention. This change is designed to prevent the abusive police practice of arresting a "suspicious" person for no other reason than to investigate the potential violation of immigration, rather than criminal, law.

Table 10.1 State and local law enforcement agencies with memoranda of agreement (MOA) to enforce federal immigration law

STATE	LAW ENFORCEMENT AGENCY	DATE OF MOA
AL	Alabama State Police	9/10/2003
AL	Etowah County Sheriff's Office	7/8/2008
AR	Benton County Sheriff's Office	9/26/2007
AR	City of Springdale Police Department	9/26/2007
AR	Rogers Police Department	9/25/2007
AR	Washington County Sheriff's Office	9/26/2007
AZ	Arizona Department of Corrections	9/16/2005
AZ	Arizona Department of Public Safety	4/15/2007
AZ	City of Phoenix Police Department	3/10/2008
AZ	Maricopa County Sheriff's Office	2/7/2007 (rescinded 2009)
AZ	Pima County Sheriff's Office	3/10/2008
AZ	Pinal County Sheriff's Office	3/10/2008
AZ	Yavapai County Sheriff's Office	3/10/2008
CA	Los Angeles County Sheriff's Office	2/1/2005
CA	Orange County Sheriff's Office	11/2/2006
CA	Riverside County Sheriff's Office	4/28/2006
CA	San Bernardino County Sheriff's Office	10/19/2005
CO	Colorado Department of Public Safety	3/29/2007
CO	El Paso County Sheriff's Office	5/17/2007
FL	Bay County Sheriff's Office	6/15/2008
FL	Brevard County Sheriff's Office	8/13/2008
FL	Collier County Sheriff's Office	8/6/2007
FL	Florida Department of Law Enforcement	7/2/2002
FL	Jacksonville Sheriff's Office	7/8/2008
FL	Manatee County Sheriff's Office	7/8/2008
GA	Cobb County Sheriff's Office	2/13/2007
GA	Georgia Department of Public Safety	7/27/2007
GA	Hall County Sheriff's Office	2/29/2008
GA	Whitfield County Sheriff's Office	2/4/2008
MA	Barnstable County Sheriff's Office	8/25/2007
MA	Framingham Police Department	8/14/2007
MA	Massachusetts Department of Corrections	3/26/2007
MD	Frederick County Sheriff's Office	2/6/2008
MO	Missouri State Highway Patrol	6/25/2008
NC	Alamance County Sheriff's Office	1/10/2007
NC	Cabarrus County Sheriff's Office	8/2/2007
NC	Cumberland County Sheriff's Office	6/25/2008
NC	Durham Police Department	2/1/2008
NC	Gaston County Sheriff's Office	2/22/2007
NC	Henderson County Sheriff's Office	6/25/2008

STATE	LAW ENFORCEMENT AGENCY	DATE OF MOA
NC	Mecklenburg County Sheriff's Office	2/27/2006
NC	Wake County Sheriff's Office	6/25/2008
NH	Hudson City Police Department	5/5/2007
NM	New Mexico Department of Corrections	9/17/2007
OH	Butler County Sheriff's Office	2/5/2008
OK	Tulsa County Sheriff's Office	8/6/2007
SC	Beaufort County Sheriff's Office	6/25/2008
SC	York County Sheriff's Office	10/16/2007
TN	Davidson County Sheriff's Office	2/21/2007
TN	Tennessee Department of Safety	6/25/2008
TX	Carrollton Police Department	8/12/2008
TX	Farmers Branch Police Dept.	7/8/2008
TX	Harris County Sheriff's Office	7/20/2008
VA	City of Manassas Police Department	3/5/2008
VA	Herndon Police Department	3/21/2007
VA	Loudoun County Sheriff's Office	6/25/2008
VA	Manassas Park Police Department	3/10/2008
VA	Prince William County Police Department	2/26/2008
VA	Prince William County Sheriff's Office	2/26/2008
VA	Prince William-Manassas Adult Detention Center	7/9/2007
VA	Rockingham County Sheriff's Office	4/25/2007
VA	Shenandoah County Sheriff's Office	5/10/2007

A local officer also has the power to arrest without warrant (1) any foreign national entering or attempting to enter the United States unlawfully, or (2) any foreign national in the United States, if the officer has reason to believe the foreign national is present in the United States in violation of law and is likely to escape before a warrant can be obtained. A local officer also may arrest, without a warrant, a person for felonies under a federal law regulating the admission, exclusion, expulsion, or removal of immigrants.

ICE's deputization of local law enforcement has created considerable controversy and confusion. Many law enforcement leaders firmly believe that the distinction between state and federal immigration roles is critical in best serving the community. More practically, all persons should feel comfortable reporting a crime and working with local police. If the cop on the beat doubles as an immigration enforcement officer, then people (both citizens and noncitizens) may be reluctant to work with law enforcement. Moreover, local police officers lose the neighborhood trust that is necessary for them to be effective.

Local Officers' Immigration Powers

In addition to arrest powers under the MOA, the local law enforcement officer also typically possesses the power to

- serve arrest warrants for immigration violations;
- administer oaths;
- take evidence required for criminal foreign national processing (e.g., fingerprints, photographs, interviews);
- prepare affidavits for ICE supervisory review; and
- detain and transport arrested immigrants to ICE-approved detention facilities. ■

Another area of confusion lies in the moniker "sanctuary city." As we have seen, it is an extraordinary act for a local agency to submit itself to deputization by ICE. The normal condition is that federal agents enforce federal law, and nonfederal agents tend to nonfederal law. Table 10.1 shows that many localities have submitted to federal deputization for enforcement of US immigration laws. Yet many, many more localities have continued with the usual business of letting the federal agents mind the federal store. In some corners of the public imagination, however, the polarities have been reversed. As such, we hear that localities pursuing the usual path of leaving federal law to federal agents have assumed the ignoble status of "sanctuary cities" and are seen as having effectively created havens for lawbreakers.

Finally, returning to our analysis of preemption, we can say that the federal deputization of local law enforcement is generally not preempted. Federal legislation (i.e., INA § 287[g]) expressly permits coenforcement, and specific MOAs between federal and state or local agencies specify responsibilities.

Arizona's S.B. 1070

On April 23, 2010, Arizona governor Janice Brewer signed into law Arizona's Senate Bill 1070 (S.B. 1070), perhaps the biggest immigration bombshell to detonate in the last several years. S.B. 1070 aggressively targeted undocumented immigration by creating immigration-related state crimes and by assigning federal enforcement powers to Arizona law enforcement agents. After a summer of intense debate, media coverage, demonstrations, and boycotts, the US district court enjoined four sections of the statute on July 28, 2010.

Among the provisions of S.B. 1070 struck down as unconstitutional was a section that required Arizona law enforcement officers to determine the immigration status of any person stopped, detained, or arrested, if the officer had a "reasonable suspicion that the person is unlawfully present in the United States."[7] Many observed that if such a provision became law, it would empower police officers to engage in racial profiling, using Latina/o ethnicity as a proxy for immigration status. Despite the widespread use of such practices, racial profiling offends basic norms of equality and undermines the law's authority.

In spring 2011, the US Court of Appeals for the Ninth Circuit affirmed the district court injunction.[8] As this book goes to press, Arizona Governor Brewer promises to seek review by the Supreme Court of the United States.

Restricting Immigrant Access to Goods, Services, and Employment

Another class of state and local initiatives aims at regulating immigration through the side door. These initiatives attempt to deny noncitizens access to housing and social benefits or to penalize employers for hiring undocumented immigrants. Several states have, for example, authorized the revocation of business licenses from employers who knowingly hire UFNs (including Arizona, Missouri, Mississippi, South Carolina, Tennessee, Virginia, and West Virginia). Other states have tried to regulate the act of harboring or transporting UFNs (including Missouri, Oklahoma, South Carolina, and Utah).[9]

The question of whether local initiatives that regulate immigrant employment and access to services are preempted has been slowly percolating through the federal courts. Insofar as the preemption question involves state or local penalization of employers, the relevant federal law (which would preempt any state or local law with which it conflicts) is a section of the Immigration Reform and Control Act (IRCA) of 1986: "The provisions of this section preempt any State or local law imposing civil or criminal sanctions (other than through licensing and similar laws) upon those who employ, or recruit or refer for a fee for employment, unauthorized aliens."[10]

Federal courts have split over the correct interpretation of this statutory language. Courts in Oklahoma (Tenth Circuit) and Pennsylvania (Third Circuit) have found such statutes unconstitutional. Courts in Arizona (Ninth Circuit) and Missouri (Eighth Circuit) have offered limited support for such statutes. The Supreme Court has yet to clearly delineate the appropriate place of state and local regulation of immigration.

Federal courts in Arizona and Missouri have upheld the validity of ordinances, a position with which the Supreme Court agreed, that revoke or suspend business licenses of employers who employ unauthorized immigrants.[11] The courts in those cases held that because the ordinances related to the issuance of business licenses, they were licensing laws permitted by federal law. Additionally, both courts concluded that Congress could not have intended to preempt regulation in this area because Congress provided an exception to the express preemption provision.

Contrary to the Arizona and Missouri cases, a Pennsylvania district court held that a similar local ordinance was invalid because IRCA expressly preempts state and local laws concerning the employment of unauthorized immigrants.[12] The court stated that licensing, as used in the statute, refers to revoking a local license for a violation of the federal IRCA, not for a violation of local laws. Furthermore, the district court found that the dominant federal interest in the field of immigration, and the comprehensive nature of IRCA's federal regulation of employment practices concerning immigration, demonstrated congressional intent to occupy the field to the exclusion of similar state or local laws.

Two important rulings on the preemption issue came from the US Court of Appeals, one from the Ninth Circuit and one from the Tenth Circuit. The Ninth Circuit case is *Chicanos Por La Causa v. Napolitano*.[13] In this case, the court upheld an Arizona statute against a "facial" challenge to the statute's constitutionality, but left the door open as to whether the statute would be constitutional "as applied." The Supreme Court affirmed.[14]

There is an important difference in the burdens of proof between "facial" challenges and "as applied" challenges to the constitutionality of state statutes. For opponents of legislation to succeed in a facial challenge, they must convince the court that the statute would be unconstitutional in *all* its potential applications. Suppose a court concludes that a statute has one hundred possible applications. Suppose also that the court concludes that ninety-nine of those applications would be unconstitutional, and only one application would be constitutional. Under those circumstances, that court must conclude, in a facial challenge, that the statute is constitutional. Thus, the opponents of a statute bringing a facial challenge must meet a stringent burden of proof, one that generally cannot be satisfied.

In an "as applied" challenge, the burden of proof is much lower. There, the court looks at the factual record to determine whether the specific application was constitutional.

Just six months before *Chicanos Por La Causa*, the US Supreme Court had sent a strong message to the Ninth Circuit by reversing one of its opinions that had been insufficiently hard on a facial challenge.[15]

Because the bar for a successful facial challenge is set so high, it may be that we learn very little about the Arizona statute's ultimate constitutionality from the Ninth Circuit's finding that the facial challenge had failed. The Ninth Circuit's opinion expressly left the door open for future challenges of the Arizona statute "as applied" to a specific case.[16]

The Tenth Circuit decision case is *Chamber of Commerce v. Edmondson*.[17] The court held that an Oklahoma statute, placing certain burdens on employers of immigrants, was preempted by federal law and thus was unconstitutional.

With a conflict among the lower courts, the stage is set for the Supreme Court of the United States to resolve the issue.

The Oklahoma statute, called the Taxpayer and Citizen Protection Act of 2007, denies state identification cards and access to public benefits to all undocumented migrants, and makes it a felony to harbor or transport any undocumented person.[18] The act also requires employers to verify that all employees are legal residents by checking social security numbers against a federally managed database. The database is part of E-Verify, a program implemented by the federal government for employers' use in verifying the status and eligibility of job applicants.[19] Although use of E-Verify is optional under federal law, the Oklahoma law makes it mandatory for employers in the state.

Voicing concerns that the law will be invalidated on federal preemption grounds and will cost the state of Oklahoma more than it can afford in legal fees, the governor signed the bill only after it passed in the state legislature by overwhelming margins. The governor stated, "While some will undoubtedly claim this legislation is a landmark step forward, the truth of the matter is we will not effectively address immigration reform until the federal government acts."[20]

Another much-publicized incident of local regulation occurred in New Jersey. After the US district court's decision in *Lozano v. City of Hazleton*,[21] the town of Riverside, New Jersey, opted to rescind its Illegal Immigration Relief Act rather than face costly litigation.[22] Having already spent $82,000 defending the law, Riverside decided to withdraw it.

The examples of Oklahoma and New Jersey show that attempting to regulate immigration at the nonfederal level is a costly gamble. Local and state legislators must consider the cost to taxpayers of enacting anti-immigrant legislation that may ultimately be found unenforceable as an impermissible encroachment on federal preemption law.

■ Nativism, Racism, Hate

The cost of litigation in defending an anti-immigration ordinance is just the beginning. Unfortunately, racism and xenophobia arise in the debates over the local ordinances and often infect the general dialogue over immigration in the United States. Such invidious sentiments are often amplified at the state and local levels. The tone of the debate can be nothing less than hateful and frightening, particularly to immigrants and US citizens of particular national origins. Moreover, hate crimes directed at immigrants and Latinas/os, not coincidentally, have increased in recent years as public concerns over immigration have grown.

Advocates of restrictionism often seek to inflame—not calm—anti-immigrant sentiment to build support for stringent immigration measures. The works of Samuel Huntington, Victor Davis Hanson, Michelle Malkin, and Peter Brimelow exemplify the common ploy of immigrant restrictionists who seek to capitalize on public fears—racial, economic, cultural, social, environmental, and otherwise—of immigration and immigrants.[23] Such a fast-and-loose characterization of the current state of immigration plays into, and reinforces, the oft-made dire claims of an "alien invasion" of the United States, a warlike situation in which outsiders are viewed as unwanted intruders who restrictionists frequently claim deserve immediate, drastic, and almost invariably harsh treatment.

Moreover, the facts show that the alarm over the level of immigration is not justified. The nation simply is not experiencing anything like an "alien invasion." Over the last decade, somewhere in the neighborhood of a million immigrants—out of a total US population of more than 300 million (or less than 0.5 percent)—have lawfully come each year to the

United States.[24] Today, a total of roughly 12 million undocumented immigrants—approximately 4 percent of the nation's overall population—live in the United States.

The bottom line is that, although numerically much greater than past times, the percentage of immigrants in the United States today is not all that different as a percentage of the total US population from that in other periods of US history.[25] Indeed, the immigrant percentage of the total US population is equaled, and in some instances surpassed, by those seen during the early twentieth century.[26] True, as is the case today, growing pains resulted from the sizeable flow of immigrants of generations past. Nonetheless, the nation ultimately more or less succeeded in integrating the new wave of immigrants into US society. There is no reason to believe that the prospects for today's immigrants are any different in the long run.

Rather than deride immigrants and pursue steps that make their lives miserable, state and local governments should constructively take steps to encourage immigrant assimilation, such as increasing access to classes in English as a second language, facilitating access to higher education, and pursuing other measures that might promote immigrant assimilation. In the end, punishing immigrants in the United States is both unfair and counterproductive since we cannot "deport them all" or keep all of "them" from entering the country.

Still, we as a nation cannot ignore the prevalence of anti-immigrant sentiment in American society, which occasionally finds strong expression at the state and local levels. Consider the following description of an anti-immigrant rally in Hazleton, a rural town in Pennsylvania, home of a much-publicized immigration ordinance that generated national controversy:

> I'm not Latino, but the anger displayed at the rally—held in support of Hazleton's anti-immigration mayor, Lou Barletta—was enough to give anyone with a soul a serious case of the chills. . . . About 700 people attended the rally, where some in attendance tried to link illegal Mexican immigrants with the 9/11 attacks. Other speakers accused illegal immigrants of carrying infectious diseases, increasing crime and lowering property values. . . . If Alabama's late segregationist Gov. George Wallace had been present, he would have wondered who hired away his speechwriters.[27]

In a similarly troubling vein, the mayor of Valley Park, Missouri, which enacted an immigration ordinance comparable to Hazleton's, complained,

"You got one guy and his wife that settle down here, have a couple kids, and before long you have *Cousin Puerto Rico and Taco Whoever moving in*."[28] Similar examples abound. Joe Arpaio, sheriff of Maricopa County, Arizona, popularly known as "America's Toughest Sheriff," has pursued controversial immigration and other law enforcement policies—such as forcing detainees to wear pink underwear—that regularly draw the ire of the civil rights and immigrant communities.[29] The anti-Mexican, anti-immigrant campaign culminating in the landslide passage of California's Proposition 187, a measure that among other things would have denied undocumented immigrant children access to the public schools, was nothing less than an anti-immigration landmark of the 1990s.

To make matters worse, as anti-immigrant rhetoric has escalated in the last few years, along with the national debate over immigration reform, hate crimes against Latinas/os have gone up dramatically.[30] In 2008, Latino immigrants were killed in vicious attacks in rural Pennsylvania and suburban New York, two locales that in recent years had seen the emergence of visible Mexican immigrant communities (and local anti-immigration ordinances).[31] The facts surrounding the killing of a lawful Ecuadoran immigrant, Marcelo Lucero, in Long Island in 2008 are deeply troubling. A group of young men allegedly began the events of a hate-filled evening with the statement: "Let's go find some Mexicans."[32] The *New York Times* later reported: "Every now and then, perhaps once a week, seven young friends got together . . . to hunt down, and hurt, Hispanic men. They made a sport of it, calling their victims 'beaners,' . . . prosecutors said."[33]

The increase in hate crimes against Latinas/os appears to be tied to the heated, at times hateful, public debate regarding immigration, which has included the scapegoating of immigrants and Latinas/os for social ills, ranging from crime to environmental degradation to destroying "American culture."[34] It hardly seems mere coincidence that hate crimes against Latinas/os are on the rise at the same time immigrants are being blamed for just about every social problem imaginable. Consider the specific context surrounding the murder of Marcelo Lucero, a Latino immigrant. In Long Island, New York, the local county executive had railed against undocumented immigrants for months.[35] Tempers flared, and a gang of teenagers killed Lucero. Similarly, earlier in 2008, in Shenandoah, Pennsylvania, a group of young men beat to death an immigrant from Mexico. Tensions had run high in the area with passage of the anti-immigrant ordinance (which a court enjoined) in Hazleton, a rural town about twenty miles away.[36]

Local immigration measures serve as a bellwether for the racism that generally influences the formation of the federal, state, and local immigration laws and their enforcement. The animus, which is often more raw at the local level, where it tends to be less sanitized than the debate in Washington, D.C., almost inexorably animates at least some of the debate over immigration reform at the national level and influences national immigration law and policy. For example, despite its judicial invalidation, Proposition 187, with anti-Mexican animus at its core, led to aggressive federal action to tighten the border and resulted in legislation that limited benefit eligibility for lawful immigrants and dramatically increased noncitizen detention and deportation. Because such measures fail to address the root causes of undocumented immigration, undocumented immigration continues.

■ Concluding Thoughts

We have seen that local regulators of immigration must dance to the tune piped by the federal government. Federal preemption doctrine creates certain costs for state and local governments, but also stands to correct the extreme acts of local regulators.

■ Discussion Questions

1. Why might it be preferable, as a policy matter, for the federal government, rather than states and localities, to regulate immigration and immigrants?

2. Do you think it is proper or effective for state and local law enforcement agencies to enforce federal immigration law? What problems might such enforcement invite for federal officers? For local officers?

3. What do you think of the term "sanctuary city"? What does the term imply?

■ Suggested Readings

Huntington, Clare. 2008. "The Constitutional Dimension of Immigration Federalism." *Vanderbilt Law Review* 61: 788.

Johnson, Kevin R. 1995. "An Essay on Immigration Politics, Popular Democracy, and California's Proposition 187: The Political Relevance and Legal Irrelevance of Race." *Washington Law Review* 70: 629.

———. 1995. "Public Benefits and Immigration: The Intersection of Immigration Status, Ethnicity, Gender, and Class." *UCLA Law Review* 42: 1509.

Neuman, Gerald L. 1996. *Strangers to the Constitution: Immigrants, Borders, and Fundamental Law*. Princeton, N.J.: Princeton University Press.

Olivas, Michael A. 2007. "Immigration-Related State Statutes and Local Ordinances: Preemption, Prejudice, and the Proper Role for Enforcement." *University of Chicago Legal Forum* 27: 55.

Villazor, Rose Cuison 2008. "What is a 'Sanctuary'?" *SMUL Law Review* 61: 133.

■ Notes

1. 424 US 351, 354 (1976).

2. *LULAC v. Wilson*, 908 F. Supp. 755 (C.D. Cal. 1995).

3. 403 US 365 (1971).

4. *Mathews v. Diaz*, 426 US 67 (1976).

5. Ibid., 67, 77.

6. 457 US 202 (1982).

7. *United States v. Arizona*, 703 F. Supp. 2d 980 (D. Ariz. 2010).

8. *United States v. Arizona*, 641 F.3d 339 (9th Cir. 2011).

9. ImmigrationWorks USA, "State Immigration Laws That Target Employers," available at www.immigrationworksusa.org/index.php?p=96.

10. INA § 274A(h)(2), 8 USC § 1324a(h)(2).

11. *Ariz. Contractors. Ass'n, Inc. v. Candelaria*, 534 F. Supp. 2d 1036 (D. Ariz.), *affirmed*, 544 F.3d 976 (9th Cir. 2008), *as amended*, 558 F.3d 856 (9th Cir. 2009), *aff'd. sub nom., Chamber of Commerce v. Whiting*, 179 L. Ed. 2d 1031 (May 26, 2011); *Gray v. City of Valley Park*, 2008 U.S. Dist. LEXIS 7238 (E.D. Mo. Jan. 31, 2008).

12. *Lozano v. City of Hazleton*, 496 F. Supp. 2d 477, 519 (M.D. Pa. 2007), *aff'd*, 620 F.3d 170 (3d Cir. 2010), *vacated and remanded*, 2011 U.S. LEXIS 4259 (U.S. June 6, 2011).

13. 544 F.3d 976 (9th Cir. 2008), *as amended*, 558 F.3d 856 (9th Cir. 2009).

14. *Chamber of Commerce v. Whiting*, 179 L. Ed. 2d 1031 (May 26, 2011).

15. See *Washington State Grange v. Washington State Republican Party*, 128 S. Ct. 1184, 1190–91 (2008), reversing Ninth Circuit's facial invalidation of a Washington State election statute.

16. The Ninth Circuit wrote, "We must observe that [the challenge to Arizona's statute] is brought against a blank factual background of enforcement and outside the context of any particular case. If and when the statute is enforced, and the factual background is developed, other challenges to the Act as applied in any particular instance or manner will not be controlled by our decision"; citation omitted.

17. 594 F.3d 742 (10th Cir. 2010).

18. 2007 Okla. sess. Law Serv. Ch. 112 (codified in part, as amended, in scattered sections of Okla. Stat. Tit. 21, 22, 25, 56, 68, 70, 64).

19. See Julia Preston, "Government Set for a Crackdown on Illegal Hiring," *New York Times*, Aug. 8, 2007, A1.

20. See "Oklahoma Governor Signs Sweeping Immigration Reform Bill," *Joplin Globe*, May 9, 2007.

21. 496 F. Supp. 2d 477 (M.D. Pa. 2007), *aff'd in part, vacated in part,* 620 F.3d 170 (3d Cir. 2010), *vacated and remanded,* 2011 U.S. LEXIS 4259 (U.S. June 6, 2011).

22. See Ken Belson and Jill P. Capuzzo, "Towns Rethink Laws against Illegal Immigrants," *New York Times*, Sept. 26, 2007, A1.

23. See Samuel P. Huntington, *Who Are We? The Challenges to America's National Identity* (New York: Simon & Schuster, 2004); Victor Davis Hanson, *Mexifornia: A State of Becoming* (New York: Encounter Books, 2003); Michelle Malkin, *Invasion: How America Still Welcomes Terrorists, Criminals, and Other Foreign Menaces to Our Shores* (Washington, D.C.: Regnery, 2002); Peter Brimelow, *Alien Nation* (New York: Random House, 1995).

24. See US Department of Homeland Security, *US Legal Permanent Residents: 2007* (March 2008), at www.dhs.gov/xlibrary/assets/statistics/yearbook/2007/ois_2007_yearbook.pdf.

25. See Peter H. Schuck, "Alien Rumination," *Yale Law Journal* 105 (1996): 1963, 1969–78, analyzing similar claims of record highs of immigration and "invasion" of the United States by immigrants in the early 1990s.

26. See Migration Policy Institute chart, "Foreign-Born Population and Foreign Born as a Percentage of the Total US Population, for the United States: 1850 to 2009" (2009), available at www.migrationinformation.org/datahub/charts/final.fb.shtml.

27. Mike Seate, "Rage over Illegals Brings '60s to Mind," *Pittsburg Tribune Review*, June 7, 2007, emphasis added. See *Lozano v. Hazleton*, 496 F. Supp. 2d 477 (M.D. Pa. 2007), *aff'd in part, vacated in part,* 620 F.3d 170 (3d Cir. 2010), *vacated and remanded,* 2001 U.S. LEXIS 4259 (U.S. June 6, 2011), invalidating Hazleton's immigration ordinance on the grounds that it was preempted by federal law.

28. Kristen Hinman, "Valley Park to Mexican Immigrants: '*Adios,* Illegals!'" *Riverfront Times*, Feb. 28, 2007, available at www.riverfronttimes.com/content/printVersion/204874, emphasis added. See *Gray v. City of Valley Park*, 2008 US Dist. LEXIS 7238 (E.D. Mo. Jan. 31, 2008).

29. See William Finnegan, "Sheriff Joe," *New Yorker*, July 20, 2009, 42; Jacques Billeaud, "Thousands Protest US Sheriff's Immigration Efforts," *El Paso Times*, Jan. 17, 2010.

30. See US Department of Justice, Federal Bureau of Investigation, *Hate Crime Statistics 2007* (2008), available at www.fbi.gov/news/stories/2008/october/hatecrime_102708.

31. See "A Death in Patchogue," *New York Times*, Nov. 11, 2008; Sean D. Hamill, "Mexican's Death Bares a Town's Ethnic Tension," *New York Times*, Aug. 5, 2008,

A12; Regna Medina, "Attack in Shenandoah Follows Immigrant's Fatal July Beating," *Philadelphia Daily News*, Sept. 17, 2008, 3.

32. "A Death in Patchogue."

33. See Cara Buckley, "Teenagers' Violent 'Sport' Led to Killing, Officials Say," *New York Times*, Nov. 21, 2008, A26.

34. See Anti-Defamation League, *Immigrants Targeted: Extremist Rhetoric Moves into the Mainstream* (2007), available at www.adl.org/civil_rights/anti_immigrant; David Holthouse and Mark Potok, *The Year in Hate* (Southern Poverty Law Center, 2008), at www.splcenter.org/intel/intelreport/article.jsp?aid=886.

35. See "The High Costs of Harsh Words," *New York Times*, Nov. 14, 2008, A32.

36. After a jury acquitted the defendants on the most serious charges, the US government brought a hate crime prosecution, along with charges against local police, for a cover-up of the crime. See Sean D. Hamill, "Federal Charges Are Filed in Killing of Immigrant," *New York Times*, Dec. 16, 2009, A27.

11

National Security and
Immigration Law and Policy

The debate over immigration reform "is ... and I would say first and foremost about our Nation's security. *In a post-9/11 world, border security is national security.*"
—Senator John Cornyn (R—Texas)

Not one terrorist has entered the United States from Mexico.
—Peter Beinart

The events of September 11, 2001, dramatically shifted the debate over immigration law and reform in the United States. Although movement toward more liberal admission and enforcement policies had been in the political winds, the tragic events caused immigration measures to be put into place that focused on security and were ostensibly directed at Arabs and Muslims. The reforms, however, had impacts on all immigrant communities, including disproportionate effects on the largest group of immigrants to the United States—those from Mexico. This chapter tells that story.[1]

Commentators and pundits have repeated, "September 11 changed everything," so frequently that the phrase has nearly lost any meaning. One cannot deny that that fateful day, and the tragic loss of human life, has unquestionably transformed US society. As a response to the terrorist acts of September 11, 2001, the Bush administration employed extreme measures, including mass arrests, interrogations, detentions, and deportations of Arabs and Muslims. Outside the United States, in addition to wars in Afghanistan and Iraq, the US government engaged in detentions and, at times, interrogations—even torture—of prisoners. The president declared that persons whom he designated as "enemy combatants" had precious few rights under the law and had no right of judicial review of that designation, a position that even a conservative US Supreme Court flatly rejected.

When it comes to immigration law and policy, the events of September 11 had especially dramatic impacts. Fears of terrorism led to tighter immigration restrictions in many areas. These changes ranged from stricter monitoring of foreign scholars and students seeking to enter the United States on nonimmigrant (temporary) visas to new immigration requirements and procedures. Many measures, including registration requirements, mass detentions, and deportation operations, unfairly targeted Arab and Muslim noncitizens.

Ultimately, all immigrants, especially those from Mexico, felt the sting of the various security measures. A vocal group of observers and policy makers claimed that the need to avoid another September 11 required greatly increased enforcement along the southern border with Mexico and indelibly influenced the national debate over immigration reform.

In retrospect, one member of Congress aptly observed,

> **The necessary pursuit of national security should not have been used . . . to enact unrelated and radical changes in immigration laws under the guise of preventing terrorism.** *Unfortunately, members of Congress have abused arguments for national security to enact hundreds of radical changes in immigration laws. . . . Instead of enacting rational immigration reform that will indeed strengthen our national security, Congress has enacted immigration changes that have very little or nothing to do with national security.*[2]

Importantly, it should be noted that the public concern with immigration existed long before September 11. Unrealistic immigration laws in place for decades have forced millions of migrants to evade the law to enter and remain in the United States and, once here, live in the shadows of American social life. As President George W. Bush observed in calling for immigration reform in 2006, *"Illegal immigrants live in the shadows of our society. . . . [T]he vast majority . . . are decent people who work hard, support their families, practice their faith, and lead responsible lives.* They are part of American life, but they are beyond the reach and protection of American law."[3]

A number of commentators have proposed a more flexible immigration admissions system that would better ensure national security than the current regime in place. In order to improve the security of the nation, as well as to attain other goals, the United States needs to dramatically revamp this system. A body of law that better matches the political, social, and economic factors contributing to the demand for immigration and that recognizes immigration as largely a labor migration—while minimizing the incentive for undocumented immigration and thus limiting the creation and maintenance of a shadow population of millions of people—would better ensure the safety and security of the nation.

At this time in US history, a proposal to liberalize admissions to protect national security may seem counterintuitive, if not misplaced. But, a carefully crafted liberal admissions scheme that regulates labor migration could allow for a more secure and safer United States. The current system of tracking lawful immigrants and temporary visitors, which is woefully inadequate, could be vastly improved. We have many residents of the United States effectively living off the books, not subject to admissions screening of any kind. The nation deserves an immigration system that regulates admissions of noncitizens into the country and ensures that the US government has basic information about them, such as name and address. Such information is necessary for effective law enforcement—criminal as well as immigration—that will allow the nation to better protect national security and public safety.

The lack of information about the population of undocumented immigrants to the United States is no small gap. The best estimate is that somewhere in the neighborhood of 12 million undocumented immigrants live in the country today. Those who entered without inspection are not subject to any admission screening. Rather than engaging in futile efforts to close the borders, the US government needs to address the modern political, economic, and social realities currently fueling immigration to the country and contributing to the ever-growing number of people who live and work in our communities in contravention of US immigration laws.

Generations of workers from Mexico have made their way to the United States. Absent dramatic economic and social changes, immigrants from Mexico and other nations will continue to come to the United States for jobs and to reunite with family members. In modern times, migrants literally risk life and limb to come to this land of freedom and opportunity. Millions of undocumented immigrants live in the United States. Given that the efforts to seal the borders have proven to be little more than a symbolic gesture and have resulted in great human misery, it makes no sense from an immigration or national security standpoint to simply continue to throw resources at fortifying the borders and engage in futile efforts to keep all undocumented immigrants out of the country.

■ Immigration Law and Policy Since September 11, 2001: Border Enforcement and More Border Enforcement

As discussed in chapter 9, the US government has engaged in unprecedented border enforcement efforts over the last two decades. However, the increased border enforcement efforts, to the surprise of many, have been accompanied by an increase in the undocumented population in the United States. One study concluded, "There is *no evidence* that the border enforcement build-up . . . has substantially reduced unauthorized border crossings" and that "despite large increases in spending and Border Patrol resources, . . . the number of unauthorized immigrants increased to levels higher than those" before 1986 (when Congress passed the last "comprehensive" immigration reform measure, the Immigration Reform and Control Act).[4]

The fact that millions of undocumented immigrants live and work in the United States confirms what most Americans well know: US immigration laws are routinely violated and, at least as currently configured, are effectively unenforceable. Undocumented workers understand that if they are able to make the arduous journey to the United States, employers will hire them and the job will pay more than most of them would have been able to earn in their native countries.

Employers willingly hire undocumented workers and cherish this relatively inexpensive supply of labor. A short drive to a day laborer pickup point in cities across the United States demonstrates both undocumented immigrants' ability to obtain work and employers' enthusiasm for hiring them.

US border enforcement has proven to be the equivalent of tilting at windmills. The US government has simply been unable to keep migrants—so determined that they are willing to risk their lives as well as those of their families—from unlawfully entering the United States. In addition, the current computer databases in place are woefully incomplete and are not accurately tracking legal immigrants who have entered and reside in the United States. Thus, even for noncitizens who enter through legal channels, the US government lacks reliable systems and data about who is here, who is not, when they entered, and when they left. In light of the technology available in this information age, such a gap in basic information about immigrants is unacceptable and certainly doesn't inspire confidence in our immigration system.

Moreover, the US government has made precious few efforts to remove noncitizens who lawfully entered the country on temporary visas, such as students and tourists, but have overstayed their terms. Visa overstays likely constitute somewhere between 25 and 40 percent of the total undocumented population of approximately 12 million.

Over the last few years, enforcement of the immigration laws away from the border has been reduced, not increased. Indeed, until near the end of President George W. Bush's second term in office, his administration made workplace enforcement of US immigration laws one of its lowest priorities. As discussed in chapter 9, in the waning days of the Bush administration, interior immigration enforcement through workplace raids increased but have had little impact on the overall undocumented population in the United States. Still, the raids had devastating impacts on Latina/o communities, as well as on some local economies.

Even with the security measures taken by the US government after September 11—when fear of another attack brought great attention, many resources, and a flurry of activity—undocumented migration to the United States continues. The US government has done relatively little to effectively manage and regulate the migration while lashing out indiscriminately at immigrants in the name of national security. As we shall see, its North American neighbors, Canada and Mexico, have acted in much the same way.

The Warped Impact of September 11 on the Debate over Immigration Reform

In the name of national security, the highest levels of the US government engaged in a sustained effort to close the borders after September 11, 2001. At first glance, this may seem entirely appropriate. After all, noncitizens perpetrated the terrorist acts of that fateful day.[5] Because the terrorists were also Muslim, the public has overall strongly supported the government's antiterrorism efforts focusing on Muslims—whether or not the measures constitute racial, national origin, and religious profiling that, in most circumstances, run contrary to the rule of law.

In no small part because the law affords the federal government broad latitude in—or *plenary power* over—its policies toward immigration and immigrants, immigration law has served as a convenient ground zero for Congress and the president's so-called war on terror. Put differently, the near-complete lack of judicial oversight made immigration enforcement a handy, and flexible, antiterrorism tool after September 11, when the administration of President Bush felt politically compelled to act decisively in a high-profile manner. The deferential body of law surrounding immigration and immigrants facilitated hyperaggressive action by Congress and the executive branch and ensured minimal interference from the courts.

Premised on the idea that the political branches of the federal government have absolute power over immigration, the plenary power doctrine shields many executive branch and congressional immigration decisions from meaningful review by the courts. In promulgating the regulations allowing for special registration procedures for Arabs and Muslims, for example, the US government resorted to the plenary power doctrine to justify the extreme measures: *"The political branches of the government have plenary authority in the immigration area. See Fiallo v. Bell*, 430 US 787, 792 (1977); *Mathews v. Diaz*, 426 US 67, 80–82 (1976). *In the context of immigration and nationality laws, the Supreme Court has particularly 'underscore[d] the limited scope of judicial inquiry.'"*[6]

As discussed in chapter 3, the law affords considerable latitude to the US government in the realm of immigration; that latitude is at its zenith when national security is involved. Immigrants possess a smaller bundle of legal, civil, and human rights than US citizens. In the wake of September 11, the US government arrested, interrogated, detained, and removed thousands of Arab and Muslim noncitizens.[7] The government took the extraordinary step of implementing a special registration system for noncitizens in the United States from a select group of nations, resulting in many arrests, detentions, and deportations (but few, if any, based on charges of terrorism) of Arabs and Muslims. The courts failed to intervene.

Capitalizing on palpable public fears about national security, pundits, including ardent restrictionists Pat Buchanan and Michelle Malkin, made incendiary arguments about the need to close the borders to all immigrants in the crusade against terrorism.[8] Even though none of the September 11 terrorists entered without inspection, advocates of increased immigration enforcement repeatedly claim that the entry of undocumented immigrants from Mexico into the United States is a national security risk. In a comment consistent with the tenor of the current debate, Senator John Cornyn emphasized that the debate over immigration reform "is . . . and I would say first and foremost about our Nation's security. *In a post-9/11 world, border security is national security."*[9]

As Professor Enid Trucios-Haynes has generally observed,

immigration dominates policy discussions in the post–September 11, 2001 world in a manner that has distorted traditional issues and concerns relating to noncitizens. To some, the perception or reality of porous US borders requires the most strenuous methods of border enforcement. In the eyes of many, immigration reform proposals since 2001 have focused exclusively on enforcement without sufficient acknowledgment of the human consequences on the noncitizens, both authorized and unauthorized, throughout our community.[10]

Put simply, September 11, 2001, represents a crucial turning point in the debate over immigration reform in the United States. The horrible human losses of that day halted in its tracks the discussion of easing immigration restrictions. Moreover, the fear of terrorism, feeding off a general tendency among many US citizens to blame immigrants for the problems of the day, helped to foster a general "close the border" mentality that for a time commanded substantial support among the general public. As a result, politicians from across the political spectrum endorsed some form of border enforcement strategy as part of overall immigration reform, with some claiming that no other reforms could be put into place until the nation successfully improved border enforcement. The public seemed to support measures directed at improving border enforcement.

Even though Mexico had nothing to do with the tragedy of September 11, the resulting change in popular opinion had concrete impacts on immigration from Mexico. Before September 11, 2001, the US and Mexican governments were seriously discussing entering into a migration accord that would have regularized labor migration between the two nations. Similarly, immigrant rights advocates appeared to be close to convincing Congress to ameliorate some of the toughest provisions of the 1996 immigration reforms. Both reform efforts stopped on September 11, as the US government immediately became preoccupied with public safety and national security. Many leaders advocated closing the borders.

Since September 11, the focus of proposals to reform US immigration law and policy has been on fortifying the borders with fences, providing additional officers and resources to Immigration and Customs Enforcement (ICE), increasing technology and detention, and related measures. Unfortunately, regularizing the flow of migrants from Mexico to the

United States, ensuring more humane treatment of immigrants, and equitable enforcement of the immigration laws took a back seat. Public opinion has softened some since the days immediately following September 11, but only time will tell whether matters will change with a new president and Congress.

September 11 thus had serious and detrimental long-term consequences on constructive immigration reform. It completely reversed the momentum of the debate, shifting it from possible liberalization of admissions and easing of removal and detention to stricter border controls, narrower admissions criteria, and harsher detention and removal proposals. Many of the most popular proposals would have generally restricted migration and were in no way limited to excluding Arab and Muslim noncitizens and improving national security. Immigrant advocates moved from making a concerted effort at advocating for positive immigration reform to devoting energies, resources, and precious political capital toward defending against the passage of punitive immigration laws.

Since September 11, national security concerns have dominated US immigration law and policy. Recent immigration legislation, including the USA PATRIOT Act; the Homeland Security Act, which created the Department of Homeland Security (DHS) to, among other things, administer the immigration laws; the REAL ID Act; and the Secure Fence Act of 2006, focus almost exclusively on border enforcement, with little attention paid to the economic, political, and social goals of immigration law and policy.[11] The plenary power doctrine, which some commentators not long before September 11 claimed was in its death throes, was relied upon by the Bush administration, as well as the US Congress, in seeking to justify various border enforcement and national security measures.

Some activists and policy makers seized on fears over terrorism to advocate restrictionist reforms, including those directed at undocumented immigration from Mexico. Often trumpeting national security goals, the US government appears ready to commit tremendous financial resources in difficult economic times to the construction of a wall along the US border with Mexico. Other border enforcement measures have also proven to be popular with the public. Increased border enforcement is generally a part of any immigration reform package proposed in Congress.

It goes without saying that, in 2005–06, national security concerns greatly influenced the discussion of immigration reform. The Sensenbrenner Bill, passed by the US House of Representatives in December 2005, was perhaps the most extreme enforcement-only immigration reform proposal to date.[12] Among other things, the bill would have made the mere status of being an undocumented immigrant a felony subject to imprisonment as well as deportation from the United States and would have allowed for the imposition of criminal sanctions on persons who provided humanitarian assistance to undocumented immigrants. The Sensenbrenner Bill's enforcement-only approach, which provoked mass public protests in cities across the United States, is consistent with the national security emphasis prevailing in the debate over immigration in recent years.

Although national security today dominates the debate over virtually any immigration-related measure, one important fact must be highlighted. Throughout the immigration reform debates of 2005–06, in which terrorism fears often arose, there was a myopic focus on bolstering enforcement along the southern border with Mexico *despite the fact that there is no evidence of terrorists entering the United States through Mexico.* Nor is there any evidence of any special need from a national security standpoint to greatly fear migration—legal or not—from Mexico.

Indeed, a 2006 study found that, although proposals for increased border enforcement along the US southern border with Mexico are routinely claimed to improve national security, no known noncitizen accused of terrorist acts in the United States has in recent years entered the country from the south. The study concluded that "not one terrorist has entered the United States from Mexico."[13] Furthermore, "despite media alarms about terrorists concealed in the illegal traffic crossing the Mexican border," not a single person charged or convicted of terrorist acts, or killed in such acts entered the United States from Mexico.[14]

Ironically enough, the only terrorists in recent years who attempted to cross the land borders of the United States on foot were from Canada, with the so-called Millennium Bomber in December 1999 probably the most well known. This suggests a need to focus not on undocumented migration from Mexico but to a greater extent on the United States' northern border with Canada, which is far more open, and much less militarized, than the southern border. The disparate treatment of the northern and southern borders regularly provokes claims that something else besides border security, such as racial and class animus directed at persons of Mexican ancestry, is at work in the establishment of US border enforcement priorities.

As this discussion suggests, the nations of North America need to consider multilateral measures that improve security and address the difficult issues of managing and regulating—not halting—migration to the United States. To this point in time, that has not occurred. The US Congress, for example, has failed to enact comprehensive immigration reform. Rather, border enforcement and more border enforcement have carried the day time and time again. Such measures, however, fail to ensure that US immigration law and policy satisfies the multiple goals that it must if the United States wishes to remain politically, economically, and socially strong—and safe.

North America's Response to September 11

The national security responses to September 11, 2001, were not limited to those by the US government. That fateful day understandably prodded the governments of many nations to attempt to improve their security. Specifically, the governments of all the nations of North America individually responded to the terrorist acts of September 11. Canada, Mexico, and the United States worked together in small ways to improve regional security. Much more, however, remains to be done.

Within months of September 11, Canada passed its own immigration legislation designed to improve national security. In December 2001, Canada passed the Anti-Terrorism Act, which expanded the Canadian government's surveillance and other powers in fighting terrorism.[15] Although this act was less extreme than the USA PATRIOT Act, Canada evidently felt—with encouragement no doubt from the US government—that it must do something to protect itself from terrorist acts as well as to act in a way consistent with America's war on terror.

In December 2001, the United States and Canada entered into a *smart border* agreement designed to increase security while facilitating lawful cross-border movement of persons and goods between the two nations. This agreement included several measures to ensure security while facilitating the mobility of goods, services, and people. Canada and the United States also agreed to require migrants to seek asylum in the first country they enter, thereby seeking to curtail perceived abuse of the asylum system.

In March 2005, the United States, Canada, and Mexico announced the establishment of the Security and Prosperity Partnership of North America.[16] The partnership seeks through multilateral cooperation to improve the security of all of North America, strengthen internal security within each nation, and promote regional economic growth. Discussions between the three partners have continued on various initiatives, with some relatively minimal incremental measures actually implemented.

More recently, no doubt in response to pressure from the United States, Canada in August 2006 promised to take further steps to tighten border security.

Mexico also agreed to take steps consistent with the US government's counter-terrorism measures. In addition, the Mexican government, at the behest of the US government, continued to take steps to restrict immigration from the south through its territory so that fewer migrants from Central America would be able to make the journey to the United States. The leaders of the United States and Mexico regularly discuss cooperation on immigration enforcement and security issues.

As the actions of Canada and Mexico suggest, security is not an issue just for the United States but one facing North America as a whole. As globalization continues, the world slowly integrates economically and politically. Domestic reform of US immigration laws is unquestionably necessary to accommodate the global economy. Moreover, international cooperation on the related issues of migration and national security needs is essential. Multilateralism is necessary in helping the North American nations to better provide for national and regional security.

A model for regional cooperation is readily available. With the emergence of a common market with a unitary currency, Europe through the advent of the European Union (EU) is far ahead of North America in terms of the integration of political and economic institutions of various nations. Integration through the EU has dramatically changed immigration law and policy in Europe, with workers generally allowed to migrate between the member nations. Such mobility has expanded to greater numbers of workers as the EU has expanded to include more member nations.

In sharp contrast, the United States, Canada, and Mexico have accomplished only a partial integration of their economies through the North American Free Trade Agreement (NAFTA). That pact provided for the expanded free trade of goods and services in North America but failed to address pressing immigration and related regional security issues among the three member nations. In the long run, the nations of North America will need to work together to address common migration and security concerns.

In formulating NAFTA, the United States steadfastly refused to discuss, much less address, labor migration in any meaningful way. Consequently, NAFTA left critical economic and security issues off the bargaining table and, in the end, failed to provide a comprehensive, integrated regional approach to labor migration in North America.

For the time being, the United States could improve security by working more closely with Canada and Mexico on common immigration and security concerns. Canada, Mexico, and the United States have cooperated only to a limited extent. Much more will be necessary in the future to ensure regional security.

Importantly, the actions of Canada implicate the safety and security of the United States just as much, if not more so, than the actions of Mexico. The US border with Mexico has received the bulk of attention of US policy makers for many years. The northern border of the United States indeed requires more careful consideration than it has received.[17]

Future multilateral cooperation in North America will need to focus on immigration and security issues. One important move would be to allow greater internal migration within the United States, Mexico, and Canada akin to that which currently exists in the European Union. A more open system of labor migration would fit comfortably into the trade relationship that currently exists among the three nations that are party to NAFTA. Although restrictionists have criticized the development of any kind of North American Union, freer migration within North America might be more politically acceptable than a liberal admission of immigrants into the United States from the world over.

US Immigration Law and Policy Since September 11 Has Hindered Multilateral Cooperation on National Security Matters

Rather than facilitate multilateral cooperation to improve global and regional security, US immigration law and policy in the post–September 11 period has had detrimental impacts on such cooperation. The harsh treatment of Arab and Muslim noncitizens, besides alienating the Arab and Muslim communities in the United States and arguably thwarting the cooperation of those communities in the war on terror, has also alienated their home governments. Similarly, the harsh impacts of tighter immigration laws and their enforcement, as well as the incendiary terms of some of the immigration debate in the United States, have hindered relations with many other nations, including Mexico.

Indeed, US immigration law and policy has in fact regularly caused serious rifts between Mexico and the United States. When US officials unveiled Operation Blockade in El Paso, Texas, in the early 1990s, Mexican governmental officials protested vociferously, resulting in a name change to Operation Hold-the-Line. In 2005 and 2006, the Mexican government reacted negatively to the punitive border enforcement bills pending in the US Congress. Eleven Latin American countries, including Mexico, lobbied against the Sensenbrenner Bill. The border fence authorized by Congress in 2006 drew vocal protests from Mexican leaders as well.

The End Result

What is the end result of the security measures implemented after September 11, 2001? Noncitizens in the United States experienced record numbers of removals and increased immigration enforcement—and selective enforcement of the immigration laws. However, there is no evidence that any actual terrorists have been deported, and there were few terrorism convictions.

In the future, North America must reconsider the system of labor migration between Canada, Mexico, and the United States. In addition, the United States must work with other nations to secure accurate intelligence about persons seeking entry into the United States. Better coordination among law enforcement agencies of the three North American governments would much improve the United States' national security. Although some steps have been taken, much more work remains to be done to improve national security.

■ Collateral Impacts of the War on Terror on Mexican Immigrants

The war on terror has been used to rationalize a wide variety of aggressive policies tightening the immigration laws that have little to do with national security and public safety.

For example, in the name of fighting terrorism, the Department of Justice announced that it would begin enforcing a rule allowing for the deportation of immigrants who fail to report their change of address within ten days of moving. Then-attorney general John Ashcroft even threatened to deport terrorists (presumably for whom he lacked evidence to deport on grounds of terrorism) for "spitting on the sidewalk."[18] He also concluded that national security concerns justified the detention of a Haitian asylum seeker without bond even though the noncitizen in question had no links whatsoever to terrorism.[19] Along similar lines, one court of appeals invoked concerns with terrorism to justify a run-of-the-mill border check at a port of entry along the US–Mexico border that escalated into the ripping open of a spare tire in search of drugs.[20] In each of these instances, the US government employed terrorism as a rationale for harsh action in rather ordinary immigration matters that had little to do with national security.

Previously condemned in criminal law enforcement, racial, national origin, and religious profiling became a centerpiece of the US government's war on terror. Such profiling has many flaws similar to those resulting from its use in ordinary law enforcement, which has resulted in general public condemnation of the practice by local police agencies. In adopting the various security measures in the war on terror, the US government seemed to minimize, if not ignore, the many harms of profiling on minority communities.

Security checks and removal campaigns resulted in record levels of deportations, almost all of noncitizens having nothing whatsoever to do with terrorism. *Importantly, the vast majority of the record numbers of immigrants deported since September 11 have been citizens of Mexico and Central America, not known to be havens for terrorists, but who constitute a large segment of the undocumented and legal immigrant populations in the United States.*

In hindsight, it is difficult to dispute that the fear generated by the events of September 11 has served as a convenient excuse for more punitive immigration law and enforcement proposals and pursuit of a restrictionist immigration agenda, with Mexican noncitizens suffering the brunt of the new enforcement measures. Proposals for increased border enforcement along the US southern border with Mexico have been claimed to be necessary to improve national security. However, there is little evidence suggesting that there is a realistic threat of terrorism from Mexico.

While the war on terror has dominated the national and international consciousness, constructive immigration reform proposals have fallen by the wayside. Serious discussions of a bilateral agreement regularizing migration between the United States and Mexico ended abruptly on September 11. Efforts to remove the harshest provisions of 1996 immigration reform laws—thought by some observers at the time to be as draconian as any in US history—also evaporated on that day; the political climate made the sensible liberalization of the immigration laws next to impossible, at least for the short run.

President Bush's subsequent efforts to recommence discussion of immigration reform, and his advocacy of a guest worker program, faced vociferous resistance from the restrictionist wing of the Republican Party. In the end, the Mexican government was unsuccessful in its efforts to move the US government forward in jointly addressing the migration of labor between the two nations.

After years of delay, the nation in 2005–06 engaged in a fractious national debate over reform of the immigration laws, with a special focus on undocumented immigration from Mexico. While the US House of Representatives passed the Sensenbrenner Bill, the US Senate considered a more moderate proposal, which included legalization and guest worker components in addition to enforcement measures.

Ultimately, the immigration reform controversy ended with Congress failing to enact a comprehensive immigration reform proposal and agreeing only to authorize extension of a fence along the United States' southern border with Mexico. Congress did so even though there is no evidence that this—or any other measure focused only on border enforcement—will decrease the flow of undocumented immigrants to the United States.

The post–September 11 period unfortunately experienced nothing less than a serious distortion of the immigration debate. Discussion of ordinary immigration reform was hijacked by the war on terror, and any proposal that did not focus on border enforcement and increased removals faced overblown claims that it would help to put the nation's security at risk. Restrictionists effectively capitalized on the fear of terrorism in an all-out effort to persuade Congress to pass ever-tougher border enforcement measures.

In the end, although reform is necessary, truly comprehensive immigration reform has proved to be politically impossible up to this point in time. At least before the 2008 presidential election, punitive measures like border fences proved much more likely to carry the day than comprehensive approaches that addressed the United States' true immigration needs and realities. It is at best uncertain whether reform efforts will be any more successful in the near future.

■ Liberal Admissions Would Result in a More Secure United States

Historically, US immigration laws have been dramatically overbroad in attacking the perceived evils of the day, whether they be racial minorities, the poor, political dissidents, or other disfavored groups. Today, "terrorists," undocumented immigrants, and "criminal aliens" are the stated targets of immigration law and its enforcement.

To be effective in protecting the security of the United States, the war on terror should attempt to exclude from admission the true dangers to national security and public safety, rather than engage in doomed efforts to seal the borders, which have proved to be virtually impossible and have encouraged the violation of the immigration laws by millions of otherwise law-abiding people.

Even if they might encourage somewhat greater rates of migration, realistic immigration laws that regulate labor flows and are efficiently enforced might improve, not undermine, the security of the nation. Immigration laws that better fulfill the nation's labor needs, as well as laws that do not require unreasonable delays in admission to the United States, would eliminate a powerful magnet to circumvent the law by employers and migrants as well as the existence of a population of people living in this country off the books. Such laws would also dampen the incentives for human trafficking and the criminal syndicates engaged in that growing industry.

An immigration system that allows for easier migration of labor to the United States would be an important first step to meaningful immigration reform. More liberal admissions grounds allowing workers and migrants who lack family members in the United States would be an important reform measure.

A more liberal scheme could also eliminate the need for complex inquiries into migrants' family histories, incomes, and purposes for entering the country. Such inquiries today are the bread-and-butter of border enforcement officers and the bane of lengthy visa applications, consular officer interviews, immigration stops, and document checks. More liberal admissions would save time and effort in the vast majority of immigrant admissions. Finite resources would be better devoted to the relatively few cases involving serious criminal and terrorist activities—the very cases that deserve careful attention by a government seeking to protect the safety of its citizens in this troubled world.

Narrower exclusion grounds in US immigration laws would also be more realistic than the current blanket exclusions and ceilings. For example, the law currently bars the immigration of poor and working-class people from the developing world, for no other reason than that they are poor and working-class people. With a narrowing of the exclusion grounds, the nation could devote scarce enforcement resources to efforts that bar entry into the United States of criminals, terrorists, and other dangers to society. Such a true security and public safety emphasis would likely make the United States safer than the current unfocused enforcement emphasis that has pervaded US border controls and their enforcement since the early twentieth century.

Most importantly, a system in which undocumented migration is reduced—and the undocumented population in the United States is legalized—would allow for improved tracking of all noncitizens living in the United States. If undocumented migration was minimized, the nation would be far better positioned to keep records, including names and addresses, of all noncitizens in the country.

Currently, millions of undocumented immigrants live and work in this country, with little governmental knowledge about them. We know little about who they are and where they live, much less what their purposes are for being in the United States. It is difficult to see how the existence of a shadow population in the millions could in any way be in the national interest, especially in a time when national security concerns are at their zenith. Nor is there any evidence that the US government as a practical matter could end undocumented immigration under the current legal regime and circumstances.

Despite great increases in resources devoted to sealing the border, increased border enforcement has failed to reduce the undocumented immigrant population in the United States. Nor does the US government do much to enforce the immigration laws in the interior of the country.

In addition, reducing the undocumented immigrant population within the United States in any meaningful way through mass deportation campaigns seems highly unlikely. Despite record deportations in the years since September 11, the highest levels of the US government have recognized that removal of all undocumented immigrants from the country is simply not possible. In 2004, undersecretary of the DHS Asa Hutchinson candidly admitted, "It is 'not realistic' to think that law-enforcement authorities can arrest or deport the millions of illegal aliens now in the United States." He further stated that he "did not think that the American public has the 'will ... to uproot' those aliens."[21] In 2006, President George W. Bush himself acknowledged, *"Massive deportation of the people here is unrealistic. It's just not going to work."*[22]

Moreover, the costs of the massive deportation campaign needed to remove all undocumented immigrants from the United States would be astronomical and are hard to justify in a time of national economic hardship. A 2005 study estimated that it would cost *$41 billion a year for five years* to fund a serious effort to remove all undocumented immigrants from the country.[23]

Besides the fact that border enforcement and unrealistic immigration laws are simply ineffective, there are many collateral impacts. Increased border enforcement has resulted in deaths, as migrants have taken more dangerous routes to the United States to evade immigration enforcement officers and various barriers to entry. Evasion of the law by millions of undocumented immigrants has created highly organized criminal networks that pose true risks to public safety and national security. In no small part due to tighter immigration enforcement, the trafficking of human beings today is big business and a growth industry, with its tentacles reaching across the entire United States. International criminal syndicates, which dominate the trafficking market, thrive and profit handsomely from the smuggling of immigrants and circumvention of US immigration laws.

Human misery and death often directly result from human trafficking. Besides risking life and limb, some immigrants are effectively enslaved to pay off smuggling debts, with thousands of immigrant women forced into the sex industry and other exploitative work relationships. The trafficking of human beings—with its devastating impacts—flows immediately from heightened immigration enforcement. Congress has passed laws in response to human trafficking, but the problem nonetheless remains.

Immigration enforcement has more general negative labor market consequences short of trafficking and involuntary servitude. The large undocumented population harkens back to the heyday of Jim Crow in the United States, with a racial caste of workers in the secondary labor market. Indeed, outright slavery and involuntary servitude of immigrants are increasingly reported in the modern United States.

Many other adverse consequences are associated with the current immigration laws. Undocumented workers are exploited in the workplace and denied basic legal rights. Because many are people of color, the nation has in place what is effectively an exploitable racial caste labor market. This labor market operates outside the confines of law, with undocumented workers receiving few legal protections and often working for low wages in poor conditions. More realistic immigration law and policy that allow labor migration could help dry up this secondary labor market and end the immoral exploitation of undocumented workers.

■ Concluding Thoughts

As all would no doubt agree, the United States needs immigration laws that reduce the probability and harm of terrorism in this country. The nation cannot ignore that the events of September 11, 2001, demonstrated that terrorists can skillfully exploit weakness in US immigration systems.

Importantly, almost all the terrorists involved in the September 11 hijackings entered the United States lawfully on nonimmigrant visas, with some having violated the terms of their visas. Such violations suggest the need for better visa monitoring. It is therefore curious that, although monitoring of nonimmigrant visas has tightened somewhat, one of the US government's most visible responses has been to try to close the borders to undocumented immigrants from Mexico, which is not known to be a haven for terrorists. A more fortified U.S border with Mexico would not have done much, if anything, to deter the terrorist acts of September 11, 2001.

Several steps could be taken to ensure that the immigration laws and their enforcement help to minimize the threat of terrorism. The laws could be narrowed so that the noncitizens excluded are in fact threats to national security or public safety, and better security and background checks could be made before allowing any noncitizen to enter the United States. A focus on public safety considerations is more likely to be effective than the generalized efforts to limit admissions under the current immigration laws.

In addition, an immigration system that was not regularly violated by entrants lacking lawful ways to migrate would better protect the national security. As previously discussed, a liberal—and more realistic—admissions system for low- and moderately skilled workers would less likely be circumvented and violated. Better tracking of all noncitizens in the United States would also be an important first step toward improving the nation's security.

Future security measures that employ the immigration laws should scrupulously respect civil rights, avoid the appearance of racial profiling, and strive to be calculated, discerning, and rational, not arbitrary, capricious, and overly broad. Such a system would improve the public confidence—both citizen and noncitizen—in the enforcement of the laws. Again, more liberal admissions, narrower exclusions, and better tracking of immigrants would demonstrate respect for the civil rights of citizens and noncitizens.

With time, the jitters in the United States caused by the tragedy of September 11, 2001, will fade. Indeed, tempers and emotions to a certain extent have already calmed in the last few years. After several years of focusing almost exclusively on strict antiterrorism and immigration enforcement measures, the nation returned to serious consideration of immigration reform in 2005–06. However, none of the reform proposals under consideration would have done much to regularize the labor migration between the United States and Mexico or stem the widespread violation of immigration laws. At most, they offered short-term "solutions" and purported quick fixes that, just like past immigration reforms, in all likelihood will necessitate new reform efforts in a matter of years.

The United States needs immigration laws that recognize that migration from the south into this country has been continuous over many generations and is spurred by desires for economic opportunity, family reunification, and political freedom. In light of the economic disparities between the United States and Mexico and the ready availability of jobs to undocumented persons in this country, the demand for migration to this country—and the flow of migrants—does not appear to have any immediate end in sight.

When the appropriate time comes, this nation will hopefully study the important issue of regularizing the flow of labor from Mexico into the United States. One possibility is something akin to a North American Union modeled on the European Union, permitting labor migration among Canada, Mexico, and the United States. In fashioning responses to the current immigration situation that we find ourselves in, it is important to keep in mind that only truly comprehensive reform—not the incremental reforms floated about in Congress time and time again—will minimize the tragic human costs resulting from immigration restrictions in US immigration law.

A guest worker program, amnesty, issuing driver's licenses to undocumented immigrants, and better tracking systems of immigrants and nonimmigrants are just a few of the measures that have been proposed to improve our immigration laws and allow for a more secure America. At bottom, the United States needs more realistic immigration laws as well as better systems for tracking noncitizens in the country.

As recommended by the blue ribbon 9/11 Commission, better national security also requires better communication and coordination among the immigration and intelligence agencies.[24] Improved tracking of noncitizens who reside in the United States and sharing of this information among different governmental agencies is one example of reform designed to promote national security. Although not strictly an immigration concern, it is unquestionably an issue in which immigration and immigrant policy can play a role.

Unfortunately, national security has come to dominate discussion of immigration law and enforcement, as well as the thorny topic of immigration reform. However, many policy makers ignore the fact that a more liberal immigration admission system is entirely consistent with the interests of the United States in protecting itself from another terrorist attack. Indeed, the current system, which has contributed to a shadow population in the country of millions of people, makes little sense from a national security and public safety standpoint. Rather, the US government would do better to embrace an immigration system in which the admission of immigrants better approximates the demand for immigrant labor. Such a system would work better for the national economy and national security, as well as being more consistent with the national commitment to equality and justice.

In this era of globalization and an increasingly integrated world economy, the United States requires a system of immigration admissions that better comports with social, political, and economic factors contributing to immigration than the current broken system. At a fundamental level, the nation needs immigration laws that avoid the creation and re-creation of a large undocumented immigrant population. The history of failed border enforcement suggests that just adding more, and more, border enforcement simply will not work. Nor is it likely to improve the security of the nation.

■ Discussion Questions

1. The record levels of removals of noncitizens from Mexico and Central America after September 11, 2001, having nothing to do with terrorism suggests that something else was at work in ramping up immigration enforcement besides simply protecting national security. Were the tragic events of September 11 used as an excuse by the US Congress and policy makers to crack down in various ways on immigrants in the United States, not simply to impose measures to improve national security and the public safety of US citizens?

2. Why were immigrants from Mexico so dramatically affected by the various measures taken by the US government after September 11? Why were the objections to this development from the public at large so subdued? Why was immigration reform conceived by some, including Senator John Cornyn, as

seen in his quote at the beginning of the chapter, considered to be a national security issue?

3. Would the United States be more secure as a nation if its immigration laws were not violated as regularly as they are and people generally entered legally rather than unlawfully, with accurate records of entry into and exit of noncitizens from the United States? Put differently, is a population of 12 million people living without immigration records—and, in many states, driver's licenses—bad for public safety and national security? Explain your reasoning.

4. Is there a trade-off between liberty and security in immigration and other areas of law? As a free nation with constitutional guarantees of freedom and liberty, will the United States always be subject to threats of terrorism?

5. What is the future of protecting national security through US immigration laws? Is tighter border enforcement possible? Will it result in a safer nation, or simply more deaths along the US–Mexico border?

■ Suggested Readings

Akram, Susan M., and Kevin R. Johnson. 2002. "Race, Civil Rights, and Immigration Law After September 11, 2001: The Targeting of Arabs and Muslims." *NYU Annual Survey of American Law* 58: 295.

Akram, Susan M., and Maritza Kaimely. 2005. "Immigration and Constitutional Consequences of Post-9/11 Policies Involving Arabs and Muslims in the United States: Is Alienage a Distinction without a Difference?" *UC Davis Law Review* 38: 609.

Bender, Steven W. 2002. "Sight, Sound, and Stereotype: The War on Terrorism and Its Consequences for Latinas/os." *Oregon Law Review* 81: 1153.

Cole, David. 2002. "Enemy Aliens." *Stanford Law Review* 54: 953.

Human Rights Center. 2005. *Freedom Denied: Forced Labor in California*. Berkeley: University of California.

Johnson, Kevin R., and Bernard Trujillo. 2007. "Immigration Reform, National Security, After September 11, and the Future of North American Integration." *Minnesota Law Review* 91: 1369.

■ Notes

Epigraph: Senator John Cornyn 152 *Congressional Record* S2551 (Mar. 30, 2006), emphasis added; Peter Beinart, "The Wrong Place to Stop Terrorists," *Washington Post*, May 4, 2006, A25, discussing a study making this finding.

1. Parts of this chapter have been adapted from Kevin R. Johnson, "Protecting National Security Through More Liberal Admission of Immigrants," *University of Chicago Legal Forum* (2007): 157.

2. US Representative Zoe Lofgren, "A Decade of Radical Change in Immigration Law: An Insider Perspective," *Stanford Law and Policy Review* 16 (2005): 349, 377–78, emphasis added.

3. "Address to the Nation on Immigration Reform," May 15, 2006. *Weekly Compilation of Presidential Documents* 42, no. 20 (May 22, 2006), emphasis added.

4. Belinda I. Reyes et al., *Holding the Line? The Effect of the Recent Border Build-Up on Unauthorized Immigration* (Public Policy Institute of California, 2002), viii, xii, emphasis added.

5. See National Commission on Terrorist Acts Upon the United States, *The 9/11 Commission Report* (2004), 145–253, available at http://govinfo.library.unt.edu/911/report/index.htm.

6. Registration and Monitoring of Certain Nonimmigrants, 67 *Fed. Reg.* 52584, 52585 (Aug. 12, 2002), emphasis added.

7. A plethora of reports have documented the civil and human rights abuses in the "war on terror." See, for example, Asian Law Caucus/Stanford Law School Immigrants' Rights Clinic, *Returning Homes: How US Government Practices Undermine Civil Rights at Our Nation's Doorstep* (Apr. 2009), available at www.asianlawcaucus .org/wp-content/uploads/2009/04/Returning%20Home.pdf; US Department of Justice, Supplemental Report on September 11 Detainees: *A Review of the Treatment of Aliens Held on Immigration Charges in Connection with the Investigation of the September 11 Attacks* (Washington, D.C., 2003); US Office of the Inspector General, *The September 11 Detainees: A Review of the Treatment of Aliens Held on Immigration Charges in Connection with the Investigation of the September 11 Attacks* (Washington, D.C., 2003).

8. See, for example, Patrick J. Buchanan, *State of Emergency: The Third World Invasion and Conquest of America* (New York: Thomas Dunne Books/St. Martin's Press, 2006); Michelle Malkin, *Invasion: How America Still Welcomes Terrorists, Criminals, and Other Foreign Menaces To Our Shores* (Washington, D.C.: Regnery, 2002).

9. 152 *Congressional Record* S2551 (Mar. 30, 2006), emphasis added.

10. Enid Trucios-Haynes, "Civil Rights, Latinos, and Immigration: Cybercascades and Other Distortions in the Immigration Reform Debate," *Brandeis Law Journal* 44 (2006): 637, 638.

11. USA PATRIOT Act, Pub. L. No. 107–56, 115 Stat. 272 (2001); Homeland Security Act, Pub. L. No. 107–296, 116 Stat. 2135; REAL ID Act of 2005, Pub. L. No. 109–13, 119 Stat. 231; Secure Fence Act of 2006, Pub. L. No. 109–367, 120 Stat. 2638.

12. Border Protection, Antiterrorism, and Illegal Immigration Control Act of 2005, H.R. 4437, 109th Cong. (2005).

13. Peter Beinart, "The Wrong Place to Stop Terrorists," *Washington Post*, May 4, 2006, A25, discussing a study making this finding.

14. Robert S. Leiken and Steven Brooke, "The Quantitative Analysis of Terrorism and Immigration: An Initial Exploration," *Terrorism and Political Violence* 18 (2006): 1, 2, footnote omitted.

15. 2001 S.C., ch. 41 (Can.).

16. www.spp.gov.

17. See Doris Meissner, "Immigration in the Post 9-11 Era," *Brandeis Law Journal* 40 (2002): 851, 858.

18. See Philip Shenon and Don Van Natta Jr., "US Says 3 Detainees May Be Tied to Hijackings," *New York Times*, Nov. 1, 2001, A1.

19. *In re* D-J-, 23 I. & N. Dec. 572, 579 (A.G. 2003).

20. *United States v. Cortez-Rocha*, 394 F.3d 1115, 1123–24 (9th Cir), *cert. denied*, 546 US 849 (2005).

21. Jerry Seper, "Rounding Up All Illegals 'Not Realistic,'" *Washington Times*, Sept. 10, 2004, A1, quoting Hutchinson.

22. Elisabeth Bumiller, "In Immigration Remarks, Bush Hints He Favors Senate Plan," *New York Times*, Apr. 25, 2006, A22, quoting President Bush, emphasis added.

23. Rajeev Goyle and David A. Jaeger, *Deporting the Undocumented: A Cost Assessment* (Center for American Progress, July 2005), 2.

24. See National Commission on Terrorist Acts Upon the United States, *The 9/11 Commission Report*, 407–16.

Integration, Protest, and Reform

¡Sí se puede!
—Cesár Chavez and Dolores Huerta, United Farm Workers Slogan

Yes, we can!
—Presidential candidate Barack Obama, 2008

What does the future hold for Mexican migration to the United States? Predicting the future is always difficult, but it is especially perilous when we are dealing with an issue as contested as migration from Mexico to the United States. This chapter outlines some possibilities for the future, as well as sketching out a possible movement to promote social justice, changing the immigration relationship between the United States and Mexico as well as respecting the civil rights of Latinas/os in the United States. It also contemplates the possibility of reforming US immigration laws.

History has shown time and time again that courts have limited abilities to bring about meaningful social change. Political activism appears to be a promising alternative for the Latina/o community to promote social change in the future, especially as the percentage of Latinas/os continues to increase in the United States.

In considering political action, this chapter examines the potential for a new civil rights movement, with immigration reform central to its agenda. A multiracial movement, including African Americans, Asian Americans, Latinas/os, and others, employing political as well as legal tools, in the twenty-first century would most likely bring improvements in the civil rights protections of a multiracial America. In this vein, this chapter analyzes the implications of the unprecedented immigrant rights marches of 2006, in which tens of thousands of people took to the streets in cities across the United States to demand justice for undocumented immigrants.[1] We also discuss the immigration reform proposals percolating in Congress in recent years and explore possible changes to US immigration law and policy.

■ Civil Rights and the Latina/o Community

The US Supreme Court's decision in *Brown v. Board of Education*, which held that legally enforced school segregation violated the US Constitution, sparked the civil rights movement and demonstrated the potential for courts to catalyze social change.[2] Over the years, litigation by Latina/o advocacy groups, such as the Mexican-American Legal Defense and Education Fund (MALDEF) and the League of United Latin American Citizens (LULAC), have successfully secured some civil rights gains for the Latino community. *Plyler v. Doe*, which ensured a primary and secondary education for undocumented children, is a shining example.[3]

However, the evidence indicates that litigation in the courts historically has not been as successful as one might think in promoting change for the Latina/o community. Although a much-heralded victory for Latinas/os, *Plyler v. Doe* itself shows the need for solid political support to cement significant changes decreed by the courts.

A slender 5–4 majority of the Supreme Court rendered the decision in *Plyler v. Doe*. Over the next decade, a political reaction slowly brewed and erupted in dramatic fashion in California in 1994. That year, immigration restrictionists placed an initiative on the ballot that, besides denying health and social service benefits to undocumented persons, would have barred the public education of undocumented children. Their hope was to convince the Supreme Court to revisit and overrule *Plyler v. Doe*. Unfortunately, the initiative campaign was marked by anti-immigrant, anti-Mexican sentiment. Although a court invalidated most of Proposition 187 as an unconstitutional intrusion on the federal power over immigration, *Plyler v. Doe* demonstrates the need to build strong political support behind any incremental civil rights gains secured for Latinas/os through the courts.[4]

Today, a political movement has grown concerning the access to higher public education of undocumented students, many of whom came to the United States as children from Mexico without proper immigration documentation. The central issue is whether such students might be eligible, like other residents of the state, for in-state fees at public colleges and universities.

Over the last decade, Congress has considered many proposals for a law that would expressly permit states to allow undocumented students to pay in-state fees to attend public colleges and universities and to regularize their immigration status. Members of Congress almost annually

The Lemon Grove Incident

In 1931 in the small Southern California community of Lemon Grove, the board of education announced plans to build a separate school for students of Mexican ancestry. The affected community organized politically and formed the Comite de Vecinos de Lemon Grove (Lemon Grove Neighbors Committee), which organized a boycott of the new "Mexican" school. The committee made public appeals in statewide Spanish and English newspapers. The Mexican consul in San Diego provided lawyers to assist the community, who successfully challenged the planned school segregation in a lawsuit. Working with political allies, the community also defeated a bill proposed in the California legislature that would have allowed segregation of persons of Mexican ancestry in the schools. Political action, supported by litigation, allowed for the successful resistance to school segregation in Lemon Grove.

Sources: Robert R. Alvarez, Jr., "The Lemon Grove Incident: The Nation's First Successful Desegregation Case," *J. San Diego History* 32 (1986), 116; *The Lemon Grove Incident* (The Cinema Guild, 1985). ■

sponsor legislation known as the Development, Relief and Education for Alien Minors (DREAM) Act.[5] Versions of the bill have defined residency requirements for in-state tuition without regard to immigration status, provided a path to legalization for eligible undocumented students, and made undocumented students eligible for federal financial assistance (which they currently are not). Immigration restrictionists harshly criticize the many iterations of the DREAM Act, contending, among other things, that it rewards unlawful conduct and amounts to an amnesty for undocumented immigrants.

Students and activists have organized a political movement in support of the DREAM Act. This political movement has grown on campuses across the United States. Although not yet successful in securing passage of the legislation, it has effectively kept the DREAM Act on the national consciousness and kept it on the legislative agenda.

In 2007, the DREAM Act was part of a comprehensive immigration reform bill in the US Senate that ultimately failed. Several subsequent and narrower versions of the act, which would have permitted a path to legalization for undocumented high school graduates who attend college or serve in the military, later failed in the US Senate, amidst criticisms that they amounted to "amnesty" for "illegal aliens." In that same year, California governor Arnold Schwarzenegger vetoed a bill passed by the state legislature that would have permitted undocumented students to be eligible for the same state financial assistance as other California residents. Similarly, in Arizona, voters passed an initiative that barred public universities from providing undocumented students with any public benefits, including in-state fees, state financial aid, or enrollment in adult education classes.

As this discussion shows, anti-immigrant groups have to this point effectively employed political means to oppose measures like the DREAM Act, which would ease the barriers facing undocumented immigrants to public colleges and universities, opposition that negatively affects Latina/o immigrants.

■ Voting and Naturalization

A nascent political movement emerged surrounding the DREAM Act. As we shall see, a mass movement of people favoring immigrants' rights took to the streets in spring 2006. There are many indications that Latinas/os are beginning to more forcefully exercise political power. This, in part, results from the steadily increasing Latina/o population in the United States.

Latinas/os today are the largest minority group in this country, comprising approximately 44.3 million people, or roughly 14.8 percent of the total US population.[6] The Pew Hispanic Center estimated that, in 2005, about 40 percent of the Hispanic population was foreign born.[7] The rapid growth of the Latina/o population over the last few decades, which has been fueled largely by immigration from Mexico, has been much publicized. The sheer numbers of Latinas/os in the United States have made them a political force to be reckoned with nationally, as well as in states and localities across the country.

There are limits to the political cohesion of Latinas/os, however. Latinas/os are an incredibly diverse community in terms of national origin, political ideology, immigration status, physical appearance, and class, to name just a few variables. Such heterogeneity significantly affects the political cohesiveness of Latinas/os as a group. Put simply, Latinas/os in reality constitute a community of communities, which are not of a single, unified mind on political, economic, and social matters.

Important for purposes of analyzing the political power dynamics at work, many Latinas/os are not US citizens but possess a wide array of immigration statuses. Some are legal immigrants; others are undocumented. Consequently, because noncitizens constitute a significant percentage of the Latina/o community, the political power of Latinas/os is not as great as the raw number of Latina/o residents in the United States would suggest.

A recurring problem in a democracy is that a majority of the electorate may unjustly treat minorities. Historically discriminated against in the United States, African Americans are the most obvious discrete and insular minority that have been punished time and time again in the political process. In similar respects, Latinas/os have also suffered the disfavor of the majority in the political process. However, their lack of political power as a minority is exacerbated by the fact that a significant portion of the community is composed of noncitizens, who cannot vote and thus cannot defend themselves politically as effectively as their population numbers would suggest. As a group, Latinas/os are younger than other groups, further diminishing Latino political power. With as many as 40 percent not US citizens, Latinas/os as a whole are worse off politically than minorities of roughly equal numbers who are part of a community without as large a noncitizen component, such as African Americans.

In short, Latinas/os and immigrants are distinctly disadvantaged in the political process because a subset of these groups (noncitizen Latinas/os and unnaturalized immigrants) are disenfranchised and thus are limited in the political power through votes that they are able to effectively exert. We can therefore expect Latinas/os to lose more often—and by wider margins—in the political process than minority groups comprised predominantly of citizens.

Nonetheless, the fact that so many Mexican lawful permanent residents live in the United States suggests great potential benefits of a drive to convince lawful permanent residents eligible for naturalization to become citizens and participate in the political process. Some Latina/o activist groups have long pursued this tactic. The anti-immigrant, anti-Latina/o sentiment seen in recent years has sparked reinvigorated efforts at promoting naturalization. Naturalization rates have spiked, partly for fear of losing public benefits and of deportation and partly because of a desire to participate in the political process. The Clinton administration took steps to encourage the naturalization of immigrants. In light of the potential benefits, naturalization efforts, which capitalize on changing demographics in a positive way, remain a strategy worthy of exploration.

For much of US history, eligibility for citizenship through the naturalization of immigrants had a racial component. Specifically, from 1790 to 1952, only "white" immigrants were eligible for naturalization and thus enjoy a path to citizenship. The naturalization bar on nonwhites had long-term impacts on the political power of certain communities, especially Asian Americans, and on their full integration into American social life. Unlike Asian immigrants, immigrants from Mexico were permitted to naturalize because of treaty obligations between the US and Mexican governments.[8]

Currently, there are eight basic requirements for naturalization:

1. *Lawful permanent residence (LPR)*: Only persons lawfully admitted as lawful permanent residents, also known as "green carders," are eligible for naturalization.[9]

2. *Residence and physical presence*: The applicant generally must have "resided continuously" as a lawful permanent resident in the United States for five years.[10]

3. *Good moral character*: The applicant must demonstrate that he or she is of "good moral character."[11] This vague requirement offers much discretion to the agency. At a minimum, it has been interpreted to mean a limited, preferably clean, criminal record.

4. *Age*: The applicant must be at least eighteen years old.[12]

5. *English language*: To naturalize, a noncitizen must demonstrate "an understanding of the English language, including an ability to read, write, and speak words in ordinary usage."[13] There are exceptions to the English language requirement based on physical or mental disability and age.

   Even with the exceptions, the English language requirement represents the most formidable obstacle to naturalization for many immigrants. Some defend the requirement as consistent with encouraging the assimilation of immigrants. Those who oppose it not only question the premise that the English language defines or unifies the US community but also note that the English language requirement fails to achieve its unifying purpose for the substantial numbers of those who learn it for purposes of naturalization but still do not make English their primary language.

6. *Knowledge of civics*: A naturalization applicant must demonstrate "knowledge and understanding of the fundamentals of the history, and of the principles and the form of government, of the United States."[14] Persons with a medically demonstrated physical or developmental condition can be exempted from this requirement, as can persons over sixty-five years old who have lived in the United States for more than twenty years.[15]

In 2007, the US Citizenship and Immigration Services (CIS) unveiled the new citizenship test. The new test includes one hundred revised questions, from which ten are randomly selected.[16] Some criticize the new test as a meaningless barrier to naturalization that perpetuates a political and social ideology that disfavors minority groups.

7. *Political or ideological requirements*: Applicants who during the ten years before filing the application have been affiliated with communist, totalitarian, or terrorist groups or have advocated the ideals of such groups, including through speeches and publications, are not eligible for naturalization.[17] These qualifications are in tension with bedrock principles of the US Constitution, including freedom of thought, speech, and association.

8. *Attachment to US constitutional principles*: An applicant must demonstrate an attachment to the principles of the US Constitution and allegiance to the US government by taking an oath promising that the applicant supports the Constitution, renounces all foreign allegiances, is willing to defend all federal laws against all enemies, will bear true allegiance to those laws, and will bear arms for the United States if required by law.[18]

Modern Naturalization Issues

In modern times, given the demographics of modern immigration, delays in the processing of naturalization petitions have disparate racial—as well as political (because only US citizens can vote)—impacts. More than 39 percent of the naturalized citizens in 2007 were from Asia and 18.5 percent from Mexico.[19]

Cultural barriers, specifically a desire to maintain exclusive Mexican citizenship, have historically resulted in a lag in the naturalization rate of Mexican immigrants. A popular saying among Mexican immigrants is "born in Mexico, die in Mexico."

Partisan debates over naturalization have been hot and heavy, with efforts by the Clinton administration in the 1990s to facilitate immigrant naturalization subjected to harsh criticism. Some Republicans accused the president of promoting naturalization as an attempt to do nothing more than increase the number of Democratic voters.

In 2007, the Bush administration substantially increased the fees for naturalization petitions, which not surprisingly discouraged the filing of naturalization petitions by low- and middle-income noncitizens. Despite the fee hikes, which the US government promised would provide the funds necessary to enhance service to immigrants and speed the processing of petitions, petition processing has continued to be exceedingly slow. Because of the modern demographics of immigration, delays in the processing of naturalization petitions are likely to have racial, national origin, and political impacts.

Dual Nationality

Until recently, US law long disfavored dual nationality, the formal possession of citizenship or nationality in two or more nations. However, in recent years, the United States has relaxed its laws to accommodate dual nationals in many instances.

Mexico's adoption in 1998 of a constitutional grant of dual nationality on the heels of similar changes by other countries, including El Salvador, has increased the number of dual nationals living in the United States. This development has provoked renewed fervor among some sectors of the public against dual nationality. Some political scientists, for example, have argued that the dual nationality of naturalized citizens, especially Latinas/os, distances immigrants from the US political system and diminishes their loyalty to the United States.

Other Electoral Strategies

Other factors besides the lack of citizenship among a segment of the Latina/o community also dilute Latina/o political power. For example, the voting rates of Latina/o citizens have historically lagged behind those of Anglos in the United States. Among other considerations, language difference—some Latinas/os speak primarily Spanish, some are bilingual, some speak only English—has dampened Latina/o political participation. All told, the political power of Latinas/os is significantly less than the group's raw numbers might suggest.

Besides increasing the number of eligible voters, steps should be taken to reform the electoral process. Energy might be wisely focused on creative steps to improve electoral systems so that representation of minority groups is improved. At-large voting schemes in local elections, for example, have limited minority representation. Voting rights litigation may assist meaningful Latina/o participation in the political process, especially in districts that in operation exclude Latinas/os from elected office. This strategy has offered some concrete gains for Latinas/os. In Los Angeles County, for example, a successful voting rights lawsuit culminated in the election of the first Latina/o (a Chicana) to the board of supervisors.[20]

Assimilation and Integration

Naturalization amounts to the full legal assimilation of noncitizens. However, it does not address social assimilation of immigrants and their true integration—politically, socially, and economically—into US society.

Samuel Huntington's provocative book *Who Are We?: The Challenges to National Identity* raises concerns shared by some Americans about a perceived loss of national identity in the United States due to the flow of immigrants into the country. Huntington emphatically proclaims that immigration from Mexico is a threat to the national identity of the United States.[21] In his estimation, Mexican immigrants refuse to assimilate into mainstream US society and instead live and act in separatist—"un-American"—ways. Such separatism, in his view, threatens the very unity of the United States. Huntington grounds his concern with Mexican immigrants in problems raised by the changes to the nation's culture that they bring, with a particular emphasis on language (Spanish rather than English) and religion (Catholic rather than Protestant).

Contrary to the claim that a separatist Mexican nation is emerging in the United States, immigrants do in fact assimilate to a certain degree into American social life.[22] The available empirical data demonstrates that immigrants from all nations, including Mexico, overwhelmingly participate in the labor market, learn English, and participate in community life. Ethnic enclaves are often first stops that, by providing financial and social support, facilitate immigrant success in US society.

None of this is meant to suggest that stresses and tensions do not result from immigration and the presence of newcomers in the community.

However, immigrant assimilation has historically prevailed in the United States. That appears to be the case with immigrants today. However, full integration is a process that takes time, sometimes a generation or two.

It is worth recalling that assimilation of immigrants has persistently been viewed as a problem with the immigrants of any particular period in US history. Early in this nation's history, for example, the claim was that German and Irish immigrants—only to be later replaced by Chinese, Japanese, southern and eastern European, and later Mexican immigrants were racially inferior and refused to assimilate. These claims have been buttressed by the contention that *this* particular group of immigrants differed from the last group. Each successive group was viewed as failing to assimilate into mainstream US society. Despite those claims, the assimilation process has in most respects been successful in the United States, and most observers see anti-immigrant episodes as unfortunate mistakes in our history.

As was the case for Asian immigrants, immigrants from Mexico have faced a series of restrictionist immigration measures designed to limit their presence in the United States, as well as discrimination against those living in this country. Society and government at times have directed assimilationist measures at Mexican immigrants and Mexican Americans living in the United States; such measures often have been accompanied by discrimination against persons of Mexican ancestry in American social life.

Assimilation campaigns directed at persons of Mexican ancestry were popular in the 1920s. The coercive assimilationist policies of the past had an unexpected boomerang effect. Coerced assimilation helped forge a collective Latina/o identity in the United States in opposition to Anglo society. Language regulation, for example, is an issue of Latina/o concern even though most Latinas/os in the United States speak, or desire to learn, English.

Policies that promote, rather than mandate, immigrant assimilation in the modern United States would be consistent with modern civil rights sensibilities and would probably be relatively uncontroversial. For example, increasing access to English as a second language (ESL) classes so that new Americans can learn English would hardly seem debatable. ESL classes are greatly overfilled in cities across the United States, and many immigrants find it difficult to enroll in them. A commitment to ensuring access to English language instruction and promoting English language acquisition would militate in favor of devoting greater resources to ESL courses; instead, few resources are generally available for such courses.

Policies that facilitate the naturalization of immigrants are another way of promoting the integration of immigrants into US society. Citizenship allows full political participation and greater participation and membership in US social life. To avoid naturalization by fear—for example, fear of removal, loss of public benefits, or other anti-immigrant measures—steps could be taken to encourage naturalization and allegiance to the United States.

■ An Impediment to Political Action: Divisions in the Civil Rights Coalition

We have discussed the potential for Latinas/os to pursue political avenues for change, including through increased naturalization, voting, and political action. There are obviously serious impediments facing Latinas/os in the political process. However, as the changing demographics suggest, the political arena offers Latinas/os the most promise in the near future. The time of a judiciary willing to foster change through lawsuits has come and gone. In short, although imperfect, the political process appears to be the optimal investment of concentrated scarce resources.

In the 1960s, many achievements of the civil rights movement were gained through a coalition of African American, labor, Latina/o, Jewish, and other progressive organizations. Unfortunately, disagreements among members of the traditional civil rights coalition have grown over time. The fault lines become readily apparent when one broaches the topic of immigration, which each group views in a different light.

For obvious reasons, immigration has been of particular interest to Latina/o activists and organizations. Immigration law and enforcement issues greatly affect Latina/o, as well as Asian American, communities. Their communities are composed of a significant number of immigrants. As a whole, one might expect those communities to be more sensitive to immigration and immigrants than the African American community, which is composed of a relatively smaller number of immigrants (although the number of immigrants from Africa to the United States has been on the rise in recent years).

Some Latina/o activists have resisted efforts to restrict immigration and to crack down on undocumented immigration. In part, this sympathy perhaps results from a perceived kinship—sometimes exaggerated—between Mexican Americans and Mexican immigrants. These efforts also have a self-interested aspect. Restrictionist immigration policies, such as increased efforts at immigration enforcement, often have negative side effects on Latino citizens and lawful immigrants. Nonetheless, at times, concerns with immigration common to many Americans have led some Latinas/os to support restrictionist measures.

Well-publicized conflicts between immigrants and African Americans have a long historical pedigree in the United States, dating at least as far back as clashes between Irish immigrants and black migrants in the urban Northeast in the 1800s. Similarly, Chinese immigrants clashed with "American workers" in California in the late 1800s. Such conflicts have unquestionably influenced immigration law, with the Chinese exclusion laws, which were supported by organized labor, a noteworthy example. Today, some have argued that African Americans support restricting immigration because of the alleged preferences of nonminorities to hire undocumented Latinos rather than black citizens.

As history teaches, tension of this sort often comes to the fore at times of intense competition for what are perceived to be scarce economic resources. In times of economic distress, competition at the margin, the place in the market where citizens of color and recent immigrants are disproportionately represented, can be intense. People of color compete for resources that have become increasingly scarce with the economic downturn in the US economy over the last few years. New immigrants are often perceived as directly competing with the poorest, including many minority, citizens in the United States.

Professor Bill Ong Hing has recognized this phenomenon in analyzing the dynamics of the tensions between Korean Americans, including many immigrants, and African Americans in South Central Los Angeles. This conflict hit a flashpoint in 1992 with widespread violence on the streets of Los Angeles following the acquittal of Los Angeles Police Department officers in the videotaped beating of Rodney King: "The tension between the Korean American and African American communities in South Central Los Angeles was not all racial. Much had to do with economic class divisions, as demonstrated by the similar destruction of Latino and African American owned businesses [in the spring 1992 violence]. . . . Thus, *what appears to be a racial conflict may be actually a class dispute, or a mixture of racial and class elements.*"[23]

Economic conflict of this variety is not limited to citizens of color and immigrants. Tensions undeniably exist between new immigrants and working-class people in general. As organized labor's historically restrictionist bent suggests, economic competition between nonminority working-class citizens and new immigrants has been a longstanding concern. Workers fear competition in the labor market, fewer jobs, lower wages, and limited benefits often attributed to an influx of low-wage immigrant labor. Business frequently lobbies to change the immigration laws to ensure a ready supply of cheap and pliant labor. In times of relative economic hardship, working people may be inclined to blame immigrants for "taking" jobs. Anti-immigrant sentiment can be expected to thrive during these times of economic insecurity and hardship.

The position of organized labor, however, has shifted on the issue of undocumented immigration in recent years. A proponent of employer sanctions adopted by Congress in 1986, the AFL-CIO now opposes the imposition of sanctions on the employers of undocumented immigrants. Organized labor today seeks to organize undocumented workers, rather than somehow squeeze them out of the labor market.

It is against this backdrop that reconstruction of a civil rights coalition must be considered. Tensions between communities of color have hindered efforts at developing coalitions. Future political action requires that these communities work together to transcend differences. In light of the economic class sensitivity of immigration, coalition builders must address it. The goal must be to minimize any societal stress resulting from migration, especially during relatively difficult economic times.

Another issue causing tension among minority communities is the tendency of the media and politicians to frame civil rights as an almost exclusively black/white issue. Latina/o concerns are often not considered to be genuine civil rights concerns. For example, immigration is not often viewed as raising civil rights issues. (Chapters 9–11 analyze the civil rights implications of immigration enforcement.)

True, Latina/o and African American communities at times have embraced divergent political positions on civil rights. Each community as a whole has slightly different views on affirmative action, immigration, reapportionment and voting rights, welfare, criminal justice, and undoubtedly other issues. Although differences exist, it is necessary to move beyond them, build consensus when possible, develop strategies that further common goals, and address shared needs.

■ Spring 2006: Mass Marches for Immigrant Rights

The brief summary of recent civil rights history helps us understand the political dynamics of immigration and civil rights today. In spring 2006, television and newspapers featured spectacular images of masses of humanity lined up for miles in marches across the United States. Hundreds of thousands of people, US citizens as well as immigrants, peacefully marched in New York, San Francisco, Chicago, and Los Angeles, with thousands also taking to the streets in other cities across the country.

What was most startling about the marches was that they were overwhelmingly pro-immigrant. Such mass public displays of *pro*-immigrant sentiment are unprecedented in US history.

At the time of the marches, energy, enthusiasm, and a deep sense of urgency filled the air. Some activists proclaimed that the marches represented a "new" civil rights movement, bringing to mind visions of the 1960s. The first round of protests targeted the punitive bill passed in December 2005 by the US House of Representatives, known popularly by the name of its sponsor, Representative James Sensenbrenner of Wisconsin. The Sensenbrenner Bill, among other things, would have made the mere status of being an undocumented immigrant a felony subject to imprisonment as well as deportation from the United States and sought to impose criminal sanctions on persons who provided humanitarian assistance to undocumented immigrants.

The immigrant rights movement in spring 2006 initially spread like wildfire. A second wave of marches followed later in the spring. Demanding more than simple rejection of the punitive Sensenbrenner Bill, the protesters instead affirmatively sought justice for immigrants and, among other things, supported legislation allowing undocumented immigrants the opportunity to regularize their immigration status.

With the spring 2006 immigration rights marches, some activists believed that the anti-immigrant tide that had dominated the national debate since the terrorist acts of September 11, 2001, might have turned. In the heady days following the marches, positive immigration reform, including some kind of path to legalization and citizenship for millions of undocumented immigrants, actually seemed possible.

By summer 2006, however, the immigrant rights movement appeared to have lost steam. A series of marches on and around Labor Day 2006 attracted far fewer people than those just a few months before.

In the end, immigration policy proved to be too volatile an issue for Congress to address constructively in the short term. The headway made by the immigrant rights movement visibly slowed. Ultimately, after much skirmishing during the summer, Congress failed to enact any comprehensive immigration reform legislation, passing only a law appropriating funds for extension of the fence along the US–Mexico border.

The mass protests in spring 2006 represented true grassroots activism, organically generated by a loosely knit group of community activists assisted by Spanish language radio stations and the Internet. As in the 1960s, high school, college, and university students helped to energize the protests, with a commitment and enthusiasm not seen on college campuses for more than a generation.

Punitive immigration reform passed by the US House of Representatives initially spurred the immigrant rights movement into action. In this way, the nascent movement, at least at the outset, represented a reaction to the Sensenbrenner Bill, not a proactive movement seeking positive change. However, the movement, at least for a time, moved well beyond blocking the passage of one restrictionist bill and morphed into a quest for justice for immigrants.

Importantly, the marches quickly tapped into a base of mainstream appeal. Putting the imprimatur of the Catholic Church on the marches, Cardinal Roger Mahony of Los Angeles condemned the Sensenbrenner Bill and promised to instruct his priests and parishioners to continue to provide humanitarian assistance to all people in need—undocumented or not—whatever the prohibitions of the law.[24]

Politicians, including, among others, Los Angeles mayor Antonio Villaraigosa and now-disgraced former Illinois governor Rod Blagojevich, addressed the protesters, praised the contributions of immigrants to US society, and called for the just and fair treatment of noncitizens; by so doing, these and other influential politicians offered the marchers' cause the official stamp of approval. Two US senators, Barack Obama and the late Edward Kennedy, marched with the protesters. And, most important, many US citizens, as well as immigrants, joined the marches in support of immigrant rights.

The marches, without question, influenced the national debate over immigration. By summer 2006, the tough-on-immigrants Sensenbrenner Bill appeared to have lost support. Indeed, in June 2006, the US Senate considered a compromise immigration reform bill that lacked the harsher provisions of the Sensenbrenner Bill and would have created a path to citizenship for undocumented immigrants.[25] Some of the last reform proposals on the table, although flawed in certain respects, would have extended certain benefits to undocumented immigrants.

For many people, the spring 2006 mass marches evoked proud memories of the civil rights movement of the 1960s, when African Americans, Latinas/os, progressive whites, and others struggled for social justice. In the last few years, there have been signs of a nascent mass political movement—such as with respect to the DREAM Act, discussed earlier in this chapter—on the horizon.

However, times and circumstances have changed in important respects. Although masses of people participated, the 2006 immigration marches were not as broad based as might be desired. Importantly, African Americans were not visible participants in the marches for immigrant rights. In no small part, this flows from the fact that immigration has proved through much of US history to be a dividing line between Asian Americans and Latinas/os, on one hand, and African Americans on the other.

In the end, comprehensive reform efforts fell by the wayside. Politics made true immigration reform an issue that many politicians scurried to avoid. Rather, Congress could reach consensus only on another additional border security measure—nothing approaching comprehensive reform. As Congress recessed in fall 2006, the only legislation passed was directed at erecting an additional seven hundred miles of fence along the southern border.

Nonetheless, in future debates over immigration, lawmakers will not soon be able to forget the power, emotion, and sheer size of the mass marches of spring 2006, as well as the firestorm of anger, controversy, and resistance brought by the Sensenbrenner Bill's punitive immigration measures.

■ Change in the Winds?

Recent political changes may suggest the propriety of renewed optimism about the possibility for reform of US immigration laws in the near future. After years of dogging immigrants and Latinas/os on his nightly television show, protest and complaints led to the departure of one of the most influential restrictionists, Lou Dobbs, from CNN. Property owners along the Texas-Mexico border brought suits challenging the erection of the border fences on their land. After at times raucous and unpleasant confirmation hearings in the US Senate, the first Latina, Sonia Sotomayor, was appointed to the US Supreme Court. In her very first opinion for the Court, Justice Sotomayor referred to "undocumented immigrants" for the first time in a Supreme Court opinion, eschewing other more controversial terms such as "illegal alien" or worse.[26]

However, the Obama administration was slow to back a comprehensive immigration reform proposal introduced by Representative Luis Gutierrez (D-Illinois) in December 2009, although it eventually did. In addition, the secretary of the DHS, Janet Napolitano, former governor of Arizona and the Obama administration's point person on immigration reform, appeared more devoted to immigration enforcement than other immigration priorities. Indeed, DHS deported a record number (nearly 400,000) of noncitizens in fiscal year 2010.[27] In addition, 2010 was an election year in the US House of Representatives, and Congress as a whole found itself unable, after much fanfare, to pass comprehensive immigration reform that year.

The new spate of immigration activity, however, should not lead one to be overly optimistic. Repeated efforts in recent years at addressing immigration reform in the United States have been both deeply unproductive and extremely divisive.

Notably, the history of immigration reform over the last few decades offers some important—yet oft-ignored—lessons for contemporary reform efforts. As we have seen, Congress regularly amends the omnibus immigration law, the Immigration and Nationality Act of 1952. The reform efforts of the last fifteen years have tended to focus more on an amalgam of immigration enforcement and punishment of certain groups of immigrants than on the meaningful pursuit of other important goals. Nonetheless, the reforms together have failed to do much better than the last major stab at what today would be called "comprehensive immigration reform" nearly a quarter century ago.

The Immigration Reform and Control Act of 1986 (IRCA) included a series of measures that all together, it was contended, would dramatically reduce—indeed, held the promise of putting an end to—undocumented immigration as we know it.[28] An amnesty for millions of undocumented immigrants, combined with temporary worker programs, and a new feature of US law known as *employer sanctions,* that is, the imposition of sanctions on those who employ undocumented immigrants, along with a number of other enforcement measures, were supposed to solve the problem of undocumented immigration.

Despite the considerable fanfare that accompanied its passage, IRCA has failed to effectively reduce undocumented immigration to the United States. The primary reason is the act's complete and utter failure to expand avenues for legal immigration to match the US economy's continuing demand for workers. As a result, in the neighborhood of 11–12 million undocumented immigrants live in the United States today, which is millions more than did in 1986. Indeed, the undocumented population roughly doubled just from the mid-1990s to the present, even with vastly heightened immigration enforcement.

Many of the contemporary comprehensive immigration reform proposals sound remarkably similar to IRCA. Many include some form of *earned legalization* of undocumented immigrants, perhaps with fines, payment of back taxes, and similar requirements. There is also talk of possible guest worker programs. By far the most certain are increased enforcement measures, perhaps with increased enforcement in the workplace. Although a more balanced approach to the issue than those that followed over the last two decades, the proposals sound like IRCA and, in the end, may also fail to effectively address the true reasons for undocumented migration.

What the nation truly needs are changes to US immigration laws that are substantial enough so that five, ten, fifteen, or twenty years from now we do not again face the call for another "comprehensive" immigration reform bill to, among other things, legalize a new population of millions of undocumented immigrants who live and work in the United States. For immigration reform to be durable and long lasting, it must address what is at the core of immigration, that is, the increasing movement of labor across borders in an era of globalization and a rapidly integrating world economy.

Unfortunately, the intensity, volatility, and, at times, sheer irrationality of the immigration debate often destroys the opportunity for reasonable dialogue on this all-important topic. To truly bring about lasting change in the regulation of migration across the borders of the United States, we as a nation need to think practically, thoughtfully, logically, and responsibly about how to reform and improve the immigration laws. Ultimately, there are no easy answers to the thorny policy questions surrounding immigration to the United States in modern times.

Most fundamentally, the country needs the current administration and the US Congress to move beyond piecemeal enforcement-only policies to address the core reasons for migration—legal and not—to the United States. To this point, responsible political leadership on the issue of immigration has been sorely lacking.

The nation seriously needs leadership to bring forth meaningful immigration reform that squarely addresses the core issues of modern immigration in an era of globalization. For reform to be lasting, we must collectively realize that the current immigration system has helped create dual labor markets with a racial caste quality to them. One job market comprises undocumented workers, many of whom are Latina/o, with workers often paid less than the minimum wage and enjoying few health and safety protections. The other labor market comprises US citizens and lawful immigrants, with the workers enjoying the full (if not fully enforced) protections of the law.

The end result injures all workers: those in one market are exploited while workers in the other market face shrinking job opportunities as employers pursuing economic rationality shift jobs from the "legal" (more expensive) to "illegal" (and less expensive) markets. Consequently, all Americans should be deeply concerned with immigration and its labor market impacts.

To avoid a repeat of the IRCA failure, for example, we need to acknowledge that immigration—undocumented and not—is largely labor driven; only by addressing that unquestionable truth reasonably and responsibly will we be able to reform the nation's immigration laws so that they are enforceable, effective, efficient, and respected. At the same time, family unification, protection of refugees, and national security and public safety are other goals that, of course, cannot be ignored by the immigration laws. Still, those goals must be appropriately—and expressly—folded into, and carefully balanced in, an overall immigration reform package.

■ The Future of the New Civil Rights Movement

Besides the movement for immigration reform, is a broad-based civil rights movement emerging or was the mass demonstration in spring 2006 simply a one-time phenomenon? As this book goes to press, it is extremely difficult to tell. Cleavages exist and, unless addressed, are ready to divide, not unite, various communities of color. Of course, under the right circumstances, outbursts of violence protesting social conditions can be triggered by a calamitous event. Many examples, including the May 1992 uprising in

Los Angeles, in which Latina/o immigrants as well as African Americans took to the streets, come to mind.

There is one significant issue that, unless addressed, could divide minority communities. And it is the precise issue that animated the marches of spring 2006 and represents one of the social justice challenges of this generation. As discussed previously, Latinas/os and Asian Americans are generally more concerned with the excesses of immigration law and enforcement than African Americans, who may at times demand greater enforcement of the immigration law and generally reduced immigration. This may explain why African Americans, generally speaking, were conspicuously absent from the 2006 mass marches, even though many black leaders expressed support for the immigrant cause.

Some African Americans, who are disproportionately represented among poor and working people in US society, have long feared economic and political competition from Latina/o immigrants. Such competition at times contributes to tension and conflict between blacks and Latinas/os. As previously discussed, conflict over jobs—especially the perceived competition by immigrants with African Americans in the unskilled job market—has always been a lingering concern.

Moreover, African Americans and Latinas/os in recent years have increasingly competed for political power in cities across the country. Simmering black/brown tensions, which the press likes to sensationalize, have at times escalated into violence. Black and Latina/o youth gangs fight on city streets and in prisons throughout the United States.

Although not often discussed, racism, as well as economic class conflicts, afflicts the African American and Latina/o communities. Antiblack sentiment unquestionably exists among certain segments of the Latina/o community. Sadly enough, some Latinas/os discriminate against African Americans. Toni Morrison has eloquently written about how immigrant assimilation often translates into the adoption by immigrants of racist views of African Americans.[29] This does occur to a certain extent among Latina/o immigrants who embrace dominant US society's views on issues of race and racism.

Similarly, nativism directed at Latinas/os and other immigrant groups, such as Korean Americans in South Central Los Angeles, afflicts the black community. Put bluntly, anti-Latina/o sentiment exists in certain segments of the African American community.

For a wide variety of reasons, minority leaders more frequently ignore rather than address the simmering animosities between minority groups. Any future civil rights movement, however, will require much hard work between and among communities of color. Racism between minority communities cannot be ignored. A healthy and frank dialogue, along with constructive action, on this subject is long overdue. Only after such a dialogue will the trust between the groups rise to a level necessary for effective concerted action.

The gulf between African Americans and Latinas/os on immigration is not insurmountable. African Americans can appreciate that immigration enforcement—like racial profiling by local police in ordinary law enforcement—is often based on race, physical appearance, and popular stereotypes. Importantly, many African American leaders saw race as central to the refusal of the US government to grant relief to Haitians seeking asylum in the United States in the 1980s and 1990s. Perhaps a visionary leader like President Barack Obama, with an African father who studied in the United States, who has voiced support for immigrants as well as for traditional civil rights issues, could be a bridge between the communities on this potentially explosive issue.

However, a broad-based civil rights movement will not just happen. Rather, a truly multiracial civil rights movement will need to identify common ground. Minorities generally want wage and labor protections in the workplace, safe and affordable housing, equal access to education, and fair treatment by government. The congruence of interests among many segments of the African American, Asian American, and Latina/o communities on these bread-and-butter issues is clear. As a concrete matter, minorities generally stand to benefit if the billions of dollars currently wasted on border enforcement, which fails to significantly reduce undocumented immigration and results in tragic human loss, were spent instead on enforcing wage and labor protections for all workers.

A Mass Social Movement?

In thinking about a future civil rights movement, important lessons should be learned from the past. The civil rights movement of the 1950s and 1960s is generally viewed as a successful movement for social change. Many groups worked together to bring about the end of *de jure* segregation that had long dominated the United States.

Although the civil rights improvements arose from the grassroots and gained support in political institutions, a litigation strategy pursued for many years helped facilitate change through the courts. Critics complain that the legacy of discrimination continues to exist in the United States but cannot dispute that the demise of Jim Crow brought about by political and legal action represented a major transformation of US social life.

The civil rights movement of the 1960s is often viewed as a black movement or a movement for the civil rights of African Americans. That was not the case, however. Many different groups, including whites, participated in the larger quest for social justice. Mexican Americans in the Southwest sought to vindicate their rights as well during this time of ferment and unrest. Civil rights victories ultimately affected many different communities. The civil rights movement, for example, directly contributed to the congressional passage of the Immigration Act of 1965, which removed a discriminatory national origins quota system from the immigration laws and eliminated the last remnants of the laws excluding immigration from Asia.[30]

As the 1960s exemplified, many social problems require political as well as legal solutions. Political movements, in turn, require numbers, coalitions, and concerted action. In the heyday of our last great civil rights movement, coalitions of groups pursued protests, marches, voting rights drives, lawsuits, and other strategies for change.

Understanding the fundamental maxim of strength in numbers, some scholars and activists have advocated coalitions among minority groups as a strategy for political action in a new civil rights movement. Of course, coalition building faces barriers, some of which have been discussed in this chapter.

While coalitions may be helpful, it is also important that different groups press for civil rights simultaneously. Timing is all important. Various groups must maintain the pressure for change. Under this scenario, a monolithic, multiracial movement may not be necessary, but a series of synchronized actions requiring cooperation and coordinated efforts are.

In the 1950s and 1960s, a convergence of interests facilitated civil rights gains in the United States. US foreign interests militated in favor of extending civil rights to African Americans and other minorities to avoid adverse propaganda in the ongoing Cold War. The extension of civil rights was part of the fight for the hearts and minds of the world community that dominated international relations until the demise of the Soviet Union in 1989.

African Americans, who had suffered the inhumanity of chattel slavery and centuries of abuse in a form of American apartheid, were at the forefront of the 1960s civil rights movements. Images of southern police busting up peaceful civil rights marches and Ku Klux Klan members terrorizing African Americans are what many Americans remember today about that transformative period in US history. People could readily coalesce around the principles of equality and justice for African Americans and participate in the quest to end legally enforced racial segregation.

At the time, there was a more unified conception of civil rights that included, at a minimum, the absence of invidious discrimination on the basis of race. The evil, as well as the immediate cure, was clear. Jim Crow was dismantled. However, legally sanctioned and enforced segregation, and the use of law to enforce the separation of the races, is not the primary mode of racial discrimination today. Times have changed, and a future broad-based civil rights movement will need to reconceptualize the idea of "civil rights" to address modern discriminatory realities. Today, immigration law and enforcement raise important civil rights concerns that are often not thought of as core civil rights issues.

The new racial demographics of the United States have necessarily transformed the civil rights agenda. Latinas/os now constitute the largest minority group in the country, roughly 15 percent (close to 45 million) of the population. Largely due to the end in 1965 of the law limiting migration from Asia, Asian Americans have also seen an increase of their population, in excess of 11.5 million, or 4 percent of the US total.

Immigration, discrimination through proxies, such as through language, immigration status, and conceptions of merit, are the civil rights problems of the twenty-first century. Our national vision of the civil rights deserving protection must change to comport with the modern demographics of the United States.

Importantly, the civil rights movement occupied the high moral ground in the 1960s and, as such, enjoyed the support of religious as well as political leaders. The moral outrage over segregation and the second-class citizenship of African Americans in the United States, as well as the lynchings of blacks, were at the forefront of many American minds. Such a system of racial apartheid ultimately proved to be morally indefensible. *Brown v. Board of Education* and its message of equality for all people was much more in keeping with the emerging concept of America embraced by many, if not most, Americans than Jim Crow America.

The deep moral underpinnings of the 1960s civil rights movement can be seen in the prominent religious leaders who participated in it. The Reverend Martin Luther King Jr. was one of the most prominent African American civil rights leaders of his generation. Many other black religious leaders joined Dr. King. Similarly, the United Farm Workers led by César Chávez tapped into the Catholicism that predominates among many persons of Mexican ancestry, in efforts to fight for the rights of farm workers.

Although often forgotten, Mexican Americans played an important role in the litigation strategy culminating in *Brown v. Board of Education*. Chicano activist George I. Sánchez worked for decades with NAACP attorney Thurgood Marshall, later the first African American justice on the US Supreme Court, on civil rights issues, including efforts to desegregate the public schools, a common issue for both Chicanas/os and blacks. For example, the court of appeals in *Mendez v. Westminister School District* held that Mexican Americans could not legally be segregated in the public schools.[31] Appreciating the importance of the case, Thurgood Marshall filed an amicus brief on behalf of the NAACP in support of the Mexican American plaintiffs in that case.

In the 1960s, the political arenas also served as a powerful tool for social change. The civil rights movement produced much energy, great enthusiasm, and heavy pressure for change in the political process. Although they came only after a lot of struggle, Congress finally enacted the Civil Rights Act of 1964, Voting Rights Act, Fair Housing Act, and many other laws that sought to eliminate the scourge of racial discrimination from various aspects of American social life.

The successful civil rights movement of the 1950s and 1960s teaches important lessons about the struggle for civil rights in modern times. A political movement was essential to the quest for social change. Moral and political leaders promoted the civil rights movement. The courts were also often, although not always, favorably disposed and helped move the nation forward. The political movement helped sustain the courts and judicial action. Together, the political and judicial branches fueled meaningful social change in US society.

What will be key to the future creation of any mass movement for social justice is the development of common ground, with the support of political and moral leaders. African Americans, Asian Americans, and Latinas/os should be able to agree on the need to remove race from the criminal justice system as well as law enforcement generally—both ordinary criminal and immigration.

In addition, African Americans—and all workers—should be persuaded of the need to enforce wage and labor protections for *all* workers. Only by so doing will employers seeking unskilled laborers be discouraged from hiring undocumented—and relatively inexpensive—workers. In these and other instances, concrete benefits might accrue to African Americans and Latinas/os by working together in the struggle for the civil rights of immigrants, rather than blaming each other for their problems.

There are signs of an emerging civil rights movement. However, the massive immigrant rights marches in spring 2006 were relatively narrow in focus. The throngs of demonstrators were marching for immigrant rights, specifically opposing the Sensenbrenner Bill and demanding a path to citizenship for undocumented—including many Latina/o—immigrants.

Immigration reform failed to hold instant appeal to non-Latina/o minority groups. Asian Americans were not automatically attracted to support immigrants. In an effort to draw Asian Americans to the marches, Asian American civil rights organizations engaged in community education to draw parallels with immigrant rights in their communities with those in Latina/o communities. Similarly, African Americans were not visibly involved in the immigration marches, with some even protesting immigrants and their alleged negative impacts on the black community.

As previously discussed, tension between various groups creates a formidable obstacle to a new multiracial civil rights movement. There are substantial challenges to the formation of a broad-based, multi-issue civil rights movement. At the same time, however, in the aftermath of the 2006 immigration marches, many knowledgeable observers urged activists to reach out to Asian Americans and for African Americans to embrace the immigrant rights agenda. The themes advanced by the proponents of unity focused on common concerns, such as human rights and the historical experience of racial discrimination.

A broad-based civil rights movement might include antidiscrimination as well as immigrants' rights planks. It could also be multiracial, with different minority groups, including African Americans, working together to secure broad social change. The unifying goal would be social justice for all people in US society, which would enhance the coalition-building potential of the movement and would help place its goals on a high moral plane.

There are good reasons for immigrants from diverse nations, immigrant rights advocates, and African Americans to work together on a number of fronts, including immigration policy, civil rights, economic justice, workers' rights, and antidiscrimination efforts. These groups and individuals have much in common. They can gain political and moral strength by unifying their numbers and developing a common agenda. However, these groups are diverse as well, and the prospect of a consistent, unified mass movement faces many challenges.

Much of the call to African Americans to support immigrant rights is based on a call to African Americans to understand and sympathize with the plight of immigrants. Of course, understanding the similarities that African Americans have with immigrants helps. But, in reaching out to African Americans, immigrant rights advocates would do well to better understand and appreciate African American concerns with immigration.

The benefits of a new, broad-based civil rights movement begin with an appreciation of an expansive vision of a meaningful political life. Although the power of the ballot box cannot be underrated, we also have to recognize the importance of nonelectoral activities. Politics involves more than voting and registration rates, a point especially worth noting because noncitizens are ineligible to vote. The mass protest is often viewed as an important form of nonelectoral political activity, with prime examples being protest movements of the 1930s and 1960s. National in scope, each demonstrated that mass mobilization can be an effective exercise of power to change law and policy. Each movement revealed a complicated relationship between mass mobilization and electoral politics.

An almost boundless range of nonelectoral activities may qualify as meaningfully political. In focusing on national mass movements, we must not neglect regional, state, and local mobilizations, overlook smaller popular uprisings, and pass over mobilization that may not cut across class, race, or ethnic lines. Centering so much attention on mass mobilizations slights the more subtle ways in which people cope with, and challenge, conventional power.

■ Concluding Thoughts

The prospects for a mass social movement supporting social change emerging from the immigrant rights movement and the mass marches of 2006 is uncertain. The 1950s and 1960s saw a mass movement achieve much and transform the racial landscape of the United States. The legal and political climate was right to facilitate the change advocated by activists. Political and judicial institutions played important roles in that change.

The demographics of the country have changed dramatically over the last fifty years. To form a lasting civil rights movement, the issues must stretch beyond immigrant rights and must include African Americans, Asian Americans, and other minority groups. We are all in this together, and together we have a better chance of bringing about change.

A truly multiracial civil rights movement will need to identify common ground among divergent communities. For rather obvious reasons, Latinas/os and Asian Americans are generally more concerned with the excesses of immigration law and enforcement than African Americans who, as we have seen, at times demand greater enforcement of the immigration laws. To find common ground, minority groups have to look well beyond immigrant rights.

All minorities—indeed, all Americans—desire wage and labor protections in the workplace, safe and affordable housing, equal access to education (including higher education), and fair treatment by government and employers. The congruence of social and economic justice interests among African Americans, Asian Americans, Latinas/os, and, indeed, all Americans is clear. They seek full membership in American society. That is the type of high moral ground that is conducive to more lasting collaborations.

In 2006, the National Latino Congress considered the possibility of building a national Latino political movement. Although the most burning issue was to persuade the US Congress to pass comprehensive immigration reform, the conference delegates also passed resolutions backing a broad range of issues that provide a basis for collaboration with other subordinated communities: voting rights reforms; universal health care; and environmental protection. This is a start toward a broad-based agenda that may hold appeal to various different minority groups.

In the modern United States, change most likely will occur first through grassroots political activism. Change occurs slowly, and the current mass movement, if it amounts to anything, will be just the beginning. Political representative institutions may change and can be expected to respond. Courts, which change slowly, will in all likelihood be the last to respond. For example, the Supreme Court, now headed by Chief Justice John Roberts, will not likely bring significant social change to the nation for at least a generation.

In sum, although we can dream of a new civil rights movement, it is far easier to remain skeptical. Latinas/os, African Americans, and Asian Americans have too many different, and at times competing, agendas. The mass activism of spring 2006, however, offered a glimmer of hope in dark times. The nation saw what true grassroots organizing can do and what impact it can have. Increased naturalization of immigrants in the past has resulted in increased political power of Latinas/os and Asian Americans, which through political action can help promote change.

■ Discussion Questions

1. In your opinion, do immigrants from Mexico and US citizens of Mexican ancestry seek to assimilate into US society? Outline the evidence in support of your conclusions. If persons of Mexican ancestry do assimilate, why do so many live in separate ethnic enclaves, speak Spanish, and remain culturally different? Explain your reasoning.

2. The political activity and activism seen in the immigration marches in spring 2006 has slowed significantly since. What does the future hold for any movement for justice for immigrants? Is it possible that mass civil unrest might result at some point if the rights of immigrants are not paid more attention by federal, state, and local governments? Millions of disenfranchised noncitizens understandably may feel that the political process does not care about, much less represent, them. These residents are also subject to taxation, civil regulation, criminal punishment, and various other government measures without representation. They, for example, cannot serve on juries but are subject to jury verdicts in criminal and civil cases. At some point, protest—even violence—may result, perhaps triggered by an unfortunate event. Is this overly pessimistic?

3. What ways would you suggest improving respect for the civil rights of immigrants in the United States? Should some kind of litigation strategy be pursued? A political strategy? Is one political strategy to encourage increased rates of naturalization among eligible immigrants and transform immigrants into US citizens (and voters)? What other strategies might be pursued to promote social change? Should immigrant rights groups look for partners in political coalitions to bring about change? Is a possible mass movement for social justice, with immigration one component, possible? Explain your reasoning.

4. Lawyers are usually trained in law, not necessarily in political organization. What is the role, if any, for lawyers in political activism and a possible new civil rights movement similar to what the United States experienced in the 1960s? Should lawyers stand on the sidelines while political activists take the reins of a mass social movement? Should lawyers bring litigation to promote and foster a political movement?

5. What kind of immigration reform makes the most sense for the United States? A legalization program? Guest workers? More border enforcement? Free labor migration between the United States, Mexico, and Canada akin to that which currently exists among the member nations of the European Union? Consider the various themes of this book in responding to this question.

■ Suggested Readings

Anaya Valencía, Reynaldo, Sonía R. García, Henry Flores, and José Roberto Juárez Jr. 2004. *Mexican Americans and the Law*. Tucson: University of Arizona Press.

Chavez, Linda. 1991. *Out of the Barrio: Toward a New Politics of Hispanic Assimilation*. New York: BasicBooks.

Johnson, Kevin, and Bill Ong Hing. 2005. "National Identity in a Multicultural Nation: The Challenge of Immigration Law and Immigrants." *Michigan Law Review* 103: 1347.

Portes, Alejandro, and Rubén G. Rumbaut. 2006. *Immigrant America: A Portrait*. 3d ed. Berkeley: University of California Press.

Prouty, Marco G. 2006. *Cesár Chávez, The Catholic Bishops, and the Farm Workers' Struggle for Social Justice*. Tucson, Ariz.: University of Arizona Press.

Rosales, F. Arturo. 1996. *¡Chicano! The History of the Mexican American Civil Rights Movement*. Houston, Tex.: Arte Puiblico Press.

Staudt, Kathleen, and Irasema Coronado. 2002. *Fronteras No Mas: Toward Social Justice at the US-Mexico Border*. New York: Palgrave Macmillan.

Vaca, Nicolas C. 2004. *The Presumed Alliance: The Unspoken Conflict Between Latinos and Blacks and What it Means for America*. New York: Rayo.

■ Notes

1. Parts of this chapter have been adapted from Kevin R. Johnson and Bill Ong Hing, "The Immigrant Rights Marches of 2006 and the Prospects for a New Civil Rights Movement," *Harvard Civil Rights-Civil Liberties Law Review* 42 (2007): 99.

2. 347 US 483 (1954).

3. 457 US 202 (1982). See Michael A. Olivas, "*Plyler v. Doe*: The Education of Undocumented Children and the Polity," in *Immigration Stories*, David A. Martin

and Peter H. Schuck, eds. (New York: Foundation Press; Eagan, Minn.: Thomson/West, 2005), 197.

4. *League of United Latin Am. Citizens v. Wilson*, 908 F. Supp. 755 (C.D. Cal. 1995).

5. See National Immigration Law Center, *DREAM Act: Basic Information* (2007), www.nilc.org/immlawpolicy/DREAM/index.htm.

6. See US Census Bureau, *Minority Population Tops 100 Million*, at www.census.gov/newsroom/releases/archives/population/cb07-70.html.

7. See Pew Hispanic Center, *The Statistical Portrait of Hispanics at Mid-Decade* (2006), table 2, available at http://pewhispanic.org/files/other/middecade/Table-2.pdf.

8. *In re* Rodriguez, 81 F. 337, 352 (W.D. Tex. 1897).

9. Immigration and Nationality Act (INA) § 318, 8 USC. § 1429.

10. INA § 316(a), 8 USC § 1427(a).

11. INA § 316(a)(3), 8 USC § 1427(a)(3).

12. INA § 334(b), 8 USC § 1445(b).

13. INA § 312(b)(1), 8 USC § 1423(b)(1).

14. INA § 312(a)(2), 8 USC § 1423(a)(2).

15. INA § 312(b), 8 USC § 312(b).

16. See US CIS, Naturalization Test, www.uscis.gov/citizenshiptest.

17. INA § 313, 8 USC § 1424.

18. INA § 337(a), 8 USC § 1448(a).

19. See US Department of Homeland Security, Office of Immigration Statistics, *Naturalizations in the United States: 2007* (2008), table 1, at 2, available at www.dhs.gov/xlibrary/assets/statistics/publications/natz_fr_07.pdf.

20. *Garza v. County of Los Angeles*, 918 F.2d 763 (9th Cir. 1990), *cert. denied*, 498 US 1028 (1991).

21. See Samuel P. Huntington, *Who Are We? The Challenges to America's National Identity* (New York: Simon & Schuster, 2004), 221–56.

22. See T. Alexander Aleinikoff and Ruben G. Rumbaut, "Terms of Belonging: Are Models of Membership Self-Fulfilling?" *Georgetown Immigration Law Journal* 13 (1998): 1, 10: "A review of the social science research literature on immigration reveals that assimilation—whether considered intergenerationally or among the most recent waves of immigrants—appears to be progressing roughly as it always has. This is particularly the case with respect to linguistic assimilation, which is frequently seen as the most important marker of acculturation"; footnote omitted.

23. Bill Ong Hing, "Beyond the Rhetoric of Assimilation and Cultural Pluralism: Addressing the Tension of Separatism and Conflict in an Immigration-Driven Multiracial Society," *California Law Review* 81 (1993): 863, 889, emphasis added.

24. See Roger Mahony, "Called by God to Help," *New York Times*, Mar. 22, 2006, A25.

25. Comprehensive Immigration Reform Act of 2006, S.B. 2611, 109th Cong., 2d sess. (2006).

26. *Mohawk Industries v. Carpenter*, 130 S. Ct. 599, 603 (2009).

27. "Secretary Napolitano Announces Record-breaking Immigration Enforcement Statistics Achieved under the Obama Administration," DHS Press Release, October 6, 2010. Available at www.dhs.gove/ynews/releases/pr_1286389936778.shtm.

28. Pub. L. No. 99–603, 100 Stat. 3359 (1986).

29. See Toni Morrison, "On the Backs of Blacks," in *Arguing Immigration: The Debate Over the Changing Face of America* (New York: Simon & Schuster, 1994), 97.

30. Pub. L. No. 89–236, 79 Stat. 911 (1965).

31. 161 F.2d 774 (9th Cir. 1947).

■ GLOSSARY OF TERMS

aggravated felony: An aggravated felony is a crime under US immigration laws that may subject a noncitizen to detention and removal. Some of the crimes that are classified as aggravated felonies are neither "aggravated," as that word is ordinarily understood, nor "felonies" (i.e., they are misdemeanors).

alien: US immigration laws define an "alien" as a person who is not a national or citizen of the United States. The term "aliens" has negative connotations and is often used colloquially to refer to immigrants of color. See also *noncitizen.*

asylum: Asylum under US immigration laws allows a noncitizen to remain in the United States if he or she can establish past persecution or a well-founded fear of future persecution on account of race, religion, nationality, membership in a particular social group, or political opinion in his or her native country.

birth-right citizenship: The Fourteenth Amendment of the US Constitution establishes the general rule that any person born in the United States is a US citizen. The rule applies to, among others, the children of undocumented immigrants born in the United States, who are sometimes denigrated as "anchor babies."

Board of Immigration Appeals (BIA):   The BIA is the administrative board that decides appeals of the decisions of the immigration courts. The BIA is part of the Executive Office for Immigration Review, which in turn is part of the US Department of Justice. See also *Department of Justice; Executive Office for Immigration Review.*

Bracero Program: The Bracero Program was a guest worker program created with the cooperation of the US and Mexican governments during World War II. It remained in effect through the early 1960s. The program brought workers from Mexico to the United States to work temporarily. During the Bracero Program's existence, the US government granted admission to nearly 4 million Mexican *braceros,* primarily in agriculture.

***Chevron* deference:**   In the decision of *Chevron USA v. Natural Resources Defense Council, Inc.*, 467 US 837 (1984), the US Supreme Court ruled that courts generally must not second-guess and disturb an administrative agency's interpretation of a law passed by Congress. *Chevron* deference is part of a general doctrine of deference of the courts to the rulings of administrative agencies.

Chinese exclusion laws: In the late 1800s, Congress passed a series of laws that represented the first efforts by the US government to comprehensively regulate immigration. The laws sought largely to severely limit any future Chinese immigration to the United States. The Supreme Court rejected constitutional challenges to the discriminatory Chinese exclusion laws. See also *plenary power doctrine.*

Citizenship and Immigration Services (CIS):   The primary functions of CIS, an agency within the US Department of Homeland Security, are to approve applications for lawful permanent residency and citizenship. See also *lawful permanent resident; naturalization.*

Civil Rights Act of 1964:   The Civil Rights Act of 1964 is a federal law intended to give force to the civil rights guaranteed by the Fourteenth Amendment of the US Constitution. The act generally prohibits discrimination on the basis of race, color, religion, sex, or national origin in public accommodations and employment.

conditional lawful permanent resident status: When a US citizen marries a noncitizen, the noncitizen spouse may obtain conditional lawful permanent resident status under US immigration laws. Lawful permanent resident status generally will be granted after two years if the couple remains married.

Constitution: The US Constitution, among other things, establishes the powers of the federal government and the rights and freedoms guaranteed to persons in the United States. Each state also has its own constitution, which generally performs similar functions at the state level.

crime involving moral turpitude: A conviction of a "crime involving moral turpitude" may be grounds for denial of entry into, and removal from, the United States. Crimes of moral turpitude include murder, voluntary manslaughter, aggravated assault, rape, kidnapping, theft, lewd conduct, bigamy, and fraud.

Customs and Border Protection (CBP):   The CBP, an agency in the Department of Homeland Security, is a law enforcement agency that patrols the land and water borders of the United States.

decision: A decision is a judge's written explanation of a ruling. It is also referred to as an *opinion.*

Department of Health and Human Services (HHS):   The Department of Health and Human Services is a department of the US government that, among other things, screens visa applicants for serious medical conditions and diseases.

Department of Homeland Security (DHS):   The DHS is the department of the US government responsible for ensuring the security of the United States, including the enforcement and administration of US immigration laws. Congress established the department in 2002.

Department of Justice (DOJ):   Headed by the attorney general, the DOJ is a department of the US government that has primary responsibility for enforcing many federal laws, including some of US immigration laws.

Department of Labor (DOL):   The Department of Labor is a department of the US government that, with respect to immigration, serves the dual purpose of protecting the interests of US workers and supplementing the national workforce with foreign labor.

Department of State: The Department of State is a department of the US government that provides diplomatic services for the United States and foreign countries and issues visas for noncitizens who seek to enter the country.

deportation hearing: A deportation hearing is an immigration proceeding held by an administrative agency (referred to as an immigration court) in which the US government seeks to remove a noncitizen from the United States. See also *removal hearing*.

Development, Relief and Education for Alien Minors (DREAM) Act: The DREAM Act, which was proposed in different forms in the US Congress in the early part of the twenty-first century, is legislation that, generally speaking, would allow undocumented students to pay in-state resident fees to attend public colleges and universities and to regularize their immigration status. Although proposals have been introduced into Congress repeatedly, the US Congress has to this point not passed a version of the DREAM Act.

diversity visa lottery: A lottery that allows 55,000 lawful permanent residents, or about 8 percent of the annual allotment of immigrant visas, to enter the United States each year. The diversity lottery was created to increase immigration from nations that have historically sent few immigrants to the United States and thus "diversify" the stream of immigrants into the country. In operation, it has favored immigration from

Europe and Africa over that from much of the developing world, populated by people of color.

Due Process Clause: The Due Process Clause guarantees that no person may be deprived of life, liberty, or property without due process of law, meaning some kind of proceeding to challenge the governmental action. The US Constitution includes two Due Process Clauses: (1) the Fifth Amendment applying to the federal government; and (2) the Fourteenth Amendment, which applies to the states. Due Process Clauses can be found in most state constitutions.

employment-based immigration: The Immigration and Nationality Act allots 140,000 lawful permanent resident visas annually for employment-based immigration for five categories of visas: (1) immigrants with "extraordinary ability"; (2) immigrants with advanced degrees; (3) immigrants who are skilled and other workers; (4) special workers; and (5) immigrants who commit to invest and create jobs in the United States.

entrants without inspection (EWI): An EWI is a noncitizen who entered the US without lawful admission at a port of entry. See also *undocumented immigrant.*

Equal Protection Clause: The Equal Protection Clause is a provision of the Fourteenth Amendment to the US Constitution that prohibits a state from denying any person within its jurisdiction the "equal protection of the laws." The clause is often invoked by persons who claim discrimination on the basis of race, color, gender, religion, or national origin.

exclusion hearing: A proceeding in the immigration court, an administrative agency in the executive branch of the federal government, for noncitizens seeking admission into the United States. See also *removal hearing.*

Executive Office for Immigration Review (EOIR): Part of the US Department of Justice, the EOIR holds hearings on the removal of noncitizens from, and those seeking admission to, the United States. The Board of Immigration Appeals and the immigration courts are part of the EOIR.

expedited (or summary) removal: Immigration reform legislation enacted by the US Congress in 1996 created expedited removal, under which immigration officials at ports of entry have the authority to remove, without a hearing in the immigration court, a noncitizen who appears to lack a legal avenue for admission into the United States.

family-based immigration: The US immigration laws provide various means for noncitizens to join US citizens or lawful permanent residents in the United States. Immediate relatives of a US citizen, including spouses and minor children, generally can immigrate to the United States without numerical limitations. There are family preferences with numerical ceilings per year for (1) unmarried sons and daughters of US citizens; (2) spouses and unmarried sons and daughters of lawful permanent residents; (3) married sons and daughters of US citizens; and (4) brothers and sisters of US citizens.

federal preemption: Federal preemption refers to the principle derived from the Supremacy Clause of the US Constitution that a federal law supersedes, or preempts, inconsistent state and local laws. Generally speaking, the federal government has exclusive authority over the admission and removal of immigrants from the United States, and state and local governments cannot intrude on that exclusive power. See also *Constitution*; *Supremacy Clause*.

Fifth Amendment: The Fifth Amendment of the US Constitution requires, among other things, that the federal government provide persons with due process before depriving them of life, liberty, or property. See also *Due Process Clause*.

First Amendment: The First Amendment of the US Constitution guarantees the freedom of speech, religion, press, assembly, and the freedom to petition the government.

Fourteenth Amendment: Ratified in 1868, the Fourteenth Amendment recognizes the citizenship of persons born in the United States and secures all persons against any state action that would result in deprivation of life, liberty, or property without due process of law or in denial of equal protection of the law. See also *Due Process Clause; Equal Protection Clause*.

Gadsden Purchase (1853): Under the Gadsden Purchase, Mexico sold the last piece of land to the United States after the US–Mexico War of 1848. From 1836 to 1853, the United States acquired nearly two-thirds of Mexico's territory.

guest (or temporary) worker program: A guest worker program generally provides for temporary admission of foreign workers into the United States. The workers are expected to leave the country upon completion of the temporary labor. See also *Bracero Program; H-2A Visa*.

H-2A visa: H-2A visas under US immigration laws allow for the admission of temporary workers engaged in specialty occupations and in occupations in which US workers are in short supply as well as farm and agricultural workers and trainees. Fifty thousand H-2A visas are available each year.

Homeland Security Act of 2002: Among other things, this act created the Department of Homeland Security, dismantled the Immigration and Naturalization Service (INS), and transferred most INS responsibilities to the DHS.

Illegal Immigration Reform and Immigrant Responsibility Act (IIRIRA) (1996): The US Congress passed IIRIRA in 1996 to increase immigration law enforcement, limit judicial review of removal orders, create expedited removal, expand removal grounds, increase immigrant detention, and restrict eligibility of immigrants for public benefits.

Immigration Act of 1824: This Mexican law permitted foreign migration into its northern territories and resulted in a wave of American settlers into Mexico, which in turn caused the government to seek to curtail additional settlement.

Immigration Act of 1965: The Immigration Act of 1965 abolished the discriminatory national origins quota system (see *National Origins Act of 1924*). As a consequence of the change in the law, the United States, over the next few decades, saw a sharp increase in migration from Asia.

Immigration Act of 1990: In this act, the US Congress, among other things, significantly narrowed the grounds for the exclusion and deportation of noncitizens from the United States because of their political views and focused on the removal of noncitizens for "terrorist activities."

Immigration and Customs Enforcement (ICE): ICE is the immigration enforcement branch of the US Department of Homeland Security. ICE has the authority to detain and initiate removal proceedings against noncitizens.

Immigration and Nationality Act (INA) (1952): The INA is the comprehensive immigration law passed by the US Congress that deals with immigration, naturalization, removal, and exclusion of noncitizens.

Immigration and Naturalization Service (INS): Until 2002, the INS was the primary agency in the US Department of Justice that administered and enforced the Immigration and Nationality Act.

immigration courts: Part of the US Department of Justice, these administrative courts hold hearings, accept evidence, and decide removal and other immigration matters.

Immigration Reform and Control Act (IRCA) (1986): Congress passed IRCA as a comprehensive reform of the immigration laws. IRCA afforded amnesty to undocumented immigrants who met certain requirements, created employer sanctions that subjected employers of undocumented immigrants to civil penalties, and established temporary worker programs. The amnesty program granted lawful status to approximately 1 million noncitizens from Mexico.

inadmissibility grounds: The inadmissibility grounds are rules established by the Immigration and Nationality Act for denying admission to certain immigrants into the United States. A substantial number of inadmissibility grounds focus on criminal convictions, any "terrorist activities," and violation of immigration controls, such as visa fraud. See chapter 6.

Jim Crow laws: Jim Crow laws were state and local laws that discriminated against African Americans, such as laws requiring separate restrooms and public schools for blacks and whites. Jim Crow laws today violate the Equal Protection Clause of the Fourteenth Amendment.

judicial review: A judicial review is the court's power to review the actions of other branches of government. It includes the judicial power to find that legislative and executive actions violate the US Constitution.

jurisdiction: Jurisdiction is a government's general power to exercise authority over all persons and things within its territory. Jurisdiction also refers to the power of a court or administrative agency to decide a matter.

lawful permanent resident (LPR): An LPR has "been lawfully accorded the privilege of residing permanently in the United States as an immigrant" under the Immigration and Nationality Act. LPRs are also known as "green carders" because the US government once issued lawful permanent residents a card that was green in color.

memoranda of agreement (MOAs): An MOA is an agreement or contract. The US government and state and local law enforcement authorities have entered into MOAs to facilitate the apprehension and deportation of immigrants. Under the agreements, state and local officers are trained to enforce the US immigration laws. See chapter 10.

Minutemen: In the modern politics of immigration, the Minutemen are a loosely affiliated—and controversial—civilian group, whom some refer to as "vigilantes," that patrol the US–Mexico border to "assist" the US government in border enforcement.

National Labor Relations Board (NLRB): The NLRB is an independent federal board created by the National Labor Relations Act of 1935 to remedy unfair labor practices by employers and to safeguard employees' right to organize into labor unions.

National Origins Act of 1924: The National Origins Act was a law passed by the US Congress that established a discriminatory quota system for the admission of immigrants into the United States based on the 1890 census. Congress designed the system to maintain the racial and ethnic makeup of the US population, the majority of which traced its ancestry to Western Europe.

National Security Entry-Exit Registration System: This system, known as the *special registration program,* was one of the national security measures implemented by President George W. Bush after September 11, 2001. It required certain noncitizens from nations populated predominantly by Arabs and Muslims to register with the US government.

naturalization: Naturalization is the process by which the US government grants US citizenship to a lawful permanent resident.

naturalization power: Article I, section 8, clause 4 of the US Constitution expressly delegates the power to Congress to establish a uniform rule of naturalization for immigrants so that they can become US citizens.

noncitizen: A person living in the United States who is not a US citizen is called a noncitizen. US citizens generally possess many legal rights, many of which are guaranteed by the US Constitution; noncitizens have fewer rights. See also *alien.*

nonimmigrant visa: A nonimmigrant visa typically allows a person to stay in the United States for a limited time or to perform some specific task, such as to vacation, attend college, or engage in business. Lawful permanent residents are ordinarily allowed to remain indefinitely in the United States while those holding nonimmigrant visas are allowed only temporarily.

Nonrefoulement: Nonrefoulement is a French word that refers to a noncitizen's right under international law not to be returned to a nation where his or her life or liberty would be threatened.

Norteños: Norteños were Mexican citizens who moved to northern territories of Mexico during the mid-1800s. After the loss of Tejas, the Mexican government encouraged its citizens to move to its northern territories in hopes of preserving Mexican control over them.

North American Free Trade Agreement (NAFTA): Ratified by the United States in 1994, NAFTA is an agreement between the United States, Canada, and Mexico that generally provides for the free trade of goods and services among the three nations. NAFTA does not generally address labor migration.

Office of Detention and Removal Operations (DRO): Under the control of Immigration and Customs Enforcement, DRO operates detention facilities called service processing centers in the United States. It may also arrange for the detention of noncitizens in state or local jails.

Operation Gatekeeper: Operation Gatekeeper is a military-style operation on the US–Mexico border near San Diego, California, designed to reduce undocumented immigration. It channels unlawful entrants away from a major metropolitan area into remote locations, where thousands of Mexican citizens die from heat, cold, exposure, and dehydration.

Operation Streamline: In 2005, the Department of Homeland Security initiated Operation Streamline, a program whereby undocumented persons arrested along the US–Mexico border are prosecuted criminally.

Operation Wetback: The Immigration and Nationalization Service (INS) pursued Operation Wetback in 1954 to raid farms in an effort to arrest undocumented workers. By the end of the operation, the INS deported more than 1 million persons.

opinion: A written explanation prepared by a judge giving reasons for making a legal ruling is an opinion, also referred to as a *decision*.

overstay: An overstay is a noncitizen who was lawfully admitted into the United States on a nonimmigrant (temporary) visa but has violated its terms (often by staying longer than the time permitted by the visa). Examples are university students who remain without continued enrollment as university students, or tourists or business visitors who remain in the country beyond the time (usually six months) permitted by their visas.

per-country ceilings: Under US immigration laws, immigration from any one country is generally limited to about twenty-six thousand lawful permanent residents per year. The per-country ceiling requires noncitizens in certain visa categories to wait for many years before lawfully coming to the United States.

plenary power doctrine: A doctrine that affords broad power over immigration to Congress and the president and greatly limits review by the courts of the immigration decisions of those branches of government. See chapter 3.

Postville, Iowa: In May 2008, Immigration and Customs Enforcement raided a meat-processing plant in the small rural town of Postville, Iowa. The raid was one of the largest raids at a single work site in US history. Nearly four hundred people, most from Guatemala and Mexico, were arrested and detained. Many were prosecuted criminally for violation of immigration and other laws.

Proposition 187: In 1994, California voters by a wide margin passed Proposition 187, a law that would have denied public benefits, including a public education, to undocumented immigrants. It also would have required public officials to report suspected undocumented immigrants to federal authorities. Many people regard Proposition 187, which a federal court found to be unconstitutional, as a high-water mark of anti-immigrant sentiment in recent US history.

public charge exclusion: The US immigration laws allow for the denial of entry to noncitizens who are likely to become a *public charge*. The US government determines whether a visa applicant is likely to become a public charge and generally considers the age and health of the noncitizen as well as his or her ability and willingness to work and income and assets. See also *inadmissibility grounds*.

racial profiling: Racial profiling is the targeting of African Americans, Latinas/os, and other racial minorities by police and immigration officers on account of their race and physical appearance.

refugee: A refugee is defined by international law and US law as a person who is unable or unwilling to return to his or her native country because of past persecution or a well-founded fear of future persecution on account of race, religion, nationality, membership in a particular social group, or political opinion.

remittance: Remittances are sums of money sent by noncitizens in the United States to family, friends, or associations in the noncitizen's native country. Remittances by Mexican citizens in the United States to Mexico amount to billions of dollars each year.

removal hearing: A removal hearing refers to both deportation and exclusion hearings. See also *deportation hearing; exclusion hearing.*

restrictionist: Restrictionists advocate various restrictions on immigration to the United States and claim that immigrants injure US society. Restrictionists often contend, for example, that immigrants take jobs from US citizens. Proposition 187 is a well-known restrictionist measure. See also *Proposition 187.*

Social Security Administration (SSA): The SSA is an independent agency within the executive branch of the US government. SSA data are used to match a worker and a Social Security number, thus allowing the US government to determine whether a worker is legally authorized to work.

statute: A statute is a law passed by a state or federal legislature, such as the US Congress.

Supremacy Clause: The Supremacy Clause, Article VI of the US Constitution, provides that federal law, namely the Constitution and federal statutes, are the "supreme law of the land" and preempt, or supersede, conflicting state and local laws. See also *federal preemption.*

Tejas: The name of territory formerly part of Mexico but now part of the United States, known as Texas. In the early 1800s, many US citizens settled in Tejas when it was part of Mexico and declared independence in 1835.

Treaty of Guadalupe Hidalgo (1848): This treaty, which ended the US–Mexican War, ceded a vast amount of Mexican territory to the United States.

undocumented immigrant (or undocumented foreign nationals): Undocumented immigrants are noncitizens lacking legal immigration status in the United States. They include noncitizens who entered without inspection and those who overstayed their visas. "Illegal alien" is a pejorative term used colloquially by some people to refer to undocumented immigrants.

USA PATRIOT (Uniting and Strengthening America by Providing Appropriate Tools Required to Intercept and Obstruct Terrorism) Act: Passed in response to September 11, 2001, the USA PATRIOT Act affords law enforcement agencies authority to collect and share information on suspected terrorists and to detain and deport noncitizens engaged in "terrorist activities."

voluntary return: Voluntary return is a relatively quick nonjudicial process used by immigration officers to return undocumented persons apprehended entering the country in violation of the law.

withholding of removal: US law prohibits the return of a noncitizen to a country where his or her life or freedom would be threatened because of his or her race, religion, nationality, membership in a particular social group, or political opinion. Withholding affords noncitizens more limited rights then asylum. See also *asylum*.

■ INDEX

"criminal aliens," 118–19, 231. *See also* aggravated felony; criminal grounds for removal

criminal grounds for removal, 138–41; crimes involving moral turpitude, 140, 274; drug crimes, 140–41. *See also* aggravated felony

criminal inadmissibility grounds, 117–18

criminal laws, use of in immigration enforcement, 143–45. *See also* Operation Streamline

Customs and Border Protection (CBP), 77–79, 274; CBP activity, 78

Davis, Gray (California Governor), 200

deaths at the border, 185–90. *See also* border enforcement; Operation Gatekeeper

DeCanas v. Bica (US 1976), 199. *See also* federal preemption; state and local regulation of immigration

deference to administrative agencies, 62–69. *See also Chevron* deference; judicial review

Demore v. Kim (US 2003), 54

Department of Health and Human Services (HHS), 81, 275

Department of Homeland Security (DHS), 58, 74–75, 76, 100, 137–38, 224, 257, 275; offices within DHS, 75; Operation Streamline, 143–45

Department of Justice (DOJ), 62, 81–84, 275. *See also* Executive Office for Immigration Review

Department of Labor, 80, 91–92, 128, 275

Department of State, 68, 77, 79, 275. *See also* consular absolutism

deportation hearings, 51, 275. *See also* removal; removal hearing

detention of immigrants, 190–91

discrimination, history of against persons of Mexican ancestry in United States, 1–2, 170–71. *See also* border enforcement; racial profiling in immigration enforcement

diversity visa lottery, 92, 275

diversity visas, 92–93

Dobbs, Lou, xi, 5, 256

Douglas, Justice William O., 7

DREAM Act, 202, 243–44, 256, 275

drug enforcement, through immigration laws, 138–39

dual (segmented) labor markets, 15–16, 184–85. *See also* Jim Crow; labor migration

dual nationality, 248. *See also* naturalization

Due Process, 51–54, 201, 276; procedural, 51–53; substantive, 53–54

economic fears of immigration, 23. *See also* labor migration; nativism; state and local regulation of immigration

employment-based immigration, 91–92, 276; limited numbers of employment visas, 127–28. *See also* guest (or temporary) worker program; H2-A visa; immigrant visas; nonimmigrant (temporary) visas

enforcement of US immigration laws, 73–86. *See also* border enforcement; administration and enforcement of US immigration laws

entrants without inspection, 276. *See also* overstay; undocumented immigrants

Equal Protection, 56, 179, 182, 276. *See also* Fourteenth Amendment

Escondido, California, 17, 18–19. *See also* state and local regulation of immigration exclusion hearings, 67, 276. *See also* deportation hearings; expedited removal; removal hearing

Executive Office for Immigration Review (EOIR), 81, 101. *See also* Board of Immigration Appeals; immigration courts

expedited removal, 69, 135–38, 276; protection questions, 136

Fair Labor Standards Act, 164

family-based immigration, 89–91, 277. *See also* immigrant visas

Farmer's Branch, Texas, 17–18. *See also* state and local regulation of immigration

Federal Bureau of Investigation, 81–84

federal power over immigration, 43–86. *See also* plenary power doctrine

federal preemption, 164, 198–99, 277. *See also* state and local regulation of immigration; Supremacy Clause

Fifth Amendment, 51, 277

First Amendment, 54–55, 277

Ford, President Gerald, 110

Fourteenth Amendment, 179–80, 277. *See also* Equal Protection

Fourth Amendment, racial profiling and, 172. *See also* racial profiling in immigration enforcement

Gadsden Purchase (1853), 32–33, 277. *See also* land acquisition from Mexico; Treaty of Guadalupe Hidalgo; US–Mexican War

Galvan v. Press (US 1954), 54–55

Gates, Bill, 128

Graham v. Richardson (US 1971), 200–201

Great Depression, "repatriation" during, 34, 112, 170

guest (or temporary) worker program, 37, 277. *See also* Bracero Program; H2-A visa; nonimmigrant (temporary) visas

Gutierrez, US Rep. Luis, 257

H2-A visa, 35–36, 158–59, 278. *See also* guest (or temporary) worker program

Hanson, Victor Davis, 210

hate crimes, against immigrants and Latina/os, 10, 211–12. *See also* nativism

Hazleton, Pennsylvania, 15, 17; anti-immigrant sentiment, 211; immigration ordinance, 209–10, 212. *See also* state and local regulation of immigration

Hernandez, Jr., Esequiel, killing of, 185, 186. *See also* border enforcement

Hing, Professor Bill Ong, 252

Hispanic population in the United States, 39. *See also* Mexican ancestry population in the United States

Hoffman Plastic Compounds, Inc. v. NLRB (US 2002), 160–63. *See also* National Labor Relations Board; racial caste in labor markets

Homeland Security Act of 2002, 74, 224, 278. *See also* Department of Homeland Security

"huddled masses," 121–22. *See also* public charge exclusion

Huerta, Dolores, 241

human trafficking, 187–88. *See also* border enforcement

Huntington, Samuel, 210, 249

Hutchinson, Asa, 233

IDENT, 134

"illegal aliens": demonized, 7–12, 23, 189; harms of, 11–12, 169, 193; stereotypes, 23; Supreme Court views of, 12–13. *See also* "aliens"; undocumented immigrants

Illegal Immigration Reform and Immigrant Responsibility Act (1996), 37, 278

immigrant sending countries to United States, 13

immigrant visas, 87–93

Immigration Act of 1824, 29, 278

Immigration Act of 1965, 124, 262, 278

Immigration Act of 1990, 55, 278

Immigration and Customs Enforcement (ICE), 58, 79, 177–80, 203, 223, 278

Immigration and Nationality Act (INA), 5, 6–7, 45, 112, 113–29, 133, 140–41, 278; 287(g) agreements, 203–6; asylum and refugees, 99–100; definition of "alien," 5–6, 43, 88

Immigration and Naturalization Service (INS), 51–53, 57, 66, 278; reorganization after September 11, 2001, 74–75. *See also* border enforcement; Department of Homeland Security; Immigration and Customs Enforcement

immigration control inadmissibility grounds, 115–16

immigration courts, 62, 101–102, 279

immigration enforcement, modern, 180–83. *See also* border enforcement

immigration fraud, case of, 82–84

ImmigrationProf blog, xii

immigration reform, xi–xii, 59–60, 231; criminal inadmissibility grounds, 117–18; discriminatory treatment of persons of Mexican ancestry, 112–13; history of inadmissibility grounds, 110–13; immigration control, 115–16; inadmissibility, 106–32, 279; more liberal admissions, 231–34; political and national security inadmissibility grounds, 116–17; possibilities for, 241–69; post–September 11, 2001, 221–26; public health inadmissibility grounds, 120–21; racial and class impacts of inadmissibility grounds, 123–25; rights of persons seeking admission, 114–15. *See also* admissions of immigrants

Immigration Reform and Control Act (IRCA) (1986), 37, 109, 158–59, 162, 164, 207–8, 257–59, 279. *See also* Immigration and Nationality Act

immigration restrictions on Mexican migrants, 34–39

INS v. Cardoza-Fonseca (US 1987), 64. *See also* deference to administrative agencies

INS v. Elias-Zacarias (US 1992) 63–64. *See also* deference to administrative agencies

interracial conflict, 251–53, 259–61. *See also* civil rights movement

Jim Crow, 15–17, 184, 234, 262, 263, 279. *See also* civil rights movement

judicial review, 67–69, 84–85; consular absolutism, 68–69; controversy over, 65–66; "court stripping" provisions, 85; restrictions on, 66–67. *See also* plenary power doctrine

slavery, 188. *See also* human trafficking

Smith, William French (US Attorney General), 12, 169

Social Security Administration (SSA), 77, 80, 283

Social Security contributions from immigrants, 21, 22. *See also* Social Security Administration

Sotomayor, Justice Sonia, 257

state and local costs of immigration, 21–22; "fiscal disconnect," 23. *See also* state and local regulation of immigration

state and local governments' perspective on immigration and immigration policy, 22–23

state and local regulation of immigration, 198–216; Arizona's S.B. 1070, 206–7; employment and restrictions, 207–10; memoranda of agreement for state and local enforcement of immigration laws, 203–6, 279–80. *See also* federal preemption; Proposition 187

Student and Exchange Visitor Information System (SEVIS), 79. *See also* Immigration and Customs Enforcement (ICE)

Supremacy Clause, 198, 283. *See also* federal preemption

Supreme Court (US), perspectives on migration from Mexico, 12–13, 16–17

Tancredo, Tom (US Representative), 189

tax revenues from immigrants, 20–21, 22–23

Texas (Tejas): Lone Star Republic, 29–30; Tejas, 28–29, 283; US acquisition of, 28–40

Treaty of Guadalupe Hidalgo, 32–33, 106, 107–8, 283; Article VIII, 107–8; Article IX, 107–8. *See also* US–Mexican War

Trucios-Haynes, Professor Enid, 223

undocumented foreign nationals, 102–4, 148–58. *See also* undocumented immigrants

undocumented immigrants, 4, 102–4, 148–58, 283; employment by industries, 154; estimated population of, 14, 16, 102–4, 148–58; and lack of employment visas, 127–28; Mexico, 37; percentage of US population, 156–57; profile, 177–79; share of select occupations, 155; "wetbacks," 4. *See also* "aliens," "illegal aliens"

United Nations Convention Relating to the Status of Refugees (1951), 98

United Nations Protocol Relating to the Status of Refugees (1967), 98

United States v. Arvizu (US 2002), 181–82

United States v. Brignoni-Ponce (US 1975), 169, 172–73, 181–82; sanctioning reliance of "Mexican appearance" in immigration stop, 173–79, 180. *See also* racial profiling in immigration enforcement

United States v. Cortez (US 1981), 181

United States v. Montero-Camargo (9th Circuit 2000), 182

USA PATRIOT Act, 116–17, 224, 226, 284. *See also* national security and immigration

US Commission on International Religious Freedom, 138

US government perspective on immigration and immigration policy, 20–21

■ ABOUT THE AUTHORS

KEVIN R. JOHNSON is dean of the School of Law, and Mabie-Apallas professor of public interest law and Chicana/o studies at the University of California, Davis. He is the author of a number of immigration and other books and articles and is coeditor of the ImmigrationProf blog (http://law professors.typepad.com/immigration). An honors graduate of Harvard Law School, where he served as an editor of the *Harvard Law Review*, Dean Johnson earned an AB in economics from UC Berkeley. He joined the UC Davis law faculty in 1989. He has taught a wide array of classes, including immigration law, Latinos and Latinas and the law, refugee law, and critical race theory. Dean Johnson has served on the board of directors of the Mexican American Legal Defense and Education Fund, the leading Mexican American civil rights organization in the United States. In 1993, he was the recipient of the law school's Distinguished Teaching Award. In 2006, the Hispanic National Bar Association named Dean Johnson the Law Professor of the Year.

BERNARD TRUJILLO is professor at the Valparaiso University School of Law, where he has taught since 2007. He is author of several articles on immigration and is editor of the *Immigration, Refugee & Citizenship Law* eJournal of the Social Science Research Network (SSRN; www.ssrn.com). He received his AB (magna cum laude) from Princeton University and his JD from Yale Law School, where he was articles editor of the *Yale Law Journal*. His areas of teaching and research include empirical legal studies, quantitative analysis of legal systems, immigration, and Mexican migration to the United States.

Immigration Law and the US–Mexico Border is a volume in the series The Mexican American Experience, a cluster of modular texts designed to provide greater flexibility in undergraduate education. Each book deals with a single topic concerning the Mexican American population. Instructors can create a semester-length course from any combination of volumes, or may choose to use one or two volumes to complement other texts.

Additional volumes deal with the following subjects:

Mexican Americans and Health
Adela de la Torre and Antonio Estrada

Chicano Popular Culture
Charles M. Tatum

Mexican Americans and the US Economy
Arturo González

Mexican Americans and the Law
Reynaldo Anaya Valencia, Sonia R. García, Henry Flores, and José Roberto Juárez Jr.

Chicana/o Identity in a Changing US Society
Aída Hurtado and Patricia Gurin

Mexican Americans and the Environment
Devon G. Peña

Mexican Americans and the Politics of Diversity
Lisa Magaña

Mexican Americans and Language
Glenn A. Martínez

Chicano and Chicana Literature
Charles M. Tatum

Chicana and Chicano Art
Carlos Francisco Jackson

For more information, please visit
www.uapress.arizona.edu/textbooks/latino.htm